Math Lesson 3

Addition I

D1710155

SonLight Education Ministry
United States of America

A Suggested Daily Schedule

(Adapt this schedule to your family needs.)

5:00 a.m.  Arise–Personal Worship

6:00 a.m. Family Worship and Bible Class–With Father

7:00 a.m. Breakfast

8:00 a.m. Practical Arts*–Domestic Activities
                                  Agriculture
                                  Industrial Arts
(especially those related to the School Lessons)

10:00 a.m. School Lessons
(Take a break for some physical exercise during this time slot.)

12:00 p.m. Dinner Preparations
(Health class could be included at this time or a continued story.)

1:00 p.m. Dinner

2:00 p.m. Practical Arts* or Fine Arts
(Music and Crafts)
(especially those related to the School Lessons)

5:00 p.m. Supper

6:00 p.m. Family Worship–Father
(Could do History Class)

7:00 p.m. Personal time with God–Bed Preparation

8:00 p.m. Bed

*Daily nature walk can be in morning or afternoon.

The Desire of All Nations

This book is a part of a curriculum that is built upon the life of Christ entitled, "The Desire of All Nations," for grades 2-8. Any of the books in this curriculum can be used by themselves or as an entire program.

INFORMATION ABOUT THE 2-8 GRADE PROGRAM

Multi-level

This program is written on a multi-level. That means that each booklet has material for grades 2-8. This is so the whole family in these grades may work from the same books. It is difficult for a busy mother to have 2 or more children and each have a different set of books. Remember, the Bible is written for all ages.

The Bible—the Primary Textbook

The books in this program are designed to teach the parent and the student how to learn academic subjects by using the Bible as a primary textbook.

The Desire of Ages

The Desire of Ages by Ellen G. White is used as a textbook to go with the Bible. This focuses on the early life of Christ, when He was a child. Children relate best to Christ as a child and youth.

Lesson Numbers

The big number in the top right corner on the cover of this book is the Lesson Number and corresponds with the chapter number in the book *The Desire of Ages*. For example, Lesson 1 in the school program will go along with chapter 1 in *The Desire of Ages*. Usually each family starts at the beginning with Lesson 1. Most children have not had a true Bible program, therefore they need the foundation built. If there is academic material that they have already covered, they do the Bible part and review then pass quickly on.

Seven Academic Subjects

There are seven academic subjects in this program—Health, Mathematics, Music, Science–Nature, History/Geography/Prophecy, Language, Voice–Speech.

Language Program

A good, solid language program is recommended to be used along with the SonLight materials.

The Riggs Institute has a multi-sensory teaching method that accommodates every child's unique learning style. Their program is called *Writing and Spelling Road to Reading and Thinking*. Order by calling (800) 200-4840 or visit www.riggsinst.org. (Disclaimer: SonLight does not endorse the reading books recommended in the Riggs' program.)

Another option which you might find more user friendly and is similar to the Riggs program but from a Christian perspective is *Spell to Write and Read* by Wanda Sanseri. To order, call Wanda Sanseri at (503) 654-2300 or visit https://www.bhibooks.net/swr.html

"The Fullness of Time"
Lesson 3 – Alertness

The following books are those you will need for this lesson.
All of these can be obtained from www.sonlighteducation.com

The Rainbow Covenant – Study the spiritual meaning of colors and make your own rainbow book.

Health
The Heart

Math
Addition I

Music
Musical and Non Musical Sounds

Science/Nature
Stars and Constellations

A Casket – Coloring book and story. Learn how to treat the gems of the Bible.

H/G/P
Continents

Language
History of the Word

Speech/Voice
Voice Culture

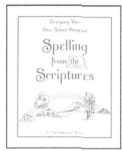

Spelling from the Scriptures

Bible Study – Learn how to study the Bible and helpful use tools.

Bible
The Desire of all Nations I
Teacher Study Guide

Student Study Guide

Bible Lesson Study Guide

Memory Verses
The Desire of all Nations I
Scripture Songs Book

and MP3 files

Our Nature Study Book – Your personal nature journal.

Table of Contents

Counsel for Parent-Teacher

1   "In the study of figures the work should be made practical. Let every youth and every child be taught, not merely to solve imaginary problems, but to keep an accurate account of his own income and outgoes.

2

"Let him learn the right use of money by using it. Whether supplied by their parents or by their own earnings, let boys and girls learn to select and purchase their own clothing, their books, and other necessities; and by keeping an account of their expenses they will learn, as they could learn in no other way, the value and the use of money.

3

"This training will help them to distinguish true economy from niggardliness [covetousness] on the one hand and prodigality [extravagance] on the other. Rightly directed it will encourage habits of benevolence. It will aid the youth in learning to give, not from the mere impulse of the moment, as their feelings are stirred, but regularly and systematically.

In the study of mathematics

4   "In this way every study may become an aid in the solution of that greatest of all problems, the training of men and women for the best discharge of life's responsibilities."

Education
238-239

Teacher Section

"And the Lord added
to the church daily
such as should be saved."
Acts 2:47

 # INSTRUCTIONS
For the Teacher

Step 1

Study the Bible Lesson and begin to memorize the Memory Verses. Familiarize yourself with the Character Quality. The student can answer the Bible Review Questions. See page 6. Use the Steps in Bible Study.

Bible Lesson

"The Fullness of Time" –
Ecclesiastes 3:1-15;
Luke 1:26-35;
Galatians 4:4-5

Memory Verses

Galatians 4:4-5; *The Desire of Ages* 32; Acts 3:22; Isaiah 61:1-3; 60:1-3; Genesis 49:10; John 3:16-17

Character Quality

Alertness – quick to understand and watching very carefully: vigilance; watchfulness; moving with celerity briskness; nimbleness; sprightliness

Antonyms – carelessness; indifference; unawareness; levity

Character Quality Verse

Mark 14:38 – *"Watch ye and pray, lest ye enter into temptation. The spirit truly is ready, but the flesh is weak."*

Step 2

Understand:

A. How to do the Spelling Cards so the student can begin to build his own spiritual dictionary.

B. How to Mark Your Bible.

C. Evaluate Your Student's Character in relation to the character quality of **alertness**.

D. Familiarize Yourself With Addition. Notice the Projects.

E. Review the Scripture References for "Addition."

F. Notice the Answer Key.

A. Spelling Cards Spelling Lists

Addition Words
Place I - II - III

addition	end
alertness	espoused (ed)
plus	faileth
sum	favour (ed)
one	forever
two	fullness
three	Galilee
four	Israel
five	Jesus
six	Joseph
seven	kingdom
eight	law
nine	made
ten	Mary
eleven	Nazareth
twelve	prolonged
	proverb

Choose spelling words from these lists

Place II - III
addend
increase

	redeem
	reign
	sent
	Son (sons)

Bible Words

adoption	stand
blessed	throne
conceive	time
David	troubled
Deliverer	under
	virgin & vision

See the booklet
Spelling from the Scriptures
for instructions about
how to make
the Spelling Cards.

B. How to Mark the Bible

1. Copy the list of Bible texts in the back of the Bible on an empty page as a guide.

2. Go to the first text in the Bible and copy the next text beside it. Go to the next one and repeat the process until they are all chain referenced.

3. Have the student present the study to family and/or friends.

4. In each student lesson there is one or more sections that have a Bible marking study on the subject studied. (See the Student Section, pages 32, 55, 72, 74, 111,133, 168, 188, 216, 239, 271, 294, 320, and 347.)

C. Evaluate Your Student's Character

This section is for the purpose of helping the teacher know how to encourage the students in becoming more **alert**. See page 8.

Placement

Place I = Grades 2-3-4
Place II = Grades 4-5-6
Place III = Grades 6-7-8

D. Familiarize Yourself With Addition
– Notice the Projects
6-arts
Projects

1. Do story problems with the family while working. (Example: add 8 rocks from the garden to the rock pile for father, 7 for mother, 5 for each child—What is the total of rocks added to the rock pile? Be **alert** to not lose the numbers. [A younger child could write the problem with a stick in the dirt.])

2. Use the addition flash cards if needed while you walk, ride, and work.

3. Explain addition in relation to your Bible story this week. Find a Bible verse that uses the word <u>add</u> in it and tells about character (Example: II Peter 1:3-11). Use II Peter verses as a story problem. How many steps on the ladder? Find two more Bible verses on addition.

4. Keep the checkbook for the family for several months. The student could also set up his own checking/savings account.

5. The student could study from the Bible information about addition. Then have him present a talk on it.

6. Next time the family goes out to eat give the child cash to pay the ticket. He can add up the slip to be sure it is correct and check to be sure the right change is made.

7. An older child can add up in his mind purchases at the store before they are paid for. Ask him for a total before you check out. How do they match up?

8. Purchase a large map of Palestine in the time of Christ. Use the enclosed Mileage chart to do addition problems following the travels of Christ through the land of His birth.

9. An activity with numbers: (1) One person thinks of a number in the Bible, such as: 6, for the days of creation. (2) When he is ready he says: "My number is six." (3) The rest think of something connected with the number from the Bible or nature. (4) Let everyone take a turn.

10. Do more research about how the people in Bible time reckoned time, the money they used, or the weights and measurements of that time.

E. Review the Scripture References for "Addition"

Teacher, read through this section before working on the lesson with the student. See the Student Section pages 32, 55, 72, 74, 111,133, 168, 188, 216, 239, 271, 294, 320, and 347.

F. Notice the Answer Key

The Answer Key for the student book is found on page 9.

Step 3

Read the Lesson Aim.

Lesson Aim

This lesson is to teach the child how addition is taught in the Bible and to practice as many problems as he needs. Help your child to be **alert** to do each problem correctly.

You should help your child understand, that by giving His Son, God made it possible for each person to

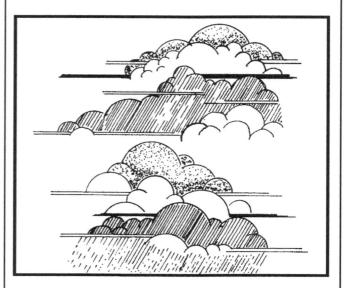

be added back into the heavenly family.

With intense interest the unfallen worlds had watched to see Jehovah arise, and subtract the inhabitants of the Earth from the universe due to their rebellion against Him. And, if God should do this, Satan was ready to carry out his plan for securing to himself the allegiance of heavenly beings. At this crisis moment, God put into operation His plan to ultimately add the inhabitants of Earth back into harmony with the rest of the universe. He sent His Son! With what **alertness** Heaven works with each soul, to add him back to God's kingdom. We also must be **alert** to watch for souls.

Jesus is coming soon, *"Therefore let us not sleep, as do others; but let us watch and be sober."* (I Thessalonians 5:6)

Step 4

Prepare to begin the Addition Lesson.

To Begin the Addition Lesson

As an introduction to the lesson, it would be helpful if the teacher could have the student add up the current ages of all family members. Then remind him how many years God has thus far been working with each soul in his family.

Step 5

Begin the Addition lesson. Cover only what can be understood by your student. Make the lessons a family project by all being involved in part or all of the lesson. These lessons are designed for the whole family.

Steps in Bible Study

1. Prayer

2. Read the verses/meditate/memorize.

3. Look up key words in *Strong's Concordance* and find their meaning in the Hebrew or Greek dictionary in the back of that book.

4. Cross reference (marginal reference) with other Bible texts. An excellent study tool is *The Treasury of Scripture Knowledge.*

5. Use Bible custom books for more information on the times.

6. Write a summary of what you have learned from those verses.

7. Mark key thoughts in the margin of your Bible.

8. Share your study with others to reinforce the lessons you have learned.

Review Questions

1. Does God have a time table? (Ecclesiastes 3:1-15)

2. To whom was the angel Gabriel sent? (Luke 1:26-27)

3. In what city did Mary live? (Luke 1:26)

4. Who was to be Mary's husband? (Luke 1:27)

5. How did the angel greet her? (Luke 1:28)

6. What did the angel say to remove her fear? (Luke 1:29-30)

7. Who did he say should be born to her? (Luke 1:31-33)

8. What does "Jesus" mean? (From the Hebrew word Joshua meaning "Yahweh is salvation")

9. What did the angel say of His throne and kingdom? (Luke 1:32-33)

10. What would He be called? (Luke 1:31)

11. When did God send His Son to this earth? (Galatians 4:4)

12. **Thought Question:** Why was it necessary for Christ to come to earth as a man to save man? (He came to fulfil what Adam failed to do—in the flesh He lived a perfect example of righteousness.)

Prophecy 36

70 Weeks, or 490 years				
457 B.C. Decree	408 B.C. Jerusalem Rebuilt	27 A.D. Jesus Anointed (Baptism)	31 A.D. Jesus' Death	34 A.D. Gospel to the Gentiles

A chart of the seventy weeks of the prophecy of Daniel as found in Daniel 9:24-27.
The period begins at 457 B.C. and extends to Stephen's death.

Mileage Map of Palestine

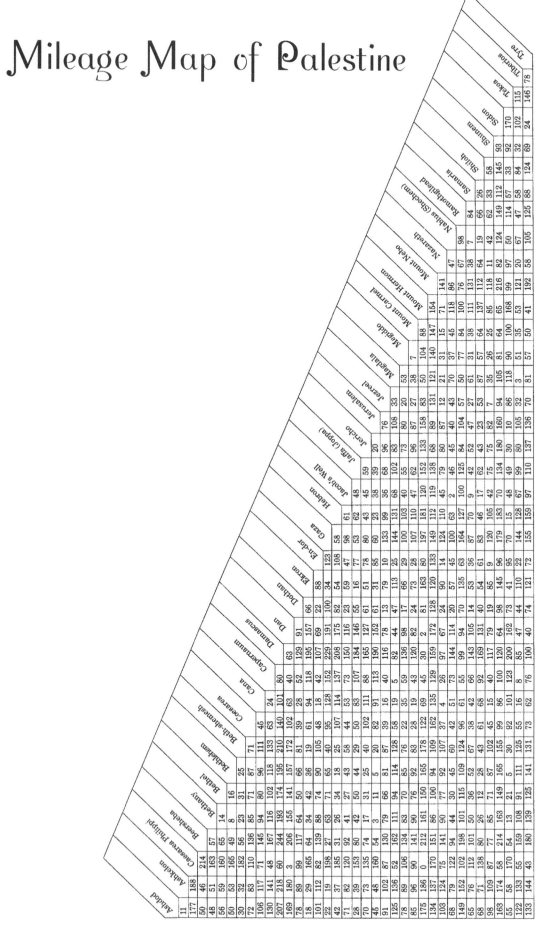

Addition 1 – Teacher – Page 7

Evaluating Your Child's Character

Check the appropriate box for your student's level of development,
or your own, as the case may be.

Maturing Nicely (MN), Needs Improvement (NI), Poorly Developed (PD), Absent (A)

Alertness

1. Does the child show **alertness** and recognize opportunities and dangers on his own?

MN NI PD A
❏   ❏   ❏   ❏

2. Is the child able to visualize the consequences of subtle dangers and act according to the wisdom of Scripture? *"A prudent man forseeth the evil, and hideth himself."* (Proverbs 22:3)

MN NI PD A
❏   ❏   ❏   ❏

3. Does the child act quickly upon command?

MN NI PD A
❏   ❏   ❏   ❏

4. Is the child sluggish in the morning?

Yes   No
❏   ❏

5. Is the child **alert** to the special needs of others about him?

MN NI PD A
❏   ❏   ❏   ❏

6. Is the child **alert** to his daily time with the Lord?

MN NI PD A
❏   ❏   ❏   ❏

7. Is the child **alert** to not listening to whisperers and talebearers?

MN NI PD A
❏   ❏   ❏   ❏

8. Is the child **alert** to use his time wisely?

MN NI PD A
❏   ❏   ❏   ❏

9. Is the child **alert** to talking with the Lord in prayer?

MN NI PD A
❏   ❏   ❏   ❏

Answer Key

Page 5

(1) Numbers, sum
(2) Addition
(3) Added, carried forward
(4) Higher
(5) Added
(6) They experience pleasure and pain, they have instincts to help them survive, and have the ability to love and serve man.
(7) Capacity of loving and serving God
(8) Man is the natural ruler and care-taker of this lower world as God is the natural ruler and care-taker of all the universe (this includes the world and man).

Page 7

Day 1, Day 2, Day 3, Day 4, Day 5
Day 6, Day 7

Page 8

1. Add
Day 1 – Light/energy
Day 2 – Atmosphere/gases
Day 3 – Solids, Plant life
Day 4 – Sun, moon, and stars
Day 5 – Living Creatures in the water, winged fowl
Day 6 – Living creatures, cattle, creeping things, beasts, and man

Page 8 continued

2. Multiply
A. moving creatures
B. fowl

A. male and female

3. Divide
light, darkness
water, water
day, night

Page 18

$$\begin{array}{r} 3\ 2\ 1 \\ +\ 1\ 1\ 1 \\ \hline 4\ 3\ 2 \end{array}$$

Page 20

Another word for zero is "cipher."

Page 21

(1)   no
1, 2, 3, 4, 5, 6
7, 8, 9, 10, 11, 12
(2)   no
337, 349, 622, 965, 737, 728
(3) N. = 133, 122, 151, 108, 125, 177
     O. = 176, 74, 93, 99, 134, 136
     T. = 1025, 614, 1162, 1572, 1231, 1611

Page 22

H. = 691, 1162, 799, 1499, 1278, 1197
I. = 547, 749, 1169, 1559, 1138, 1338
N. = 866, 1035, 1538, 1443, 1361, 1259
G. = 1096, 1369, 1290, 1493, 1299, 1069

Page 24

(1) W. = (3 + 7) + (8 + 2) + 2 =
    10 + 10 + 2 = 22

I. = 4 + 4 + 3 + 3 + 3 + 3 + 6 =
    (4 + 3) + 3 + (4 + 3) + 3 + 6 =
    (7 + 3) + (7 + 3) + 6 =
    10 + 10 + 6 = 26

T. = (5 + 5) + (3 + 7) + (9 + 1) + 10 =
    10 + 10 + 10 + 10 = 40

N. = 5 + 5 + 2 + 10 + 1 + 9 + 8 =
    10 + 10 + (9 + 1) + (2 + 8) =
    10 + 10 + 10 + 10 = 40

E. = 3 + 3 + 2 + 7 + 7 + 2 + 6 =
    (3 + 7) + (3 + 7) + (2 + 2) + 6 =
    10 + 10 + (4 + 6) =
    10 + 10 + 10 = 30

S. = 9 + 1 + 1 + 3 + 10 + 4 + 10 +
    2 + 6 =
    (9 + 1) + (4 + 6) + 10 + 10 +
    (1 + 3) + 2 =
    10 + 10 + 10 + 10 + (4 + 2) =
    10 + 10 + 10 + 10 + 6 = 46

S. = (8 + 2) + 8 + 10 + 2 + 10 =
    10 + (8 + 2) + 10 + 10 =
    10 + 10 + 10 + 10 = 40

Page 32

1.
I, first
I, first
I
I, Alpha, first
first
I, Alpha, beginning, first

2. Genesis

3. Light (energy)

4. *"Thou shalt have no other gods before me."*

5. Body, Spirit, hope of your calling, Lord, faith, baptism, God and Father of all

Page 33

6. Genesis 1:9

7. She was created from one of Adam's ribs.

8. *"One language, and of one speech"*

9. Teacher, check.

Other Bible Firsts

• *"And God blessed them, and God said unto them, Be fruitful, and multiply, and replenish the earth, and subdue it: and have dominion over the fish of the sea, and over the*

Other Bible Firsts continued

fowl of the air, and over every living thing that moveth upon the earth."
• *"Ye shall not surely die."*
• Cain
• Enoch
• Jabal
• Jubal
• Tubal-cain
• Adam
• Ararat
• Hagar
• Esau and Jacob
• Moses
• Aaron, Nadab, Abihu, Eleazar, and Ithamar
• Saul

Page 36

(1) 2, 3, 4, 5, 6, 7
     8, 9, 10, 11, 12, 13
One spelled out several times.

Page 37

(2) 10, 6, 3, 7, 12, 4
    2, 9, 13, 5, 8, 11

(3) 2, 8, 5, 4, 10
    8, 4, 6, 7, 9
    6, 5, 9, 3, 7

Adam lived 130 years before Seth was born.

1 = <u>hundreds</u>   3 = <u>tens</u>   0 = <u>ones</u>

Page 38

(4) 7, 10, 12, 4, 6, 13
    9, 3, 11, 5, 8, 2
    5, 11, 2, 8, 6, 3
    12, 10, 7, 4, 13, 9

(5) 2, 3, 4
    5, 6, 7
    6, 7, 8
    9, 9, 10
    11, 12, 13

Page 39

(1) Divine nature combined with human nature to give sinful man a Saviour.

    23, 27, 28, 29, 29, 26
    36, 36, 34, 38, 41, 44
    49, 47, 51, 49, 49, 53
    62, 60, 60, 66, 61, 63
    70, 75, 70, 75, 76, 78

Page 40

81, 86, 91, 84, 88, 86
96, 95, 99, 97, 100, 101

(2) 18, 21, 18   27, 30, 27
    16, 23, 15   30, 25, 23
    17, 20, 21   37, 42, 39
    26, 27, 27   39, 44, 45

(3) 10, 30, 50, 60, 70, 90, 100, 110
    130, 140, 150, 170, 180, 200

Page 41

Teacher, check.

Page 42

(1) F. = (8 + 2) + (6 + 4) + 5 =
     10 + 10 + 5 = 25
     2 x 10 = 20 + 5 = 25

   A. = (7 + 3) + (9 + 1) + 5 =
     10 + 10 + 5 = 25
     2 x 10 = 20 + 5 = 25

   M .= (6 + 4) + 10 + (6 + 3) =
     10 + 10 + 9 = 29
     2 x 10 = 20 + 9 = 29

   I. = (9 + 1) + 11 + 4 + 3 + 5 =
     10 + 11 + 4 + 3 + 5 = 33

   L. = 10 + (8 + 2) + (1 + 9) +
        (12 + 4) =
     10 + 10 + 10 + 16 = 46
     3 x 10 = 30 + 16 = 46

   Y. = (5 + 5) + (7 + 3) + (9 + 1) +
        (11 + 8) + 6 =
     10 + 10 + 10 + (19 + 6) = 55
     3 x 10 = 30 + 25 = 55

F   A   M   I   L   Y

Page 43

(2) A. = 30, L. = 30, E. = 45, R. = 60,
    T. = 65

(3) S. = (5 + 4 + 1) + (7 + 3) + (7 + 3) =
     10 + 10 + 10 = 30
     3 x 10 = 30

  E. = (9 + 1) + (8 + 2) + (6 + 6) + 3
     10 + 10 + (12 + 3) = 35
     2 x 10 = 20 + 15 = 35

  T. = (7 + 3) + (2 + 8) + (6 + 5)
     10 + 10 + 11 = 31
     2 x 10 = 20 + 11 = 31

  H. = (4 + 6) + (11 + 12) + (3 + 2) =
     10 + 23 + 5 = 38

  E. = (2 + 8) + (7 + 3) + (6 + 5)
     10 + 10 + 11 = 31
     2 x 10 = 20 + 11 = 31

  N. = (5 + 4 + 1) + (6 + 3) + 2 =
     10 + 9 + 2 = 21

  O. = (5 + 3 + 2) + (7 + 3) + 4 =
     10 + 10 + 4 = 24
     10 x 2 = 20 + 4 = 24

  C. = (9 + 1) + (8 + 2) + (7 + 3) +
        (6 + 4) + 5 =
     10 + 10 + 10 + 10 + 5 = 45
     10 x 4 = 40 + 5 = 45

Page 44 continued

H. = (9 + 1) + (7 + 3) + (5 + 5) +
        (7 + 6) + 2
      10 + 10 + 10 + 13 + 2 = 45
      3 x 10 = 30 + (13 + 2) =
      30 + 15 = 45

Page 45
(1) 1, 8, 8, 9
(2) 1, 3, 3, 3

Page 46

(1) 22, (2) 24, (3) 15, (4) 80

1. Shem   5. Noah's wife
2. Ham   6. Shem's wife
3. Japheth   7. Ham's wife
4. Noah   8. Japheth's wife

Page 47

(1) Teacher, check.
(2) 34
(3) Cain, Abel, Seth, Seth
(9 + 1) + (6 + 12) + (9 + 14) + 8 = 59
10 + 18 + 23 + 8 = 59

Friends—Teacher, check.

Page 49

3, 4, 5

Page 55

1. *"In the beginning God created the heaven and the earth. And the earth was without form, and void; and darkness was upon the face of the deep."*

2. Exodus

3. Genesis 1:16

4. Lamech

5. Two by two

6. Sodom

7. Laban

Page 56

8. *"Two tables of testimony, tables of stone"*

9. In two parts

10. The man who had two sons and asked each one to go work in his vineyard.

A man who gave to each of his servants a different number of talents.

The creditor which had two debtors.

11. Revelation 13:11

Page 58

(1) 3, 4, 5, 6, 7, 8
   9, 10, 11, 12, 13, 14
   Two spelled out several times.

Page 59

(2) 6, 12, 8, 4, 10, 13
   7, 11, 3, 14, 9, 5
   7, 10, 14, 3, 6, 4
   12, 9, 5, 11, 13, 8

Page 60

4, four; 7, seven; 11, eleven; 2, two
6, six; 8, eight

Page 63

(1) 9, 11, 6, 11, 4, 1
   9, 3, 7, 13, 6, 3
   7, 10, 10, 14, 4, 8
   12, 5, 8, 2, 12, 5
(2) 10
(3) 3

Page 64

Page 65

(1) 4, 55, 61, 71, 20, Total = 211
The average was 8.44 (211 ÷ 25)

Page 66

(2) 27, 35, 41, 28, 35, 34, Total = 200
11 homes were not visited (211 - 200)

Page 68

Adam, Seth, Enoch, Noah

Page 71

One who gives testimony of a fact or event.

Page 74

1. Dry land—earth, seas, grass, the herb yielding seed, the fruit tree yielding fruit whose seed is in itself.

2. Jonah was in the belly of the fish 3 days and on the 3rd day the fish *"vomited out Jonah upon the dry land."* So Christ was in the tomb for 3 days and on the 3rd day rose from the dead.

3. *"It was the third hour, and they crucified him"*

4. Leviticus

Page 75

5. Holy, holy, holy

6. God and 2 angels

7. *"Three measures of fine meal"* made into cakes

8. *"A bullock a meat offering of three tenth deals of flour mingled with half an hin of oil."*

9. Offering

10. *"The kingdom of heaven is like unto leaven, which a woman took, and hid in three measures of meal, till the whole was leavened."*

11. Feast of unleavened bread, feast of harvest, and feast of ingathering

12. *"Three days' journey into the desert"*

13. One cluster of grapes, pomegranates, and figs

14. *"All the words which the LORD hath said will we do."*

Page 76

15. Jordan

16. The fig tree that did not bare any fruit and was going to be cut down.

Page 76 continued

17. The widow of Nain's son, a certain ruler's daughter, Lazarus

18. King, Priest, Prophet

19. One hundred men at Gilgal, four thousand men beside women and children at Bethsaida, and five thousand men beside women and children at a later time.

20. God's friend

21. Christian/s

Page 77

22. Greek, Latin, and Hebrew

23. *"a great sheet...Wherein were all manner of fourfooted beasts of the earth, and wild beasts, and creeping things, and fowls of the air."*

24. *"And now abideth faith, hope, charity, these three; but the greatest of these is charity."*

Page 80

(1) 4, 5, 6, 7, 8, 9
10, 11, 12, 13, 14, 15
5, 8, 13, 10, 4, 11
6, 9, 12, 15, 7, 14

Page 81

(1) 7, 1, 0, 2, 7, 1
    7, 9, 9, 5, 8, 1
    6, 5, 3, 2, 1, 5
    2, 8, 2, 8, 1, 9
    3, 4, 3, 1, 5, 4

Page 82

(2) 5, 5
    5, 9
    5, 7
    2, 1
    9, 5

Page 84

(1) P. = 63, 48, 79
    E. = 96, 113, 102
    R. = 99, 172, 131
    F. = 123, 133, 103
    E. = 121, 175, 122
    C. = 30, 89, 45
    T. = 41, 73, 64

    W.= 159, 81, 120
    I. = 60, 47, 60
    T. = 124, 120, 111
    N.= 133, 101, 118
    E. = 118, 118, 99
    S. = 85, 151, 128
    S. = 69, 95, 68
c o m p l e t e n e s s
e n t i r e n e s s

Page 85

Century

Page 87

15, 13, 12
Shem, faith

Page 88

(1) 4, 9, 6, 2, Shem

Page 89

(2) 2, 3, 4, 4, 17

Page 90

(3) 2, 3, 4, 6, 8, 17

Page 91

(4) 11, 7, 3, 10, 5, 13
    8, 2, 9, 12, 4, 6
    5, 13, 8, 10, 3, 6
    14, 9, 4, 7, 11, 12
    7, 12, 15, 10, 8, 13
    5, 11, 9, 6, 14, 4

Three spelled out at least three (3) times.

Page 92

8, 12, 6	14, 15, 11
8, 8, 12	4, 7, 7
5, 3, 15	13, 13, 5
4, 9, 10	9, 3, 12
12, 6, 4	7, 10, 6
11, 5, 2	11, 13, 10
9, 11, 10	13, 8, 15

Page 93

(5) 13, 8, 6, 13, 4, 10
    9, 5, 13, 7, 10, 4
    7, 11, 12, 7, 5, 9
    11, 2, 10, 4, 15, 8
    9, 12, 6, 5, 11, 14
    3, 8, 3, 14, 12, 6
    3, 3, 4, 4, 5, 5
    3, 4, 5
    3, 4, 5

Page 94

(1)

41	14	10	12	18	34
17	11	21	36	20	22
+31	+33	+64	+21	+41	+43
89	58	95	69	79	99

76	11	24	10	12	13
13	23	51	46	32	14
+10	+42	+13	+43	+55	+22
99	76	88	99	99	49

40	24	55	45	35	25
42	51	22	31	14	12
+17	+14	+21	+13	+20	+50
99	89	98	89	69	87

15	23	35	42	16	65
32	45	31	15	32	24
+51	+21	+33	+43	+51	+12
98	89	99	100	99	101

The divine nature and human nature combined.

Page 94 continued

(2) 89, 81, 70,
    61, 94, 85
    87, 98, 102
(3) Teacher, check.

Notes

Page 96

(1) D. = 33 + 13 = 46   17 + 85 = 102   78 + 52 = 130
    E. = 44 + 84 = 128 76 + 72 = 148   34 + 25 = 59
    L. = 18 + 12 = 30   73 + 45 = 118   80 + 58 = 138

    I. = 40 + 46 + 42 = 128   30 + 32 + 35 = 97
    V. = 12 + 33 + 47 = 92   47 + 27 + 63 = 137
    E. = 45 + 52 + 33 = 130   41 + 13 + 58 = 112
    R. = 61 + 22 + 37 = 120   37 + 55 + 82 = 174
    E. = 13 + 28 + 75 = 116   57 + 41 + 75 = 173
    R. = 33 + 15 + 32 = 80   87 + 42 + 72 = 201

    W.= 35 + 48 + 97 = 180   79 + 63 + 96 = 238
    I. = 55 + 36 + 42 = 133   87 + 64 + 81 = 232
    L. = 43 + 14 + 35 = 92   92 + 42 + 62 = 196
    L. = 23 + 60 + 48 = 131   28 + 71 + 35 = 134

    C. = 36 + 70 + 49 = 155   39 + 82 + 46 = 167
    O.= 47 + 60 + 50 = 157   40 + 93 + 57 = 190
    M. = 35 + 58 + 23 = 116   46 + 69 + 34 = 149
    E. = 17 + 38 + 57 = 112   27 + 46 + 37 = 110

"The days are prolonged, and every vision faileth."

Page 97

Innumerable
Countless
Numerous
Infinite
Unnumbered
Incomputable
Abundant
Profuse
Plenteous
Bountiful

Page 98

(1) Row 1 has 6 seeds.
    Row 2 has 6 seeds.
    Row 3 has 6 seeds.

Page 99

(2) Row 1 has 12 or 18 ears.
    Row 2 has 12 or 18 ears.
    <u>Row 3 has 12 or 18 ears.</u>
    Total   36 or 54 ears.

(3) Isaac

Page 100

(4) 7

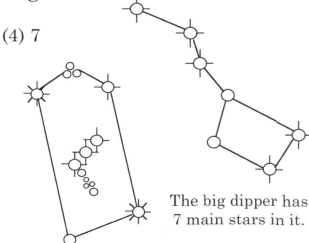

Orion has 15
main stars in it.

The big dipper has
7 main stars in it.

Page 101

(1) 4 + 23 + 22 = 49
(2) 16 + 14 + 7 = 37
(3) 29

Page 102

(1) 114 light years
(2) Rigel is in the constellation Orion. 1190 light years
(3) 376 light years

Page 109

Creation

Page 110

Jacob, Esau

Page 111

1. Sun, moon, and stars

2. Cherubims

3. Teacher, check.

4. Numbers

5. The Sabbath

6. Miriam, Deborah, Huldah, Noadiah

7. Daniel, Hananiah, Mishael, and Azariah

Page 112

8. Hananiah (Shadrach), Mishael (Meshach), Azariah (Abednego), and Jesus

9. Nebuchadnezzar, Belteshazzar, Darius, and Cyrus

10. Dragon, old serpent, devil, Satan

11. Fowl, vulture, lion's whelps, fierce lion

12. Ants, conies, locusts, and the spider

13. The way side, stony places, among thorns, good ground

14. The best robe, a ring, shoes, and the fatted calf

15. *"Carry neither purse, nor scrip, nor shoes: and salute no man by the way."*

16. Signs, wonders, divers miracles, and gifts of the Holy Ghost

17. Eve

18. Troubled on every side, perplexed, persecuted, and cast down

Page 117

(1) 5, 6, 7, 8, 9, 10
    11, 12, 13, 14, 15, 16
    14, 12, 10, 5, 9, 15
    11, 6, 8, 13, 7, 16
    10, 7, 16, 12, 9, 6
    14, 13, 11, 5, 15, 8

Four spelled out four (4) times.

Page 118

(2) 3, 2, 6, 2

Page 119

2, 2
(3) 0, 1, 2, 3, 4, 5, 6
    7, 8, 9, 10, 11, 12, 13
    14, 15, 16, 17, 18, 19, 20
       21 numbers

Page 120

(4) 5, 4, 6, 4, 7, 4
    5, 6, 7
    5, 6, 7
(5) 7, 14, 13, 10, 5, 15
    12, 8, 11, 16, 6, 9
    15, 8, 6, 13, 9, 14
    10, 5, 12, 16, 7, 11

Page 121

(6) 10, 6, 7   15, 8, 13
    13, 12, 14   5, 11, 16
    11, 9, 12

Page 121 continued

(7) 0
    1, 2, 3, 4
    5, 6, 7, 8
    9, 10, 11, 12

Page 122

(8) 4, 12, 4, 12, 8, 12
    4, 8, 12, 8, 8, 16
    13, 5, 13, 5, 13, 5
    13, 9, 5, 9, 9, 9
    10, 6, 10, 15, 10, 2
    14, 10, 6, 6, 14, 6
    7, 11, 11, 3, 11, 7
    11, 15, 7, 14, 3, 7

Page 124

See pages 21-23 of the "Answer Key" for the answers to these problems.

Page 125

(1)
C. = 164, 188, 172, 196, 204, 163
R. = 157, 747, 1330, 539, 1101, 1176
E. = 306, 1937, 1912, 1347, 2155, 2647

Page 126

A. = 1841, 2100, 1720, 1976, 2087, 1513
T. = 562, 1578, 1026, 1324, 952, 1212
I. = 3054, 5143, 4386, 2611, 3398, 3606
O. = 2898, 3963, 3097
N. = 3232, 3887, 4526, 3011

Teacher, check for correct set-up like the problems set up on page 125 and 126 C, R, E, A, T, or I.

Page 124

(1) D. 316 pounds
     + 400 pounds
       716 pounds

____

E. (1) 229 yards 165 inches
        + 53 yards 356 inches
        282 yards 521 inches

(2)   14 yds. r 17 in.
    36 inches) 521 inches
                36
                161
                144
                17 remainder

3)   229 yards 165 inches
    + 53 yards 356 inches
      282 yards 521 inches
    + 14   17 inches
      296 yards 17 inches

____

F. (1) 133 weeks 85 days
       + 96 weeks 45 days
        229 weeks 130 days

(2)   18 wks. r 4 days
    7 days) 130 days
             7
             60
             56
             4 remainder

(3) 133 weeks 85 days
    + 96 weeks 45 days
     229 weeks 130 days
    + 18 weeks   4 days
      247 weeks   4 days

Page 124 continued

(2)   (1)   6 years   9 months   (2)   1yr. r 1 mo.

           +   3 years   4 months   12 mo.)13 mo.

             9 years   13 months   12

       (3) +   1 year   1 month   1 remainder

            10 years   1 month

N.   (1)   4 days   12 hours   *No conversion necessary as

           +   9 days   7 hours   19 hours is smaller than 24

             13 days   19 hours   hours. 24 hours = 1 day.

---

       (1)   18 gallons   6 quarts   (2)   2 gal. r 2 qts.

           +   3 gallons   4 quarts   4 qts.)10 qts.

             21 gallons   10 quarts   8

       (3) +   2 gallons   2 quarts   2 remainder

             23 gallons   2 quarts

---

       (1)   17 feet   8 inches   (2)   1 ft. r 2 in.

           +   9 feet   6 inches   12 in.)14 in.

             26 feet   14 inches   12 in.

       (3) +   1 foot   2 inches   2 remainder

             27 feet   2 inches

I.   (1)   47 pounds   6 ounces   (2)   1 lb. r 2 oz.

           + 18 pounds   12 ounces   16 oz.)18 oz.

             65 pounds   18 ounces   16 oz.

       (3) +   1 pound   2 ounces   2 remainder

             66 pounds   2 ounces

---

       (1)   9 gallons 10 quarts   (2)   4 gal. r 0 qts.

           +   7 gallons   6 quarts   4 qts.)16 qts.

             16 gallons 16 quarts   16

       +   4 gallons   0 quarts   0 remainder

             20 gallons   0 quarts

Page 124 continued

T.

(1)
```
    22 feet      18 inches
  + 17 feet       5 inches
    39 feet      23 inches
(3) +  1 foot    11 inches
    40 feet      11 inches
```

(2)
```
            1 ft. r 11 in.
12 in. ) 23 in.
            12
            11 remainder
```

(1)
```
    19 yards      8 feet
  + 13 yards      4 feet
    32 yards     12 feet
(3) +  4 yards    0 feet
    36 yards      0 feet
```

(2)
```
            4 yds. r 0 in.
3 ft. ) 12 ft.
            12
            0 remainder
```

E.

(1)
```
    21 yards      5 feet
  + 18 yards      3 feet
    39 yards      8 feet
(3) +  2 yards    2 feet
    41 yards      2 feet
```

(2)
```
            2 yds. r 2 ft.
3 ft. ) 8 ft.
            6
            2 remainder
```

(1)
```
    11 hours    25 minutes
  +  9 hours    16 minutes
    20 hours    41 minutes
```

*No conversion necessary as 41 minutes is less than 60 minutes. 60 minutes = 1 hour.

(3) Teacher, check.

Page 126 continued

Creation

Page 133

1. "...Whales, and every living creature that moveth, which the waters brought forth abundantly, after their kind, and every winged fowl after his kind...."

Page 133 continued

2. Deuteronomy

3. Head of gold, breast and arms of silver, belly and thighs of brass, legs of iron, feet part of iron and part of clay

4. Smooth stones

Page 133 continued

5. *"And five of you shall chase an hundred, and an hundred of you shall put ten thousand to flight: and your enemies shall fall before you by the sword."*

Page 139

(1) 6, 7, 8, 9, 10, 11
    12, 13, 14, 15, 16, 17
(2) 9, 14, 12, 7, 13, 8
    11, 16, 10, 17, 15, 13
    6, 13, 16, 7, 9, 12
    8, 11, 15, 10, 17, 14

Page 140

(3) 13, 10, 15   14, 11, 16
    18, 16, 6   15, 8, 6
    11, 9, 14   12, 7, 9
    13, 14, 13   16, 14, 15
    17, 9, 10   11, 17, 12
    8, 7, 12

Page 141

(4)
1. beginning, divine unity
2. difference, fullness of testimony
3. reality, completeness, entireness
4. creation
5. grace, favor
(5) 15, 10, 11, 13, 6, 12
    3, 5, 13, 9, 7, 8
    4, 12, 14, 10, 11, 7
    8, 12, 9, 5, 16, 6
    10, 11, 13, 7, 4, 8

Page 142

15, 5, 9, 17, 11, 6
16, 12, 8, 5, 6, 14
10, 3, 6, 14, 8, 14
10, 13, 9, 9, 12, 2
13, 7, 7, 4, 15, 11

Page 143

(6)   6, 6, 7, 7
     8, 8, 9, 9
     5, 5, 6, 6
     7, 7, 8, 8, 4, 4
     4, 5, 6, 6, 7, 7

Page 145

(1)
A. = 12 in. , 4 ft. x 12 in. = 48 in.
L. = 3 ft., 8 yds. x 3 ft. = 24 ft.
E. = 4 qts., 6 gal. x 4 qts. = 24 qts.
R. = 2 gal. x 8 pts. = 16 pts., 4 gal. x
    8 pts. = 32 pts.
T. = 16 oz., 6 lbs. x 16 oz. = 96 oz.
F. = 2,000 lbs., 4 tons x 2000 lbs. =
    8000 lbs.
A. = 60 min., 3 hrs. x 60 min. = 180 min.
M. = 12 mo., 7 yrs. x 12 mo. = 84 mo.
I. = 12 items, 5 doz. x 12 = 60 items
L. = 6 ft. x 12 in. = 72 in. + 4 in. =
76 in. 4 gal. x 4 qts. = 16 qts. + 2 qts.
    = 18 qts.
I. = 5 gal. x 8 pts. = 40 pts. + 4 pts. =
44 pts. 3 lbs. x 16 oz. = 48 oz. + 9 oz. =
    57 oz.
E. = 6 hrs. x 60 min. = 360 min. +
    25 min. = 385 min.
S. 5 yrs. x 12 mo. = 60 mo. + 6 mo. =
    66 mo.

Page 146

(1)
F. = 177, 206, 208, 179, 179, 155
A. = 219, 195, 233, 186, 132, 125
V. = 181, 195, 60, 215, 122, 214
0. = 273, 251, 220, 174, 163, 153

Page 147

R. = 219, 195, 167, 187, 166, 244
G. = 2137, 3077, 2039, 1993, 2781, 2488
R. = 3401, 2694, 2749, 2201, 1755, 2423
A. = 25637, 18180, 9100, 22760, 13060
C. = 23027, 30528, 24042, 29199, 24412

Page 148

E. = 26090, 32387, 361439, 342867

Notes

Page 149

(1)   8
(2)   4
(3)   12

Page 150

(1)   60
(2)   405

Page 151

Jacob Family = 45
Heh Family = 40
Johnson Family = 83 going right;
        62 going left
Hurley Family = 57

Page 152

(1)   2, 3, 4, 5, 6, 7
        8, 9, 10, 11, 12, 13
        3, 4, 5, 6, 7, 8
        9, 10, 11, 12, 13, 14
        4, 5, 6, 7, 8, 9
        10, 11, 12, 13, 14, 15

Page 153

        5, 6, 7, 8, 9, 10
        11, 12, 13, 14, 15, 16
        6, 7, 8, 9, 10, 11
        12, 13, 14, 15, 16, 17
(2)   11, 10, 15, 4, 6, 5
        12, 9, 8, 9, 9, 13
        11, 6, 3, 8, 13, 12
        4, 14, 10, 8, 16, 8

Page 154

17, 5, 13, 13, 7, 15
6, 2, 9, 11, 11, 11
7, 13, 5, 7, 7, 16
9, 8, 6, 10, 14, 10
12, 3, 15, 4, 12, 5
14, 10, 6, 12, 7, 14

Page 155

(3)   14, 14, 14
        fourteen, fourteen, fourteen

Page 156

(4)   14, 28, 23, 26, 28, 42, 42
(5)   5, 4, 5, 14, 7, 2, 9

Page 157

(6)   19
        14
        28
        14   28   42
        42

Five spelled out five (5) times

Page 158

(1)
2 yrs. x 12 mo. = 24 mo. + 9 mo. = 33 mo. / 4 yrs. x 12 mo. = 48 mo. + 6 mo. = 54 mo.
3 wks. x 7 days = 21 days + 5 days = 26 days / 22 days
18 wks / 5 wks. x 7 days = 35 days + 4 days = 39 days
1 hr. x 60 min. = 60 min. + 35 min. = 95 min. / 3 hrs. x 60 min. = 180 min. + 20 min. =
    200 min.
28 hrs. / 12 ft. x 12 in. = 144 in. + 7 in. = 151 in.
9 ft. x 12 in. = 108 in. + 8 in. = 116 in. / 3 lbs. x 16 oz. = 48 oz. + 14 oz. = 62 oz.
4 lbs. x 16 oz. = 64 oz. + 6 oz. = 70 oz. / 15 lbs.

Page 159

(2)
19 qts. / 98 in. / 66 mo. / 67 oz.
20 ft. / 110 mo. / 72 days / 100 in.
44 in. / 131 min. / 12 ft. / 21 gal.
57 oz. / 44 ft. / 42 days / 25 ft.
93 mo. / 50 in. / 305 min. / 31 qts.
(Teacher check for correct conversion. Use answers in (1) above as examples.

Page 160

(1)
1464, 1615, 2611, 14694, 28889
25808, 17999, 26024, 208454
19533, 123979, 252743, 745263

Page 168

1. *"...The beast of the earth after his kind, and cattle after their kind, and every thing that creepeth upon the earth after his kind...."* Also, man and woman.

2. Serpent, adder, viper, asp, cockatrice, fiery flying serpent

Page 168 continued

3. Labour, and do all thy work

4. *"Thou shalt not kill."*

5. Solomon

6. *"And thou shalt set them in two rows, six on a row, upon the pure table before the LORD."*

7. Abraham

8. That He had a devil in Him

Page 169

9. Scribes, Pharisees, Sadducees, disciples, others, Jews

10. Pilate, Herod, Judas, Pilate's wife, thief on the cross, centurion

Page 172

(1) 7, 8, 9, 10, 11, 12
13, 14, 15, 16, 17, 18
(2) 14, 8, 12, 7, 8, 13
11, 7, 9, 16, 15, 12
10, 8, 17, 14, 18, 13
9, 12, 16, 11, 18, 15

Page 173

(3) 14, 11, 18
17, 16, 7
12, 10, 15
14, 15, 14
18, 10, 11
13, 9, 8
15, 12, 18
17, 9, 7
10, 8, 13
17, 15, 16
13, 17, 12

Six spelled out six (6) times.

Page 174

(1) 1. All nations under one government
2. One language was widely spoken
3. Jews in other countries came to Jerusalem to annual feasts from all lands
4. People longed to know God

(2) 1. Many nations united in United Nations
2. The English language is the universal language
3. Travel is quick and easy throughout the world, many countries are friendly with one another
4. People are longing today to know God

Page 175

See answers for page 177 on the next page.

Page 176

(1) T. = when the great clock of time pointed to that hour
I. = 1. all nations under one government
2. one language was widely spoken
3. Jews in other countries came to Jerusalem to annual feasts from all lands
4. people longed to know God
M. = yes

Page 175 (3)

T.	3 min.	13 sec.	4 hrs.	16 min.
	+ 5 min.	42 sec.	+3 hrs.	35 min.
	8 min.	55 sec.	7 hrs.	51 min.

I.	5 hrs.	48 min.	2 min.	43 sec.
	+ 2 hrs.	53 min.	+6 min.	56 sec.
	7 hrs.	101 min.	8 min.	99 sec.
		- 60 min.		- 60 sec.
	8 hrs	41 min.	9 min.	39 sec.

M.	6 min.	53 sec.	3 hrs.	39 min.
	+ 4 min.	41 sec.	+1 hr.	51 min.
	10 min.	94 sec.	4 hrs.	90 min.
		- 60 sec.		- 60 min.
	11 min.	34 sec.	5 hrs.	30 min.

E.	1 hr.	19 min.	7 min.	52 sec.
	+ 3 hrs.	45 min.	+6 min.	17 sec.
	4 hrs.	64 min.	13 min.	69 sec.
		- 60 min.		- 60 sec.
	5 hrs.	4 min.	14 min.	9 sec.

C. = 16 hrs. 33 min.
O. = 22 min. 21 sec.
M. = 10 hrs. 10 min.
E. = 76 min. 27 sec.

Teacher, check students work in arriving at these answers. These must be worked out like the above examples.

Page 176 continued

E. 1. many nations united in United Nations
2. the English language is the universal language
3. travel is quick and easy throughout the world many countries are friendly with one another
4. people are longing today to know God

Page 177

(2)
J. = 1406, 2146, 2416, 3086, 2054, 2755
E. = 25945, 14756, 25426, 31152, 21433
S. = 336193, 197713, 201663, 233482,
     250722
U. = 33457, 37938, 27166, 27450, 29114
S. = 115547, 80392, 208100, 132660,
     182690

Page 178

(1) 5
(2) 7

Page 180

(1)   6:15 am   (5)   10:00 am
(2)   7:15 am   (6)   12:00 pm
(3)   7:30 am   (7)   Teacher,
(4)   1 1/2 hours   check.

Page 181 (1)   90 + 88 + 92 + 91 + 94 + 99 + 97 = 651 (there are 7 addends)

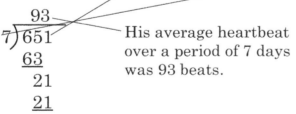

His average heartbeat over a period of 7 days was 93 beats.

```
    93
7)651
   63
   21
   21
    0 remainder
```

(2)   5,655,000
(3)   28
       51
      127
      206

Page 182

(1) Teacher, check.
(2) six, eight

Page 188

1. Judges

2. God and all of His creation rested. *"And God blessed the seventh day, and sanctified it...."*

3. Enoch

4. Every clean beast

5. The animals went into the ark.

6. Jacob. Laban.

7. *"And Pharaoh said unto Joseph, In my dream, behold, I stood upon the bank of the river: And, behold, there came up out of the river seven kine, fatfleshed and well favoured; and they fed in a meadow: And, behold, seven other kine came up after them, poor and very ill favoured and leanfleshed, such as I never saw in all the land of Egypt for badness: And the lean and the ill favoured kine did eat up the first seven fat kine: And when they had eaten them up, it could not be known that they had eaten them; but they were still ill favoured, as at the beginning. So I awoke."*

Page 189

8. *"...All the waters that were in the river...."*

9. Fish, cucumbers, melons, leeks, onions, and garlic. Wheat, barley, vines, fig trees, pomegranates, oil olive, and honey.

10. Jericho

11. Delilah

12. The house of the LORD

13. Child, son, no name

14. Naaman

15. Nebuchadnezzar

16. (1) Ehud, (2) Shamgar, (3) Deborah, (4) Jael, (5) a certain woman whose name is not mentioned, (6) Gideon, (7) Samson.

Page 190

17. (1) Jacob hid the strange gods and earrings of his household under the oak.

(2) Deborah, Rebekah's nurse, died and she was buried beneath Bethel under an oak.

(3) Saul and his sons' bones were buried under a tree.

Page 190 continued

(4) *"Joshua wrote these words in the book of the law of God, and took a great stone, and set it up there under an oak."*

(5) Absalom's head was caught between the branches of a great oak.

(6) *"And there came an angel of the LORD, and sat under an oak...."*

(7) A man of God was found sitting under an oak.

18. (1) Water turned to wine

(2) The nobleman's son healed

(3) The impotent man healed

(4) Over five thousand fed

(5) Blind man restored to sight

(6) Lazarus raised from the dead

(7) An abundance of fish caught during the day

Page 191

19. Seven loaves and a few little fishes

20. Mary Magdalene

21. (1) The sower

(2) The man which sowed good seed in his field and while he slept his enemy came and sowed tares

(3) A grain of mustard seed

(4) The leaven

(5) Hidden treasure

(6) Pearl of great price

(7) The net

22. Stephen, Philip, Prochorus, Nicanor, Timon, Parmenas, and Nicolas

23. Once every seven years

24. "...*On the tenth day of the seventh month....*" Forty-nine.

25. "...*The seventh month, on the tenth day of the month....*"

26. (1) Loins girt about with truth, (2) breastplate of righteousness, (3) feet shod with the preparation of the gospel of peace, (4) shield of faith, (5) helmet of salvation, (6) the sword of the Spirit—which is the word of God, and (7) "*Praying always with all prayer and supplication in the Spirit....*"

27. (1) Evil thoughts, (2) murders, (3) adulteries, (4) fornications, (5) thefts, (6) false witness, (7) blasphemies

28. (1) Prophecy, (2) ministry, (3) teacheth, (4) exhorteth, (5) giveth, (6) ruleth, and (7) showeth mercy

29. (1) Body, (2) Spirit, (3) hope, (4) Lord, (5) faith, (6) baptism, (7) God and Father

30. (1) Pure, (2) peaceable, (3) gentle, (4) easy to be entreated, (5) full of mercy and good fruits, (6) without partiality, and (7) without hypocrisy

31. (1) Virtue, (2) knowledge, (3) temperance, (4) patience, (5) godliness, (6) brotherly kindness, and (7) charity

32. Teacher, check.

Page 194

(1)   8, 9, 10, 11, 12, 13
       14, 15, 16, 17, 18, 19
(2)   15, 9, 13, 8, 9, 14
       12, 8, 10, 17, 16, 13
       11, 9, 18, 15, 19, 14
       10, 13, 17, 12, 19, 16

Page 195

(3)   15, 12, 19
       18, 17, 8
       13, 11, 16
       15, 16, 15
       19, 11, 12
       14, 10, 9
       16, 13, 19
       18, 10, 8
       11, 9, 14
       18, 16, 17
       14, 18, 13

Seven spelled out
seven (7) times

Page 196

(4)   8, 8, 9, 9, 10, 10
       11, 11, 12, 12, 13, 13
(5)   7, 7, 7, 7, 7, 7
       7, 7, 7, 7, 7, 7
(6) 14 (7) 16 (8) 10 (9) 19

Page 197

(10) 11, 5, 9, 10, 3, 13
      14, 12, 11, 15, 6, 15
      12, 7, 14, 10, 13, 12
      12, 8, 3, 11, 5, 16
      9, 11, 2, 13, 10, 10
      7, 17, 8, 6, 15, 9
      6, 18, 11, 8, 10, 16
      4, 7, 9, 14, 9, 16

Page 198

12, 10, 15, 14, 4, 15
19, 8, 14, 11, 17, 14
18, 13, 8, 8, 9, 16
16, 13, 8, 13, 12, 8
7, 9, 13, 5, 17, 14
10, 13, 12, 16, 13, 12
14, 11, 14, 14, 8, 15
4, 14, 10, 12, 12, 6

Page 199

L.   3 days   9 hrs.
    + 2 days   8 hrs.
      5 days   17 hrs.
(No conversion necessary as
17 hrs. is less than 24 hrs.
24 hrs. = 1 day)

      3 wks.   4 days
    + 2 wks.   6 days
      5 wks.   10 days
                − 7 days
      6 wks.   3 days

A.   2 yrs.   116 days
    + 1 yr.   214 days
      3 yrs.   330 days
(No conversion necessary as
10 mo. is less than 12 mo.
12 mo. = 1 yr.)

      4 yrs.   10 mo.
    + 2 yrs.   6 mo.
      6 yrs.   16 mo.
                − 12 mo.
      7 yrs.   4 mo.

N.   1 yr.   6 mo.
    + 2 yrs.   4 mo.
      3 yrs.   10 mo.

      2 days   12 hrs.
    + 3 days   18 hrs.
      5 days   30 hrs.
                − 24 hrs.
      6 days   6 hrs.

G.   5 wks.   5 days
    + 1 wk.   4 days
      6 wks   9 days
                7 days
      7 wks.   2 days

      1 yr.   328 days
    + 1 yr.   224 days
      2 yrs.   552 days
                − 365 days
      3 yrs.   187 days

Page 200

U.
```
    3 yrs.   7 mo.     4 days
    1 yr.    6 mo.     5 days
    4 yrs. 13 mo.      9 days
          – 12 mo.
    5 yrs.   1 mo.     9 days
```

A.
```
    1 day   10 hrs.    45 min.
    3 days  15 hrs.    25 min.
    4 days  25 hrs.    70 min.
         – 24 hrs.  – 60 min.
    5 days   1 hr      10 min.
           + 1 hr
    5 days   2 hrs.    10 min.
```

G.
```
    1 lb.      15 oz.
   +2 lb.      10 oz.
    3 lb.      25 oz.
             – 16 oz.
    4 lb.       9 oz.
```

E.
```
    8 qts.     2 pts.
   +1 qt.      3 pts.
    9 qts.     5 pts.
             – 4 pts.
   11 qts.     1 pt.
```

Page 201

(1)
L. = 2270, 1948, 1483, 1573, 1741, 1611
A. = 2867, 2122, 2763, 2819, 3497, 2560
N. = 136939, 116233, 140959, 171611, 91979
G. = 8515, 11329, 10012, 6901, 10505

Page 202

U. = 31213, 36452, 29860, 24728, 40456
A. = 326769, 310689, 387658, 220793, 319629
G. = 289433
E. = 148055

Page 203

(1)
```
    4      addend
  + 1      addend
    5      sum
```

(2)
```
   14      addend
 +  7      addend
 +  1      addend
   22      sum
```

(3)
```
    5      addend
 + 22      addend
   27      sum
```

Page 204

(1)
```
    2 hrs.    15 min.
  + 1 hr.     45 min.
    3 hrs.    60 min
            – 60 min.
    4 hrs.     0 min.
```

(2)
```
    1hr.      53 min.
  + 1hr.      53 min.
    2 hrs.   106 min.
            – 60 min.
    3 hrs.    46 min.
```

(3)
```
    4 hrs.     0 min.
  + 3 hrs.    46 min.
    7 hrs.    46 min.
```

Page 205

(1)
47% + 22% + 8% + 5% + 4% +
4% + 4% + 3% + 2% + 1% = 100%

Page 206

(2)   8, 28, 4 (40)

Page 216

1. Eight. Noah, Shem, Ham, Japheth, Noah's wife, and the three wives of his sons.

2. He was circumcised

3. David

4. Jesus

5. (1) The son of a widow

(2) The son of the widow of Nain

(3) The son of the Shunammite

Page 217

(4) The daughter of the ruler of the synagogue

(5) The man who was cast on the bones of Elisha

(6) Lazarus

(7, 8) Dorcus, Eutychus

Page 217 continued

6. Feast of Tabernacles

7. (1) He smote the waters and they parted so that he could pass over.

(2) Healed these waters.

(3) He cursed 42 rebellious children and *"there came forth two she bears out of the wood, and tare"* them.

(4) *"...There came water by the way of Edom, and the country was filled with water."*

(5) The oil poured from that one jar continued to flow till all the vessels were filled so that the widow could pay her debt and support her family.

(6) The son of the Shunammite raised from the dead.

(7) Healed the poisoned pottage.

(8) Elisha fed one hundred men with the present brought to him when to all appearances it was not sufficient.

(9) Naaman healed from leprosy.

(10) Gehazi made a leper for his deception.

Page 217 continued

(11) The axhead brought to the surface of the water.

(12) The eyes of the young man were opened and he saw the mountain full of horses and chariots of fire round about Elisha.

(13) A great host smitten with blindness.

(14) The army followed Elisha to another city and then their eyes were opened.

(15) Foretelling the coming of a messenger.

(16) The dead man who was cast on the bones of Elisha revived, and stood up on his feet.

Page 220

(1)   9, 10, 11, 12, 13, 14
       15, 16, 17, 18, 19, 20

(2)   14, 10, 12, 9, 16, 15
       14, 17, 11, 18, 9, 13
       16, 15, 19, 12, 20, 10
       13, 14, 20, 11, 18, 17

Page 221

(3)   9, 13, 18
       19, 20, 16
       14, 12, 17
       16, 17, 16

Page 221 continued

    20, 12, 15
    13, 11, 10
    17, 10, 20
    19, 11, 9
    12, 14, 15
    19, 17, 18
    15, 19, 14

Eight spelled out eight (8) times.

Page 222

(4)   8, 1, 8, 2, 8, 3
       8, 4, 8, 5, 8, 6
(5)   8, 8, 8, 8, 8, 8
       8, 8, 8, 8, 8, 8

Page 223

(6)   15, 20, 13, 12, 17, 13
       16, 19, 16, 13, 9, 9
       17, 17, 16, 17, 19, 15
       11, 15, 14, 16, 12, 19
       12, 18, 16, 14, 15, 16
       14, 14, 13, 17, 18, 16

Page 224

(7)   90, 30, 70, 110, 90, 150
       100, 70, 29, 23, 26, 28
       29, 29, 26, 29, 34, 36
(8)   6, 13, 17, 12, 13, 10
       16, 19, 11, 11, 20, 7
       9, 14, 10, 11, 14, 9
       10, 12, 14, 9, 16, 6

Page 225

    17, 17, 15, 10, 17, 10
    15, 16, 5, 10, 16, 13
    8, 15, 7, 9, 18, 9
    12, 16, 9, 12, 16, 11
    12, 17, 16, 17, 19, 14
    17, 16, 13, 17, 13, 18
    11, 8, 18, 13, 7, 8

Page 226

(1) 389, 879, 896, 138, 676, 577
(2)

F. =	164	39
	20365	732
	8	4234
	4192	

E.=	232100	481
	3694	5241
	76	22
	374	

A. =	16	335267
	432	72866
	3	
	162	
	689	

S. =	325876	63294
	2347535	31
	39	58

T. =	3498	432
	378	78
	14874	3624
	9	

Page 228

(1)

F. =	126, 131, 91, 60, 98, 110
E. =	139, 172, 113, 100, 102, 93
A. =	102, 105, 108, 140, 82, 153
S. =	92, 111, 105, 91, 70, 136
T. =	140, 173, 139, 126, 190, 162
S. =	261, 155, 226, 214, 231, 199

Page 229

(1)
$$\begin{array}{r} 7 \\ +\ 7 \\ \hline 14 \end{array}$$
addend
addend
sum

(2)
$$\begin{array}{r} 10 \\ +\ 6 \\ \hline 16 \end{array}$$
addend
addend
sum

(3)
$$\begin{array}{r} 14 \\ +\ 5 \\ \hline 19 \end{array}$$
addend
addend
sum

"...The Fullness of the Time..."

Page 230

```
(4)    8          3  addend
     + 3        + 8  addend
      11         11  sum

(5)    8         12  addend
     + 12       + 8  addend
      20         20  sum

(6)    8          7  addend
     + 7        + 8  addend
      15         15  sum
```

Page 231

```
(1) 26      24   (2)    20   (3)      9
            26          50           30
          + 26          70           70
            76         100          200
                       300          600
                     + 400        + 800
                       940         1709
```

Page 232

(1)   9, 30, 50 (answer = 89)
(2)   7, 20, 70, 100 (answer = 197)
(3)   975 + 888 + 87 = 1950

Page 239

1. Genesis 5:5

2. *"Thou shalt not bear false witness against thy neighbour."*

3. The 99 sheep that were safe in the fold while 1 was missing in the wilderness.

4. He healed nine lepers.

5. *"...Unto the ninth hour."*

6. *"My God, my God, why hast thou forsaken me?"*

7. An angel of God came to tell him to send for Peter so that he could hear the truth.

Page 240

8. A topaz

9. (1) Shelomith's son

(2) A man that gathered sticks upon the sabbath day

(3) Achan

(4) Abimelech

(5) Adoram

(6) Naboth

Page 240 continued

(7) Zechariah

(8) Stephen

(9) Paul

10. (1) Tamar

(2) The woman of Tekoah

(3) A woman of the tribe of Naphtali whose son was filled with wisdom, and understanding, and cunning to work all works in brass.

(4) Zeruah

(5) The woman of Zarephath

(6) The woman with two mites

(7) Anna

(8) The woman of Nain

(9) The woman in the parable who troubled the judge

Page 241

11. (1) The men of Sodom

(2) Isaac

(3) Israel (Jacob)

(4) Samson

Page 241 continued

(5) Eli

(6) Ahijah

(7) The company of Syrian soldiers

(8) Zedekiah

(9) Saul (Paul)

12. (1) Moses

(2) Miriam

(3) Naaman

(4) Gehazi

(5)-(8) four men

(9) Azariah

Page 244

(1)   10, 11, 12, 13, 14, 15
      16, 17, 18, 19, 20, 21
(2)   11, 15, 13, 16, 17, 10
      15, 12, 18, 19, 14, 10
      13, 11, 20, 17, 21, 16
      12, 18, 21, 14, 19, 15

Page 245

(3)   15, 13, 19
      20, 20, 18
      10, 18, 17
      18, 14, 11

Page 245 continued

20, 11, 16
14, 13, 17
17, 12, 19
21, 15, 16
16, 18, 10
20, 12, 21
13, 21, 15

Nine spelled out nine (9) times

Page 246

(4) 10, 10, 11, 11, 12, 12
13, 13, 14, 14, 15, 15
16, 16, 17, 17, 18, 18
(5) 9, 9, 9, 9, 9, 9
9, 9, 9, 9, 9, 9
(6) 18
(7) 10
(8) 11
39

Page 247

(9) 11, 17, 17, 15, 16, 13
9, 16, 13, 19, 16, 18
17, 13, 15, 14, 11, 15
18, 8, 17, 15, 19, 12
14, 16, 16, 10, 10, 18
19, 17, 14, 12, 20, 10
17, 15, 14, 20, 12, 15
12, 16, 16, 16, 14, 15

Page 248

21, 13, 17, 9, 13, 13
18, 15, 18, 10, 12, 16

Page 248 continued

17, 14, 14, 17, 10, 12
11, 21, 18, 14, 11, 16
8, 15, 13, 17, 21, 10

Page 249

(10) Isaiah 53, Genesis 3:15 etc.

8, 14, 14, 16, 10, 18
12, 18, 18, 12, 15, 17
11, 16, 13, 17, 9, 16
19, 15, 15, 11, 19, 13
14, 12, 18, 12, 20, 10
17, 16, 14, 20, 10, 16

Page 250

(11) 170, 130, 140, 150, 150, 150
120, 110, 120, 130, 140, 150
120, 180, 700, 900, 1000, 600
700, 900, 1600, 1000, 3000,
11000

Page 251

(12) 5, 8, 7, 7, 2, 8
12, 7, 6, 8, 11, 4
7, 8, 2, 9, 8, 8
12, 6, 6, 6, 10, 4

Page 252

6, 7, 5, 6, 3, 6
6, 9, 6, 8, 8, 9
8, 3, 10, 5, 9, 6
8, 9, 8, 8, 2, 7

Page 253

(1)   348   = 3 hundreds 4 tens 8 ones = 300 + 40 + 8
       540   = 5 hundreds 4 tens 0 ones = 500 + 40 + 0
       888   = 8 hundreds 8 tens 8 ones = 800 + 80 + 8 = 888

       914   = 9 hundreds 1 tens 4 ones = 900 + 10 + 4
        84   = 0 hundreds 8 tens 4 ones = 000 + 80 + 4
       998   = 9 hundreds 9 tens 8 ones = 900 + 90 + 8 = 998

       650   = 6 hundreds 5 tens 0 ones = 600 + 50 + 0
       328   = 3 hundreds 2 tens 8 ones = 300 + 20 + 8
       978   = 9 hundreds 7 tens 8 ones = 900 + 70 + 8 = 978

       735   = 7 hundreds 3 tens 5 ones = 700 + 30 + 5
       143   = 1 hundreds 4 tens 3 ones = 100 + 40 + 3
       878   = 8 hundreds 7 tens 8 ones = 800 + 70 + 8 = 878

       623   = 6 hundreds 2 tens 3 ones = 600 + 20 + 3
       373   = 3 hundreds 7 tens 3 ones = 300 + 70 + 3
       996   = 9 hundreds 9 tens 6 ones = 900 + 90 + 6 = 996

       526   = 5 hundreds 2 tens 6 ones = 500 + 20 + 6
       273   = 2 hundreds 7 tens 3 ones = 200 + 70 + 3
       799   = 7 hundreds 9 tens 9 ones = 700 + 90 + 9 = 799

Page 254

(2)   125, 121, 55, 114, 105, 102, 50
(3)   B = 61, 64, 107, 92, 92, 61
       I = 63, 100, 123, 78, 60, 73
       B = 82, 117, 107, 83, 74, 53
       L = 106, 125, 97, 104, 87, 95

Teacher, check for correct breakdown on student's paper
on above problems. See answers for (1) page 256.

Page 255

E. = 105, 126, 97, 93, 88, 83
B. = 103, 106, 106, 113, 116, 135
O. = 91, 88, 114, 96, 94, 74
O. = 142, 111, 133, 125, 126, 115
K. = 142, 80, 63, 80, 73, 101
S. = 107, 97, 76, 130, 126, 108

Page 256

(1) S. = 91, 112, 120, 114, 126, 153
     C. = 140, 155, 173, 79, 172, 80
     R. = 191, 179, 237, 191, 168,
                                   218
     I. = 194, 200, 203, 159, 195, 111
     P. = 166, 151, 186, 167, 180,
                                   199

Page 257

T. = 206, 174, 141, 184, 147, 136
U. = 270, 164, 138, 138, 256, 206
R. = 216, 221, 131, 151, 110, 207
E. = 202, 196, 146, 193, 192, 181

Page 261

(1)	2 + 3 5	(3)	11 + 6 17
(2)	17 + 11 28	(4)	28 +17 45

Page 262

(6) $9 + 8 = 17$
(7) $8 + 9 = 17$
(8) $17 + 17 = 34$

(1) $39 + 27 = 66$
(2) $73 + 77 = 150$
(3) $88 + 88 = 176$

$$22 \overline{)\, 176 }$$
8 verses in each section

Page 271

1. Exodus 20:3-17;
Deuteronomy 5:7-21

2. The tenth of all our income

3. The smallest weight and coin among the Hebrews.

4. 10 plagues, 7 last plagues

5. Sockets

6. (1) Pharaoh, (2) Balaam, (3) Achan, (4) Saul, (5) David, (6) Shimei, (7) Hezekiah, (8) Job, (9) Micah, (10) Nehemiah

Page 272

7. *"Because they met you not with bread and with water in the way, when ye came forth out of Egypt; and because they hired against thee*

Page 272 continued

Balaam the son of Beor of Pethor of Mesopotamia, to curse thee."

8. (1) The sower

(2) The man which sowed good seed in his field and while he slept his enemy came and sowed tares

(3) A grain of mustard seed

(4) The leaven

(5) Hidden treasure

(6) Pearl of great price

(7) The net

(8) The man without a wedding garment

(9) Ten virgins

(10) The talents

9. The ten virgins

10. (1) In Egypt, (2) In the wilderness, (3) Plains of Jericho, (4) Hezekiah's (5) Josiah's, (6) Ezra's (7) When our Lord was twelve years of age, (8) John 2:13, (9) John 6:4, and (10) Matthew 26:2

Page 272 continued

11. (1) Sisera, (2) Abimelech, (3) Sheba, (4) a child, (5) prophets of the LORD, (6) Naboth, (7) a son, (8) all the seed royal, (9) Haman's ten sons, (10) John the Baptist

Page 278

(1)   11, 12, 13, 14, 15, 16
        17, 18, 19, 20, 21, 22
(2)   18, 16, 11, 17, 12, 14
        19, 13, 11, 20, 15, 16
        21, 18, 14, 12, 22, 17
        22, 19, 13, 15, 16, 20

Page 279

(3)   16, 14, 20
        21, 13, 19
        11, 19, 18
        19, 15, 12
        21, 12, 17
        15, 14, 18
        18, 13, 20
        22, 16, 17
        17, 19, 11
        21, 13, 22
        14, 22, 16

Ten spelled out ten (10) times.

Page 280

(4)   4, 7, 2
        1, 6, 11
        9, 12, 10
        3, 5, 8

Page 281

(1)
1540, 1426, 1637, 1666, 1657, 1535
1055, 1028, 1263, 1432, 1322, 1384

Teacher, check for correct breakdown on student's sheet.

Page 282

(2)
P. = 1057, 1443, 1481, 1254, 1442, 1454
R. = 1433, 1478, 1314, 1930, 1531, 1172
O. = 1614, 1902, 1453, 1942, 925, 1805
M. = 833, 1247, 983, 485, 1622, 1586

Page 283

I. = 1006, 1176, 1948, 755, 1693, 1709
S. = 1167, 1041, 1455, 1348, 1711, 1236
E. = 1456, 1653, 1433, 1676, 1322, 1234
S. = 1306, 1154, 1153, 1324, 1135, 1534

Page 284

(1)
S. = 91, 112, 120, 124, 126, 131
E. = 140, 154, 173, 92, 174, 92
C. = 163, 131, 119, 104, 101, 95
O. = 196, 189, 188, 228, 204, 189
N. = 203, 158, 195, 131, 164, 140
D. = 166, 164, 180, 181, 196, 175

Page 285

C. = 143, 207, 160, 179, 261, 164
O. = 148, 138, 256, 207, 188, 224
M. = 155, 150, 143, 200, 226, 198

Page 285 continued

I. = 146, 200, 172, 153, 237, 144
N. = 182, 168, 137, 234, 138, 203
G. = 146, 192, 143, 162, 114, 208

Page 286

(1)   10 oz. + 9 oz. = 19 oz.
(2)   12 + 12 = 24
(3)   90 + 78 = 168

Page 287

(4)   16 + 0 = 16
        8 + 8 = 16
        9 + 7 = 16
(5)   11 + 1 = 12
        7 + 5 = 12
        6 + 6 = 12

Page 288

(1)   C = 30
        O = 29
        M = 34
        E = 50
(2)   30 + 29 + 34 + 50 = 143

Page 289

(1) 92 (2) $119.94; $220.81; $168.80; $389.61

Page 294

1. (1) Duke Timnah, (2) Duke Alvah, (3) Duke Jetheth, (4) Duke Aholibamah, (5) Duke Elah, (6) Duke Pinon, (7) Duke Kenaz, (8)

Page 294 continued

Duke Teman, (9) Duke Mibzar, (10) Duke Magdiel, and (11) Duke Iram.

2. Joseph

3. Eleven days

4. Jehoiakim

5. Zedekiah

6. Ezekiel

7. Judas, Matthias

8. The king who made a wedding for his son and had to go into the highways in order to find guests to come in just in time for the feast.

The man who paid the same amount to those who worked from the eleventh hour as the ones who had been working all day.

9. 33 years (3 x 11)

10. (1) Pharaoh, (2) Balak, (3) Jeroboam, (4) king of Israel (Ahab), (5) Naaman, (6) Asa, (7) Joash, (8) Uzziah, (9) Jehoiakim, (10) Zedekiah, and (11) Herod

Page 295

11. 30 − 2 = 28 − 17 = 11 years. Joseph.

Page 297

Dove, Lamb,
Light, Bread,
Water – (or any other symbol
of Christ in the Bible)

Page 298

(1)   12, 13, 14, 15, 16, 17
       18, 19, 20, 21, 22, 23
(2)   12, 17, 15, 18, 13, 19
       22, 14, 23, 21, 16, 20
       15, 18, 22, 13, 14, 19
       16, 20, 23, 12, 21, 17

Page 299

(3)   15, 17, 21
       23, 22, 20
       20, 12, 19
       13, 16, 20
       22, 18, 13
       16, 15, 19
       14, 19, 23
       21, 18, 17
       12, 18, 20
       23, 15, 22

Page 299 continued

Eleven spelled out eleven (11)
times.

Page 300

(4)   16, 19, 21, 18, 20, 17
       15, 12, 14, 22, 13, 23
(5)   2, 11, 11, 1, 11, 11
       3, 11, 10, 9, 11, 12

Page 301

(6)   one, two, three
       four, five, six
       seven, eight, nine
       ten, eleven, twelve

(7)   E T W O L V E O N X I
       L S F N E V E S E S I
       F I V E I N I N E V E
       V X E E G E L E V E N
       F O U R H E V L E W T
       V E N H T E N T W E L
       T H E T F O U S R T H

Page 302

(1)
C. = 1782, 2310, 2488, 2440, 2669,
                                    2598
O. = 16646, 18081, 17699, 14353,
                                    14987
M. = 257, 320, 315, 334, 293, 304
P. = 15444, 14676, 13681, 14215,
                                    22254

Page 303

L. = 3455, 3724, 3801, 3733, 3534, 3011
E. = 20992, 18428, 21605, 30413, 26503
T. = 179969, 230869, 190684, 222530, 279939
E. = 251416, 250942, 39939, 14244, 259527

Page 304

(1)

C. =	68.5	35.9
	54.3	5.3
	95.9	63.8
	218.7	105.0

O. =	52.0	8.7
	88.9	47.8
	85.0	8.9
	225.9	65.4

M. =	83.7	21.3
	78.0	59.6
	43.5	7.0
	205.2	87.9

(2)

P. =	71.10	39.35	62.84	8.78	31.60
	63.46	75.94	85.00	64.20	8.01
	32.81	48.30	4.15	41.17	23.54
	53.67	82.14	45.80	4.30	88.70
	221.04	245.73	197.79	118.45	151.85

Page 305

L. =	961.580	19.180	382.700	8.830
	56.341	577.500	6.716	413.110
	105.250	65.000	217.268	2.286
	68.134	552.267	56.300	68.687
	1191.305	1213.947	662.984	492.913

Page 305 continued

(3)
$$
\begin{array}{r}
\text{E.} = 47.125 \\
66.540 \\
649.000 \\
\underline{98.800} \\
861.465 \\
\end{array}
$$

$$
\begin{array}{r}
91.440 \\
15.700 \\
\underline{24.859} \\
131.999 \\
\end{array}
$$

$$
\begin{array}{r}
\text{T.} = 26.160 \\
79.000 \\
44.487 \\
\underline{7.320} \\
156.967 \\
\end{array}
$$

$$
\begin{array}{r}
537.596 \\
89.000 \\
\underline{23.140} \\
685.736 \\
\end{array}
$$

$$
\begin{array}{r}
\text{E.} = 76.000 \\
52.410 \\
106.800 \\
\underline{34.077} \\
269.287 \\
\end{array}
$$

$$
\begin{array}{r}
24.850 \\
9.000 \\
7.681 \\
\underline{259.000} \\
300.531 \\
\end{array}
$$

Page 308

11 worlds   11 worlds
+ 1 world   + 2 worlds
12 worlds   13 worlds

11 worlds   11 worlds
+ 3 worlds   + 4 worlds
14 worlds   15 worlds

11 worlds   11 worlds
+ 5 worlds   + 6 worlds
16 worlds   17 worlds

11 worlds   11 worlds
+ 7 worlds   + 8 worlds
18 worlds   19 worlds

11 worlds   11 worlds
+ 9 worlds   + 10 worlds
20 worlds   21 worlds

Page 309

11 worlds   11 worlds
+ 11 worlds   + 12 worlds
22 worlds   23 worlds

11 worlds   11 worlds
+ 13 worlds   + 14 worlds
24 worlds   25 worlds

11 worlds   11 worlds
+ 15 worlds   + 16 worlds
26 worlds   27 worlds

11 worlds   11 worlds
+ 17 worlds   + 18 worlds
28 worlds   29 worlds

11 worlds   11 worlds
+ 19 worlds   + 20 worlds
30 worlds   31 worlds

Page 310

```
S R A T S R L M I L K Y
O T E L E S C O P E J E
U A A W I D S U A T O M
L D R O X S U N L S O U
S E T W A Y O T O L A V
T V H E L P A L O M A R
R A T A A S I J E S U S
S S H R G N W O R L D S
S I N L E S S L E T O M
```

   (1)   1026
   (2)   3131
   (3)   24322

Page 312

(1)   49.4 gallons
(2)   75.1 miles
(3)   111.6 miles

Page 320

1. Twelve

2. *"And he made the breastplate of cunning work, like the work of the ephod; of gold, blue, and purple, and scarlet, and fine twined linen. It was foursquare; they made the breastplate double: a span was the length thereof, and a span the*

breadth thereof, being doubled. And they set in it four rows of stones: the first row was a sardius, a topaz, and a carbuncle: this was the first row. And the second row, an emerald, a sapphire, and a diamond. And the third row, a ligure, an agate, and an amethyst. And the fourth row, a beryl, an onyx, and a jasper: they were enclosed in ouches of gold in their enclosings. And the stones were according to the names of the children of Israel, twelve, according to their names, like the engravings of a signet, every one with his name, according to the twelve tribes" (Exodus 39:8-14).

3. *"Fine flour,"* *"upon the pure table [of shewbread]* *before the LORD"*

4. Twelve fountains of water

5. Twelve stones. "These stones were to be set up as a monument in the first camping place beyond the river." (*Patriarchs and Prophets* 484)

6. Twelve stones

7. Plowing with twelve yoke of oxen

8. Went to Jerusalem for the feast

9. Twelve disciples

Page 320 continued

10. Twelve full baskets

11. Jairus' daughter

Page 321

12. (1) There were sealed twelve thousand from each tribe

(2) A crown of twelve stars

(3) Twelve gates

(4) Twelve angels at the gates

(5) The names written on the gates are the twelve tribes

(6) Twelve foundations

(7) In the foundations are the names of the twelve apostles of the Lamb

(8) The twelve gates were twelve pearls

(9) The tree of life bares twelve manner of fruits

Page 328

(1)   13, 14, 15, 16, 17, 18
       19, 20, 21, 22, 23, 24
(2)   14, 13, 20, 18, 16, 19
       18, 21, 15, 22, 17, 13
       16, 20, 23, 19, 24, 14
       17, 21, 24, 18, 22, 15

Page 329

(3)   18, 16, 22
       23, 23, 21
       13, 21, 20
       21, 17, 14
       23, 14, 19
       17, 16, 20
       20, 15, 22
       24, 18, 19
       19, 21, 13
       23, 15, 24
       16, 24, 18

Twelve spelled out twelve (12) times.

Page 330

(4)	12	12	12	12
	+ 1	+ 2	+ 3	+ 4
	13	14	15	16
	12	12	12	12
	+ 5	+ 6	+ 7	+ 8
	17	18	19	20
	12	12	12	12
	+ 9	+ 10	+ 11	+ 12
	21	22	23	24

(5)   14, 19
       23, 17
       13, 15
       21, 18
       24, 16
       14, 22

Addition 1 – Teacher – Page 50

Page 331

(1)

R. =	53.40	74.20	.573	4.36	.140	71.30
	7.48	53.10	43.100	32.60	2.340	5.42
	31.10	4.07	3.260	.23	.548	3.10
	91.98	131.37	46.933	37.19	3.028	79.82

I. =	6.120	19.20	.541	6.52	32.20	25.12
	23.560	7.40	16.200	3.61	2.32	5.20
	.234	2.53	4.350	.06	6.53	20.46
	29.914	29.13	21.091	10.19	41.05	50.78

(2)

G. =	73.50	4.33
	46.21	87.41
	259.70	21.34
	379.41	113.08

Page 332

H. =	7.40	27.40	T. =	6.60	2.62
	561.60	2.12		23.42	12.00
	32.29	93.50		0.29	27.34
	601.29	123.02		30.31	41.96

T. =	24.52	41.25	I. =	22.70	27.40
	3.30	7.46		9.26	2.32
	81.20	12.50		0.35	2.40
	109.02	61.21		32.31	32.12

Page 332 continued

M. =	2.43	4.310
	4.13	9.240
	0.16	0.121
	6.72	13.671

E. =	32.20	3.16	7.100	0.076	0.32	9.52
	5.26	47.10	0.572	1.500	0.41	3.20
	0.12	2.20	12.300	6.430	2.50	0.45
	37.58	52.46	19.972	8.006	3.23	13.17

Page 333

(1)　G. = $12.43, $18.43, $10.95, $14.71, $18.88
　　　O. = $241.53, $247.89, $169.71, $177.33, $181.12
　　　V. = $141.38, $221.48, $250.26, $167.27, $205.82
　　　E. = $2714.08, $1837.99, $2031.08, $2461.95

Page 334

(2)　R. = $118.53
　　　N. = $81.28
　　　M. = $50.77
　　　E. = $18.55
　　　N. = $562.79
　　　T. = $4.64
　　　S. = $104.35

Page 336

(1)　16
(2)　12 + 0 = 12
　　　6 + 6 = 12
　　　9 + 3 = 12
　　　7 + 5 = 12
(3)　12

Page 337

(4)　4
(5)　4

　　2 parts time latitude
　+ 2 parts longitude
　　4 parts of the world

6 months	12 hours	30 minutes
+ 6 months	+12 hours	+30 minutes
12 months	24 hours	60 minutes
or 1 year	or 1 day	or 1 hour

Page 338

(1)　16.2 hours
(2)　$13.06
(3)　$19.34

Page 339

(1)　$11.65
　　　no
(2)　$63.81
(3)　$19.00
　　　yes

Page 341

(1)　12, 20, 18, 15, 22, 8
　　　23, 13, 18, 17, 24, 16
　　　12, 19, 13, 9, 18, 14
　　　13, 17, 19, 16, 14, 21
　　　11, 14, 14, 20, 13, 17
　　　20, 10, 15, 19, 18, 15
　　　16, 14, 11, 10, 19, 12

Page 342

15, 9, 21, 18, 16, 20
17, 22, 12, 15, 10, 13
15, 19, 11, 16, 21, 17
17, 17, 23, 14, 21, 19
16, 15, 12, 11, 23, 19

Page 343

(1)   Teacher, check.

(2)

3.53 + 2.25	2.06 + 3.85	6.30 + 9.86
1.36 + 24.30	12.49 + 2.10	7.52 + 0.49
3.670 + 0.432	3.22 + 2.25	12.50 + 4.16
0.791 + 0.102	53.5 + 78.3	8.92 + 53.20
7.42 + 62.30	0.621 + 42.300	75.30 + 6.58
34.700 + 0.347	8.94 + 32.20	24.50 + 6.32
9.57 + 4.63	38.2 29.7	0.596 0.423
1.341 + 31.500	3.32 + 35.50	17.100 + 0.139
0.35 + 34.00	0.234 + 3.540	54.60 + 3.26

Page 344

(1)
 1 = beginning, divine unity
 2 = difference, fulness of testimony
 3 = reality, completeness, entireness
 4 = creation
 5 = grace, favor
 6 = man
 7 = spiritual perfection
 8 = new beginning
 9 = divine completeness
10 = perfection of divine order or judgment
11 = incompleteness, disorder, imperfection
12 = perfect government

(2) **Alert** - quick to understand and watching very carefully: vigilance; watchfulness; moving with celerity; briskness; nimbleness; sprightliness.

(3) As a nation, Israel desired the advent of the Messiah, but their hearts and lives were separated from God. They did not understand the character or mission of the promised Deliverer.

Notes

Music

God Made Them

'Tis Almost Time for the Lord to Come

G. W. Sederquist   G. W. Sederquist

"...The fullness of the Time..."

Waiting and Watching

S. M. H.

Will H. Pontius

1. We know not the time when He com - eth, At
2. I think of His won - der - ful pit - y, The
3. O Je - sus, my lov - ing Re - deem - er, Thou

ev - en, or mid - night, or morn; It may be at deep - en - ing
price our sal - va - tion hath cost: He left the bright man - sions of
know - est I cher - ish as dear The hope that mine eyes shall be -

twi - light, It may be at ear - li - est dawn. He
glo - ry To suf - fer and die for the lost. And
hold Thee, That I shall Thine own wel - come hear! If to

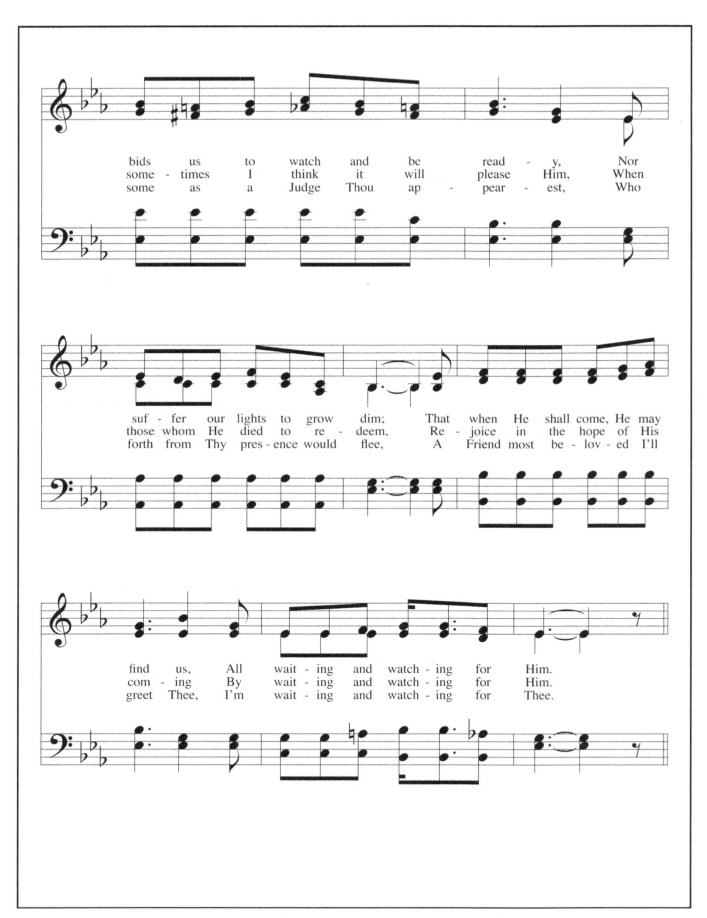

Praise God,
From Whom All Blessings Flow

Thomas Ken

Guillaume Franc

Praise God, from whom all bless - ings flow; Praise
Him, all crea - tures here be - low; Praise Him a - bove, ye
heav'n - ly host; Praise Fa - ther, Son, and Ho - ly Ghost.

Ready to do His Will

S. E. L.

Charlie D. Tillman

1. Read-y to suf-fer grief or pain, Read-y to stand the test;
2. Read-y to go, read-y to bear, Read-y to watch and pray;
3. Read-y to speak, read-y to think, Read-y with heart and brain;
4. Read-y to speak, read-y to warn, Read-y o'er souls to yearn;

Read-y to stay at home and send, Oth-ers if He sees best.
Read-y to stand a-side and send give, Till He shall clear the way.
Read-y to work where He sees fit, Read-y to bear the strain.
Read-y in life, read-y in death, Read-y for His re-turn.

Chorus

Read-y to go, read-y to stay, Read-y my place to fill;

Read-y for serv-ice, low-ly or great, Read-y to do His will.

Like a Little Candle

Happy the Home

How Shall We Stand
In the Judgement

Harriet B. M'Keever

Jno. R. Sweney

1. When———— Je - sus shall gath - er the na - tions, Be -
2. Shall we hear, from the lips of the Sav - iour, The
3. He will smile when He looks on His chil - dren, And
4. Then———— let us be watch - ing and wait - ing, With
5. Thus———— liv - ing with hearts fixed on heav - en, In

fore Him at last to ap - pear, Then———— how shall we stand in the
words "faith - ful serv - ant, well done," Or———— trem - bling with fear and with
sees on the ran - som'd His seal; He will clothe them in heav - en - ly
lamps burn - ing stead - y and bright; When the Bride - groom shall call to the
pa - tience we wait for the time When the days of our pil - grim - age

Judg - ment, When sum - mon'd our sen - tence to hear?
an - guish, Be ban - ished a - way from His throne?
beau - ty, As low at His foot - stool they kneel.
wed - ding O may we be read - y for flight!
end - ed, We'll bask in the pres - ence di - vine.

Joy to the World

O Brother, Be Faithful

Scripture References
"Addition"

Synonyms

(1) joining, uniting, combining, adding, attaching, annexing, appending.

(2) increase, enlargement, extention, expansion, continuation.

Psalm 139:17 *"How precious also are thy thoughts unto me, O God! how great is the sum of them!"*

Character

II Peter 1:5-8 *"And beside this, giving all diligence, <u>add</u> to your faith virtue; and to virtue knowledge;*

"And to knowledge temperance; and to temperance patience; and to patience godliness;

"And to godliness brotherly kindness; and to brotherly kindness charity.

"For if these things be in you, and abound, they make you that ye shall neither be barren nor unfruitful in the knowledge of our Lord Jesus Christ."

Wisdom – I Kings 10:7-8 *"Howbeit I believed not the words, until I came, and mine eyes had seen it: and, behold, the half was not told me: thy wisdom and prosperity <u>exceedeth</u> the fame which I heard.*

"Happy are thy men, happy are these thy servants, which stand continually before thee, and that hear thy wisdom."

Proverbs 1:5 *"A wise man will hear, and will <u>increase</u> learning; and a man of understanding shall attain unto wise counsels:"*

Proverbs 9:9 *"Give instruction to a wise man, and he will be yet wiser: teach a just man, and he will <u>increase</u> in learning."*

Proverbs 16:23 *"The heart of the wise teacheth his mouth, and <u>addeth</u> learning to his lips."*

Ecclesiastes 1:16, 18 *"I communed with mine own heart, saying, Lo, I am come to great estate, and have gotten more wisdom than all they that have been before me in Jerusalem: yea, my heart had great experience of wisdom and knowledge.*

"For in much wisdom is much grief: and he that <u>increaseth</u> knowledge <u>increaseth</u> sorrow."

Ecclesiastes 2:9 *"So I was great, and increased more than all that were before me in Jerusalem: also my wisdom remained with me."*

Praise – Psalm 71:14 *"But I will hope continually, and will yet praise thee <u>more</u> and <u>more</u>."*

Strength to Strength – Job 17:9 *"The righteous also shall hold on his* *way, and he that hath clean hands shall be* <u>stronger</u> *and* <u>stronger</u>.*"*

Counsel

Reproof – Jeremiah 36:32 *"Then took Jeremiah another roll, and gave it to Baruch the scribe, the son of Neriah; who wrote therein from the mouth of Jeremiah all the words of the book which Jehoiakim king of Judah had burned in the fire: and there were* <u>added</u> *besides unto them many like words."*

Teaching – Luke 19:11 *"And as they heard these things, he* <u>added</u> *and spake a parable, because he was nigh to Jerusalem, and because they thought that the kingdom of God should immediately appear."*

Asking God – I Samuel 23:4 *"Then David inquired of the Lord yet* <u>again</u>. *And the Lord answered him and said, Arise, go down to Keilah; for I will deliver the Philistines into thine hand."*

People

Days and Years

Days – II Kings 20:6 *"And I will* <u>add</u> *unto thy days fifteen years; and I will deliver thee and this city out of the hand of the king of Assyria; and I will defend this city for mine own sake, and for my servant David's sake."*

Years – Isaiah 38:5 *"Go, and say to Hezekiah, Thus saith the Lord, the God of David thy father, I have heard thy prayer, I have seen thy tears: behold, I will* <u>add</u> *unto thy days fifteen years."*

Proverbs 9:11 *"For by me thy days shall be multiplied, and the years of thy life shall be* <u>increased</u>.*"*

Children – Genesis 30:24 *"And she called his name Joseph; and said, The Lord shall* <u>add</u> *to me another son."*

Nations – Isaiah 26:15 *"Thou hast* <u>increased</u> *the nation, O Lord, thou hast* <u>increased</u> *the nation: thou art glorified: thou hadst removed it far unto all the ends of the earth."*

Census – II Samuel 24:3 *"And Joab said unto the king, Now the Lord thy God* <u>add</u> *unto the people, how many soevever they be, an hundredfold, and that the eyes of my lord the king may see it: but why doth my lord the king delight in this thing?"*

Size – Matthew 6:27 (Luke 12:25) *"Which of you by taking thought can* <u>add</u> *one cubit unto his stature?"*

Law

Galatians 3:19 *"Wherefore then serveth the law? It was <u>added</u> because of transgressions, till the seed should come to whom the promise was made; and it was ordained by angels in the hand of a mediator."*

Proverbs 3:1-2 *"My son, forget not my law; but let thine heart keep my commandments:*
For length of days, and long life, and peace, shall they <u>add</u> to thee."

People Called

Isaiah 29:19 *"The meek also shall <u>increase</u> their joy in the Lord, and the poor among men shall rejoice in the Holy One of Israel."*

Isaiah 37:31 *"And the remnant that is escaped of the house of Judah shall again take root downward, and bear fruit upward:"*

Acts 2:41, 47 *"Then they that gladly received his word were baptized: and the same day there were <u>added</u> unto them about three thousand souls.*
"Praising God, and having favour with all the people. And the Lord <u>added</u> to the church daily such as should be saved."

Acts 5:14 *"And believers were the more <u>added</u> to the Lord, multitudes both of men and women.)"*

Acts 11:24 *"For he was a good man, and full of the Holy Ghost and of faith: and much people was <u>added</u> unto the Lord."*

I Samuel 3:6, 8 *"And the Lord called yet <u>again</u>, Samuel. And Samuel arose and went to Eli, and said, Here am I; for thou didst call me. And he answered, I called not, my son; lie down again.*
"And the Lord called samuel <u>again</u> the third time. And he arose and went to Eli, and said, Here am I; for thou didst call me. And Eli perceived that the Lord had called the child."

Sin

Genesis 37:5, 8 *"And Joseph dreamed a dream, and he told it his brethren: and they hated him yet the <u>more</u>.*
"And his brethren said to him, Shalt thou indeed reign over us? or shalt thou indeed have dominion over us? And they hated him yet the <u>more</u> for his dreams, and for his words."

Deuteronomy 29:19 *"And it come to pass, when he heareth the words of this curse, that he bless himself in his heart, saying, I shall have peace, though I walk in the imagination of mine heart, to <u>add</u> drunkenness to thirst:"*

I Samuel 12:19 *"And all the people said unto Samuel, Pray for thy servants unto the Lord thy God, that we die not: for we have <u>added</u> unto all our sins this evil, to ask us a king."*

II Chronicles 28:13 *"And said unto them, Ye shall not bring in the captives hither: for whereas we have offended against the Lord already, ye intend to <u>add</u> more to our sins and to our trespass: for our trespass is great, and there is fierce wrath against Israel."*

Ezra 10:10 *"And Ezra the priest stood up, and said unto them, Ye have transgressed, and have taken strange wives, to <u>increase</u> the trespass of Israel."*

Job 34:37 *"For he <u>addeth</u> rebellion unto his sin, he clappeth his hands among us, and multiplieth his words against God."*

Psalm 69:27 *"<u>Add</u> iniquity unto their iniquity: and let them not come into thy righteousness."*

Isaiah 30:1 *"Woe to the rebellious children, saith the Lord, that take counsel, but not of me; and that cover with a covering, but not of my spirit, that they may <u>add</u> sin to sin:"*

Hosea 13:2 *"And now they sin <u>more</u> and <u>more</u>, and have made them molten images of their silver, and idols according to their own understanding, all of it the work of the craftsmen: they say of them, Let the men that sacrifice kiss the calves."*

Luke 3:20 *"<u>Added</u> yet this above all, that he shut up John in prison."*

Adding to what was wrongfully taken

Leviticus 5:16 *"And he shall make amends for the harm that he hath done in the holy thing, and shall <u>add</u> the fifth part thereto, and give it unto the priest: and the priest shall make an atonement for him with the ram of the trespass offering, and it shall be forgiven him."*

Leviticus 6:5 *"Or all that about which he hath sworn falsely; he shall even restore it in the principal, and shall <u>add</u> the fifth part more thereto, and give it unto him to whom it appertaineth, in the day of his trespass offering."*

Things

Creation – See Genesis 1. (Added new things each day of creation)

Temple – I Chronicles 22:14 *"Now, behold, in my trouble I have prepared for the house of the Lord an hundred thousand talents of gold, and a thousand thousand talents of silver; and of brass and iron without weight; for it is in abundance: timber also and stone have I prepared; and thou mayest <u>add</u> thereto."*

Kingdom – Daniel 4:36 *"At the same time my reason returned unto me; and for the glory of my kingdom, mine honour and brightness returned unto me; and my counsellors and my lords sought unto me; and I was established* in my kingdom, and excellent majesty was <u>added</u> unto me."

Cities

Levites – Numbers 35:6 *"And among the cities which ye shall give unto the Levites there shall be six cities for refuge, which ye shall apoint for the manslayer, that he may flee thither: and to them ye shall <u>add</u> forty and two cities."*

Refuge – Deuteronomy 19:9 *"If thou shalt keep all these commandments to do them, which I command thee this day, to love the Lord thy God, and to walk ever in his ways; then shalt thou <u>add</u> three cities more for thee, beside these three:"*

Seek God – Matthew 6:33 (Luke 12:31) *"But seek ye first the kingdom of God, and his righteousness; and all these things shall be <u>added</u> unto you."*

Seeds to soil – Proverbs 11:24 *"There is that scattereth, and yet <u>increaseth</u>; and there is that withholdeth more than is meet, but it tendeth to poverty."*
See Matthew 13:3-9; 18-23.

Harvest increase – Leviticus 19:25 *"And in the fifth year shall ye eat of the fruit thereof, that it may <u>yield</u> unto you the <u>increase</u> thereof: I am the Lord your God."*

Matthew 13:23 *"But he that received seed into the good ground is he that heareth the word, and understandeth it; which also beareth fruit, and <u>bringeth</u> <u>forth</u>, some an hundredfold, some sixty, some thirty."*

Trials

Jeremiah 45:3 *"Thou didst say, Woe is me now! for the Lord hath <u>added</u> grief to my sorrow; I fainted in my sighing, and I find no rest."*

Ezekiel 5:16 *"When I shall send upon them the evil arrows of famine, which shall be for their destruction, and which I will send to destroy you: and I will <u>increase</u> the famine upon you, and will break your staff of bread:"*

Philippians 1:16 *"The one preach Christ of contention, not sincerely, supposing to <u>add</u> affliction to my bonds:"*

Burdens – I Kings 12:11, 14 *"And now whereas my father did lade you with a heavy yoke, I will <u>add</u> to your yoke: my father hath chastised you with whips, but I will chastise you with scorpions.*

"And spake to them after the counsel of the young men, saying, My father made your yoke heavy, and I will <u>add</u> to your yoke: my father also chastised you with whips, but I will chastise you with scorpions."

II Chronicles 10:14 *"And answered them after the advice of the young men, saying, My father made your yoke heavy, but I will <u>add</u> thereto: my father chastised you with whips, but I will chastise you with scorpions."*

Proverbs 10:22 *"The blessing of the Lord, it maketh rich, and he <u>addeth</u> no sorrow with it."*

Do not add to God's Word

Deuteronomy 4:2 *"Ye shall not <u>add</u> unto the word which I command you, neither shall ye diminish ought from it, that ye may keep the commandments of the Lord your God which I command you."*

Deuteronomy 5:22 *"These words the Lord spake unto all your assembly in the mount out of the midst of the fire, of the cloud, and of the thick darkness, with a great voice: and he <u>added</u> no more. And he wrote them in two tables of stone, and delivered them unto me."*

Deuteronomy 12:32 *"What thing soever I command you, observe to do it: thou shalt not <u>add</u> thereto, nor diminish from it."*

Proverbs 30:6 *"<u>Add</u> thou not unto his words, lest he reprove thee, and thou be found a liar."*

Revelation 22:18 *"For I testify unto every man that heareth the words of the prophecy of this book, If any man shall <u>add</u> unto these things, God shall <u>add</u> unto him the plagues that are written in this book:"*

Notes

Gardening Sheet

Lesson __Three__ **Subject** ___Mathematics___

Title ___"Addition I"___

In Season	Out of Season

In Season

Plants need nitrogen. The earth (you) needs the Son of God. In about every acre (.4 hectares) of land or sea there hangs 37,500 tons (1,800 metric tons) of nitrogen, for 78 percent of the air we breathe is nitrogen. Yet in the midst of this plenty, garden crops—requiring hardly more than 50 pounds of nitrogen, all told—have been known to starve for lack of nitrogen! **Alertness** is needed! Our plants cannot make use of nitrogen in the air directly as a plant food. It has to be processed. The micro-organisms assist in this process.

Legumes (peas, beans, lentils, alfalfa, sweet clover, etc.) need nitrogen. The organisms that work with nitrogen grow on the roots of their legume hosts, to transform the atmosphere's nitrogen (taken from the rain) into complex nitrogen compounds forming part of their own bodies. To do this, living conditions in the soil must be right for the bacteria, right for the legume

Out of Season

God assists man in giving the soil nitrogen.

A really good bolt of lightning may turn a hundred pounds (45 kg.) of nitrogen into a form available for plants all in a flash! Just as God provides nitrogen for the plants from the air above, so He sent His Son from above to earth to **alert** men to their spiritual needs.

The chemical symbol for nitrogen is N. Two nitrogen atoms are bound (added) together to form a molecule. The chemical formula is: N_2.

Practice doing addition problems by adding nitrogen atoms.

$$\begin{array}{r} 2 \\ + 2 \\ \hline 4 \end{array} \begin{array}{l} \text{nitrogen atoms} \\ \text{nitrogen atoms} \\ \text{nitrogen atoms} \end{array}$$

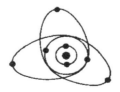

Gardening Sheet

"Addition I," continued

with which a specific bacteria must be associated. The soil must be just right!

Farmers can also supply nitrogen to their fields by rotating crops. An example is, a field is planted with corn one year and legumes the next.

Plants are eaten by animals. In the final stage, the decay of animal wastes and of dead plants returns nitrogen compounds to the soil. <u>Add</u> fertilizer to your garden with these natural wastes.

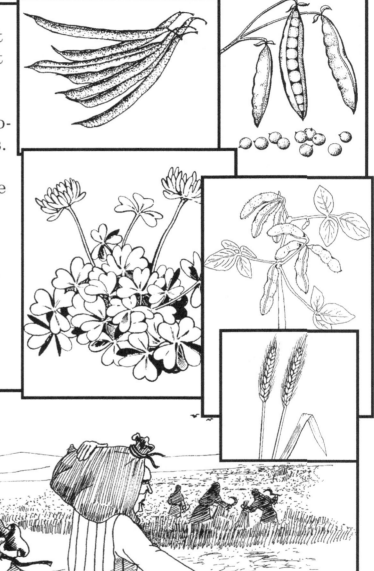

United States Conversion Chart

Length

12 inches = 1 foot
36 inches = 1 yard
3 feet = 1 yard
5,280 feet = 1 mile
1,760 yard = 1 mile

Capacity

4 cups (c.) = 1 quart (qt.)
2 cups = 1 pint (pt.)
2 pints = 1 quart
8 pints = 1 gallon (gal.)
4 quarts = 1 gallon
3 teaspoons (tsp.) = 1 tablespoon
(Tbls.)
8 fluid (fl.) ounces (oz.) = 1 cup
16 fluid ounces = 1 pint
32 fluid ounces = 1 quart
128 fluid ounces = 1 gallon
8 quarts = 1 peck (pk)
4 pecks = 1 bushel (bu)

Time

60 second = 1 minute
60 minutes = 1 hour
24 hours = 1 day
7 days = 1 week
365 days = 1 year
12 months = 1 year
4 weeks = 1 months

Units

1 dozen = 12 units or items

Weight

16 ounces (oz.) = 1 pound (lb.)
2,000 pounds = 1 ton

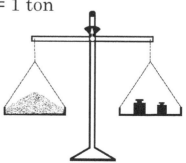

Metric Conversion Chart

Length and Distance

1 inch = 25 millimeters
1 inch = 2.5 centimeters
1 foot = .3 meters
1 foot = 30 centimeters
1 yard = .9 meters
1 mile = 1.6 kilometers

Volume and Capacity (liquid)

1 fluid ounce = 30 milliliters
1 pint (U.S.) = .47 liters
1 quart (U.S.) = .95 liters
1 gallon (U.S.) = 3.8 liters

Weight and Mass

1 ounce = 28 grams
1 pound = .45 kilograms
1 ton = .9 metric tons

Surface or Area

1 acre = .4 hectares

Temperature

$F° - 32 (5/9) = C°$

$C° \times (9/5) + 32 = F°$

Student
Section

"...And much people
were added
unto the Lord."
Acts 11:24

Introduction
Addition 1

Research
In the Beginning

"In the beginning God [is plural] created the heaven and the earth."

Genesis 1:1

Addition in this world began on the first day of creation when God <u>added</u> light or energy to the darkness of *"the earth [which] was without form and void"* (Genesis 1:2). *"And God said, Let there be light: and there was light"* (Genesis 1:3).

The next thing God did after He <u>added</u> light to the darkness was to <u>divide</u> the light from the darkness. *"And God divided the light from the darkness. And God called the light Day, and the darkness he called Night. And the evening and the morning were the first day"* (Genesis 1:4-5).

This simple story teaches us a deep spiritual lesson about how God saves the soul. God graciously <u>adds</u> spiritual light to a person living in the darkness of sin. As the person responds and is enlightened, a <u>division</u> must take place. The soul must choose between light and darkness, between good and evil. Light represents good, for it is written, *"And God saw the light [energy], that it was good"* (Genesis 1:4). As a person separates or <u>divides</u> himself from the darkness of sin, he becomes identified with the light. Of all who do this it may be said, *"Ye are all children of light, and the children of the day: we are not of the night, nor of darkness"* (I Thessalonians 5:5).

Note: When God said the word *"light"* He was creating electromagnetic energy (light, heat, sound, electricity, magnetism, x-ray, etc.) as well as gravitational energy and the nuclear energies in the atoms themselves, all began to function. All of the created elements and energies next were organized into a vast array of complex systems—atoms, molecules, and compounds.

$$1 \ x \ 1 \ x \ 1 = 1$$

| Father | Son | Holy Spirit | God |

Before beginning this math lesson go to page 9 and 10 and read the instructions about the activity.

This union in Arithmetic reminds us of addition. Why? Because it is the uniting of two or more numbers in one sum. It is a very important process to understand well because it forms the basis for all higher, more complicated mathematics. It will require **alertness** to learn all the facts thoroughly.

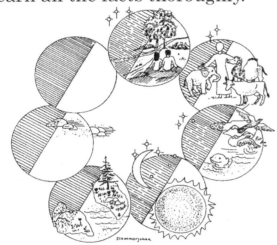

First Things First
+ ÷ x

One of the first things to learn in Mathematics is addition; then further advancement can be made. God also follows this method of advancing from the simple to the complex. His created works reveal a definite order in development. We also see this idea, in the first chapter of Genesis that addition comes before division (verse 4) or multiplication (verse 22).

God's Methods

"But when the fulness of the time was come, God sent forth his Son, made of a woman, made under the law."

Galatians 4:4

In giving unity to His created works, God has two methods. One is the method of addition and the other, that of development. God practices addition as He passes onward and upward, from one step to another during creation week. At each step He added something new, but He also carried forward, either in itself or in its results, all that had gone before. In like manner, as you learn to add bigger and bigger numbers you will need to learn how to carry numbers forward. You will also need to carry forward all the facts you have learned in addition when the time comes for you to study more complicated mathematics. Higher ideas are not reached without the simpler ones preparing the way.

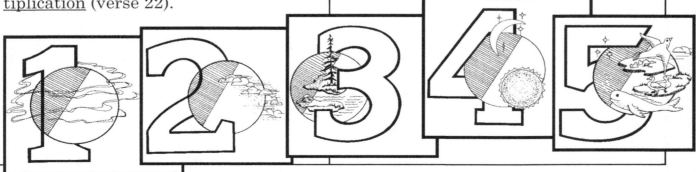

This can remind you of our Bible lesson and how certain things had prepared the way for the first Advent. Then, when the *"fullness of the time"* was come, Jesus was <u>added</u> to the human family so that more development could take place in the plan of salvation. Only those who had been spiritually **alert** before Jesus came would be prepared to perceive further light as soon as it unfolded.

Simple to Complex

God planned for the developments of creation week to happen in a certain order. For example, the animal life that was brought into being on the fifth and sixth days of the creation week could not have been sustained without the previous steps of the creation of air and plant life.

God continued <u>adding</u> more complex systems on each day of creation and each was dependent on what had happened before they came along. Each step of <u>addition</u> carried the creation process to a higher level. The animals which were created at the end of the week were more complex than the plants which had been created earlier in the week. The beasts of the earth, in <u>addition</u> to being able to experience pleasure and pain and having instincts that helped them survive, were given the <u>added</u> ability to love and serve man.

After the animals were created, there was one more crowning step to <u>add</u>. A being was made to which was <u>added</u> the capacity of loving and serving God! He would have spiritual **alertness** which none of the animals could possess.

1 + 1 + 1 + 1 + 1 + 1 = 6

Man was subject to all the physical laws of life, like the plants and animals were, but, because of the higher gifts of reason and conscience, he only reflected the *"image of God"* (Genesis 1:27). So you see, an advanced development had occurred. Creation had passed from that which was subject to law, to that which also understood law. This is why man takes his rightful position on the top of the pyramid of the lower works and is fitted to link himself with that which is above. He is the natural ruler and caretaker of this lower world, having alone the ability to <u>sum</u> up and give expression to the voiceless praise which goes up from the earth and its creatures to its Creator.

Steps that led to the development of *"the fulness of the time."*

Providence had directed:

(1) the movements of nations,

(2) the tide of human impulse and influence until

(3) the world was ripe for the coming of the Deliverer.

(4) The nations were united under one government.

(5) One language was widely spoken.

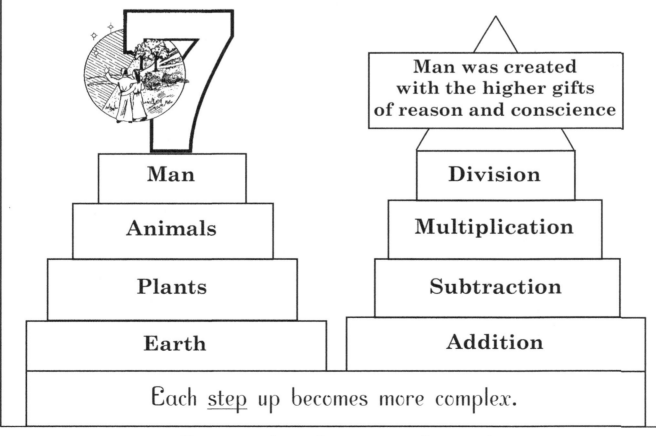

Man
Animals
Plants
Earth

Man was created with the higher gifts of reason and conscience

Division
Multiplication
Subtraction
Addition

Each <u>step</u> up becomes more complex.

Review

1. Addition is the uniting of two or more _____ in one _____ .

2. Circle which process came first during creation week.

    division   addition   subtraction

3. At each step during creation week, God _____ something new, but He also _____ _____ all that had gone before.

4. _____ ideas are not reached without simpler ones preparing the way.

5. When *"the fulness of the time was come"* Jesus was _____ to the human family.

6. In what way are the beasts of the earth more complex than the plants?

7. What very special thing was <u>added</u> to man that the animals do not have?

8. Explain how man's position in this world is like God's position in the universe.

Reinforce

1. As you work at memorizing your memory verse, be reminded how you are adding a simple piece of information into your mind that you can build on to help you understand the more complex and deep things of God later on.

2. As you are doing your chores, be **alert** to how important it is that development take place in a certain order.

(For example: When you are baking bread, what would happen if you waited to put the yeast in until it was time to knead it? Or if you are working in the garden, think how important it is that the soil be prepared before the seeds are planted and not afterwards.)

3. Discuss as a family the idea of God's order in family life and the church. Are there certain things that God has told us to get in order before we try to take on more complex duties? For instance, does it do much good for a family to try to witness to others if their own lives are not in order?

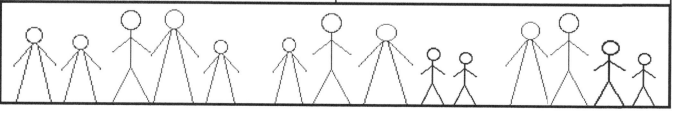

$$3 + 1 = 4$$
$$1 + 2 = 3$$

Creation

$$5 + 1 = 6$$

$$4 + 1 = 5$$

"God's Mathematics"

$$6 + 1 = 7$$

1. God desired to <u>add</u> to the family of heaven, so He *"created the heavens and the earth."* (Genesis 1:1)

2. God <u>added</u> light to the darkness of the earth which was *"without form and void."* (Genesis 1:3)

3. *"God <u>divided</u> the light from the darkness."* (Genesis 1:4)

4. God <u>added</u> the firmament. (Genesis 1:6)

5. God <u>divided</u> *"the waters from the waters."* (Genesis 1:6)

6. God <u>added</u> the waters together *"unto one place."* (Genesis 1:9)

7. God <u>divided</u> the waters from the dry land. (Genesis 1:9)

8. God <u>added</u> plant life, which would <u>divide</u> and <u>multiply</u> by producing seed. (Genesis 1:11-12)

9. God <u>added</u> lights in the firmament to <u>divide</u> the day from the night, season from season, and year from year. (Genesis 1:14-18)

10. God <u>added</u> fish to the sea and fowl to the air. These <u>multiplied</u> after their kind, which showed that a <u>division</u> must be maintained between kinds. (Genesis 1:21-22)

11. God <u>added</u> the beasts and the creeping things, which were also to <u>multiply</u> and maintain <u>divisions</u> between kinds. (Genesis 1:24-25)

12. God <u>added</u> man who was made in His own image (having the <u>addition</u> of a conscience). And God <u>divided</u> man and made a woman. *"And God blessed them, and God said unto them, Be fruitful and <u>multiply</u>, and replenish the earth, and subdue it."* They were given *"dominion over the fish of the sea and over the fowl of the air and over every living thing that moveth upon the earth."* (Genesis 1:28) This put a <u>division</u> between them and the lower created beings.

Then God <u>added</u> the Sabbath day, on which man could <u>sum</u> up all the blessings of the past week. *"How great is the <u>sum</u> of them!"* (Psalm 139:17)

Added • Subtracted • Multiplied • Divided

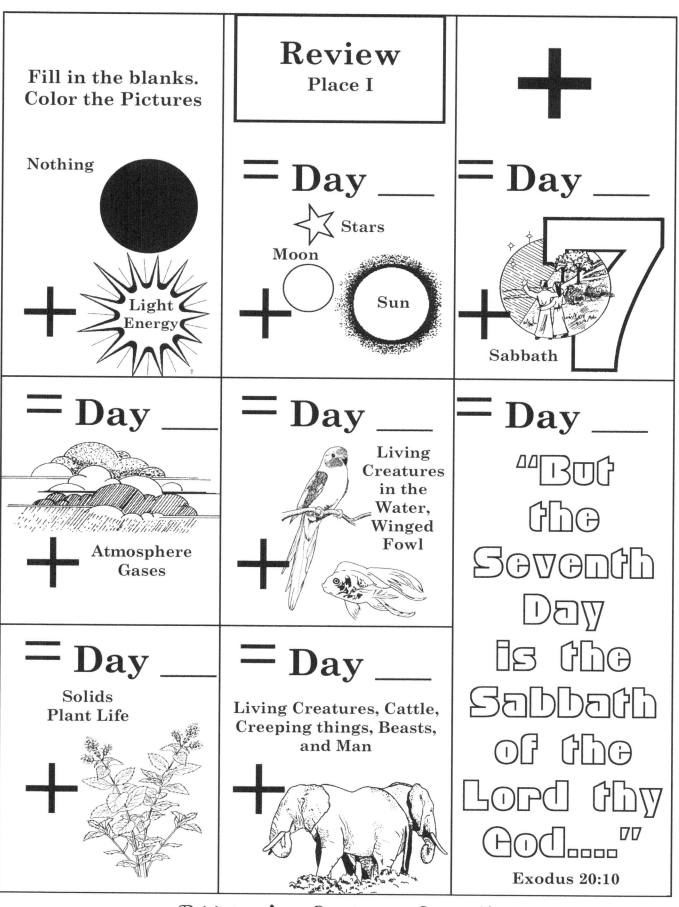

Fill in the blanks.
Color the Pictures

Nothing

+ Light Energy

Review
Place I

= **Day** ___

Stars
Moon
Sun

+

+

= **Day** ___

Sabbath

7

= **Day** ___

+ Atmosphere Gases

= **Day** ___

Living Creatures in the Water, Winged Fowl

+

= **Day** ___

+

"But the Seventh Day is the Sabbath of the Lord thy God...."

Exodus 20:10

= **Day** ___

Solids Plant Life

+

= **Day** ___

Living Creatures, Cattle, Creeping things, Beasts, and Man

+

Addition 1 – Student – Page 7

Review

Place II - III

1. What did God add on day 1-6?

Day 1 _____

Day 2 _____

Day 3 _____

Day 4 _____

Day 5 _____

Day 6 _____

2. What did God multiply?

"Be fruitful, and multiply"

A. _____ _____

B. _____

"Be fruitful and multiply"

A. _____ and _____

Adam and Eve <u>added</u> one more thing that changed the beauty of creation.

"...She took of the fruit thereof, and did eat, and gave also unto her husband...."
Genesis 3:6

3. What things did God divide?

"...Divided the _____ from the _____."

"...Divide the _____ from the _____."

"...Divide the _____ from the _____."

Sin changed nature.

Reinforce
Finding Knowledge in Nature Activities

"Bow down thine ear, and hear the words of the wise, and apply thine heart unto my knowledge."

Proverbs 22:17

Information:
Remember, each day of the week <u>adds</u> one or more things as the creation week unfolds and then you have the final <u>sum</u> of the matter.

Instructions:
1. Begin this math lesson on a Sunday. Find the texts in the next column. First read the texts together as a family. Next meditate on the words and discuss them together. Finally go on a nature walk or work in the garden or yard.

2. Use "Our Nature Study Book" and a pencil.

3. Each day find one or more items that expresses what was created that day of the very first week of this world's history and how it teaches addition. What are the spiritual lessons?

4. This exercise is to help the family members to think and then come up with objects and lessons about God in nature and addition.

Week's Schedule of Nature Walks

Sunday – **Day 1** – Light—energy (Ge 1:3-5; Ps 27:1; Jn 1:6-8) +

Monday – **Day 2** – Atmosphere—Gas (Ge 1:6-8; Ps 19:1) +

Tuesday – **Day 3** – Solids and plant life (Ge 1:9-13; Is 53:1-2) +

Wednesday – **Day 4** – Sun, moon (stars appear) (Ge 1:14-19; Mal 4:2; Ps 84:11) +

Thursday – **Day 5** – Living creatures in the water, winged fowl (Ge 1:20-23; Mt 6:25-26; Lu 12:24; Jonah 1:17; 2:10) +

Friday – **Day 6** – Living creatures, cattle, creeping things, beasts, man (Ge 1:24-31; Ps 50:9-12; Ge 2:7; Ps 103:13-15; Ec 12:7) +

―――――――――――

= Saturday – Sabbath – **Day 7** – Rest (Ge 2:1-2)

THE SUM
OF CREATION

Example 1: (Day 1) Light—energy

Reread on page 1 the box that says "Note." What was spoken into existence the first day of creation? *"And God said, Let there be light* [energy]: *and there was light* [energy]*"* (Genesis 1:3). Read also Psalm 27:1 and John 1:6-8. Discuss.

Lesson: Possible objects to find on the nature walk—sticks. Talk while you walk!

+ The light <u>adds</u> energy to the plant. (See *Light and Heat* Nature Lesson 8.) It grows and produces into a tree. When the tree dies you can use it as fuel to warm yourself. You can eat the fruit from the plant or tree and receive energy from it.

+ From where does this energy originate? What do the texts state? Feel the ground, is it warm or cold? Why?

+ The light or energy helps you see that you may pick up the sticks. Light <u>adds</u> energy to the fruit from the plant you eat which <u>adds</u> energy to you to carry wood to burn in the stove.

+ In the same way Christ is the energizing force in your life. He <u>adds</u> moment-by-moment the power you need to overcome sin—if you <u>will</u>!

Example 2: (Day 5) Living creatures in the water, winged fowl

Read the verses in Genesis 1:20-23; Matthew 6:25-26; Luke 12:24; and Jonah 1:17; 2:10. What was added on the 5th day of creation?

Lesson: Look for fowls or their feathers when walking or working.

+ Who cares for them or <u>adds</u> food to their plate each day? (Draw a picture of the bird in "Our Nature Study Book" or find a feather—in winter old bird's nests are a good source of feathers.)

+ God has ordained natural laws that operate to produce food (Job 38:41; Psalm 145:15-16; 147:9). The food is there but the birds must go and get it.

+ You must go to the Word (John 1:1) each day to receive your spiritual nourishment (Jeremiah 15:16). God then adds an abundance of tasty morsels to your plate!

Sing the hymn, "God Made Them."

God's Design in Mathematics

In the next several mathematic's lessons the numbers 1-12 will be studied with a few other numbers. It will be discovered that God has established a <u>design</u> in the use of them both in the <u>works of God</u> and in the <u>Word of God</u>.

The study of the numbers formed by the letters of the words themselves is called by the ancients *Gematria*. This is the use of the letters of the alphabet instead of figures. Arabic numerals being a comparatively modern invention were not, of course, known to, and could not have been used by, the most ancient nations.

The Hebrews and Greeks, therefore, used their alphabets as follows:

The **Hebrew** alphabet consists of 22 (2 x 11) letters, so the 5 finals were added to make up three series of 9, or 27 in all.

Aleph	א = 1	Yod	י = 10	Koph	ק = 100
Beth	ב = 2	Kaph	כ = 20	Resh	ר = 200
Gimel	ג = 3	Lamed	ל = 30	Shin	ש = 300
Daleth	ד = 4	Mem	מ = 40	Tau	ת = 400
He	ה = 5	Nun	נ = 50	Koph	ך = 500 ⎫
Vau	ו = 6	Samech	ס = 60	Mem	ם = 600 ⎪
Zayin	ז = 7	Ayin	ע = 70	Nun	ן = 700 ⎬ Finals.
Cheth	ח = 8	Pe	פ = 80	Pe	ף = 800 ⎪
Teth	ט = 9	Tsaddi	צ = 90	Tsaddi	ץ = 900 ⎭

The **Greek** letters were 24, and the required number, 27, was made up by using the final "Ϛ" or Ϛ (called Stigma) for 6, and adding two arbitary symbols called respectively Koppa, for 90, and Sampsi, for 900.

Alpha	α = 1	Iota	ι = 10	Rho	ρ = 100
Beta	β = 2	Kappa	κ = 20	Sigma	σ = 200
Gamma	γ = 3	Lambda	λ = 30	Tau	τ = 300
Delta	δ = 4	Mu	μ = 40	Upsilon	υ = 400
Epsilon	ε = 5	Nu	ν = 50	Phi	φ = 500
Stigma	ς = 6	Xi	ξ = 60	Chi	χ = 600
Zeta	ζ = 7	Omicron	ο = 70	Psi	ψ = 700
Eta	η = 8	Pi	π = 80	Omega	ω = 800
Theta	θ = 9	*Koppa*	Ϙ = 90	*Sampsi*	ϡ = 900

Reinforce
Scribes Copying the Word of God

One scribe reading, what he has copied from the Hebrew Scriptures, while the other is checking his work with the original manuscript.

In ancient Israel, the vocation of the scribe was highly regarded. While writing Scriptures, the scribe exercised great care. His ink had to be black and indelible; the parchment had to be especially prepared from an animal permitted to the Jews as food.

Exactness in spelling, crowning certain letters, dotting others, and following prescribed regulations as to spacing for sections was mandatory.

Before writing the names of God, he recited a prayer. An error in writing God's sacred name required discarding of the entire sheet; erasures were forbidden. If three or more errors were found on one page, the scroll was not to be used.

Color this picture.

*"How do ye say,
We are wise,
and the law of the Lord
is with us?
Lo, certainly in vain
made he it; the pen
of the scribes is in vain."*
Jeremiah 8:8

How thankful we are for their **alertness** to details that we might have the book of Genesis, which tells the history of Creation and carries on to the death of Joseph, a period of more than 2,000 years.

Their faithfulness preserves not only the Old Testament but the New Testament as well, which gives to us the story of Jesus coming to this earth as a baby.

+ + + Addition + +

Research
"The Fulness of the Time"

"Father, the hour is come; glorify thy Son, that thy Son also may glorify thee."

John 17:1

The way had been prepared. The <u>time</u> was right. *"But when the fulness of the <u>time</u> was come, God sent forth his son...to redeem them that were under the law, that we might receive the adoption of sons"* (Galatians 4:4-5).

God prepared the way for the first advent or addition of Christ to the human family even as today the way is being prepared for His second coming.

Was Israel **alert** to the <u>time</u>? As a nation, Israel desired the advent of the Messiah, but their hearts and lives were separated from God. They did not understand the character or mission of the promised <u>Deliverer</u>. He would not come as a conqueror to break the yoke of the Roman power. The Saviour would come to <u>deliver</u> the people of Israel from the bondage of sin. **Alertness** was important as they studied the prophecies and followed the steps necessary in preparing for the coming One.

"...The Fullness of the Time..."

Would Israel be **alert** and prepared to accept the coming <u>Deliverer</u>?

"He came unto his own,
and his own received
him not."
John 1:11

What was wrong? Had they not been told about the coming of the Deliverer?

Yes, they had been told long before. In fact, Adam and Eve (1 plus 1 equals 2) were told about the Saviour's coming in Eden after they had sinned.

"And I will put enmity
between thee
and the woman,
and between thy seed
and her seed;
it shall bruise thy head,
and thou shalt
bruise his heel."
Genesis 3:15

What does this verse mean?

Reflect

God, the Creator, became a Baby!

"For verily
he took not on him
the nature of angels;
but he took on him
the seed of Abraham."
Hebrews 2:16

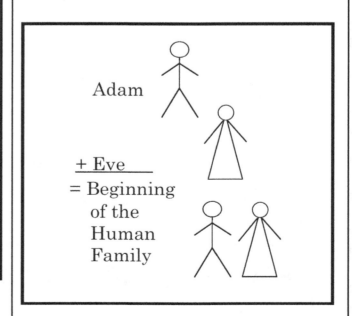

Adam

+ Eve
= Beginning
of the
Human
Family

Reflect

1. *"I will put enmity between thee and the woman,"* means I will send a <u>Deliverer</u>.

2. *"Between thy seed and her seed,"* means that there will be a struggle between Satan's followers and God's followers.

3. *"It shall bruise thy head,"* means Christ would crush the serpent's head, or overcome Satan.

4. *"And thou shalt bruise his heel,"* means Christ will ever carry the marks of His sacrifice, the *"bruise."* (See Habakkuk 3:4.)

When Adam and Eve (1 plus 1 equals 2) first heard the promise they expected it to be quickly fulfilled. The first baby (Cain) was born into the home of Adam and Eve (2 plus 1 equals 3). They hoped he would be the <u>Deliverer</u>. He was not! Another child (3 plus 1 equals 4) was born to Adam and Eve whom they named Abel. More and more babies came to live in the home of Adam and Eve. None of these babies were the <u>Deliverer</u>!

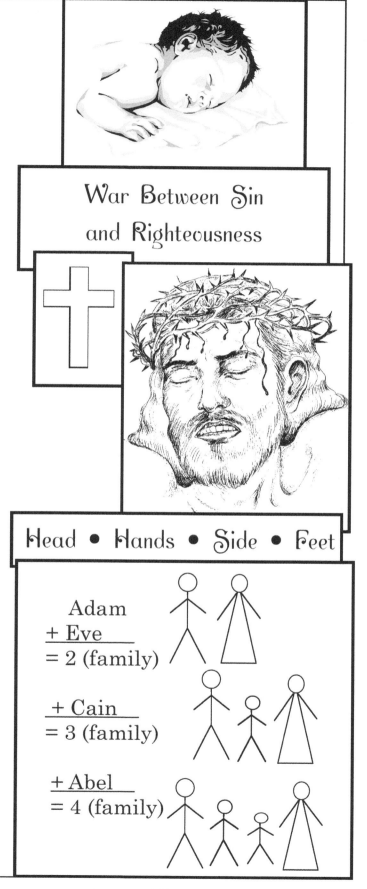

War Between Sin and Righteousness

Head • Hands • Side • Feet

Adam
<u>+ Eve</u>
= 2 (family)

<u>+ Cain</u>
= 3 (family)

<u>+ Abel</u>
= 4 (family)

Reinforce

Adam and Eve and Their First Children

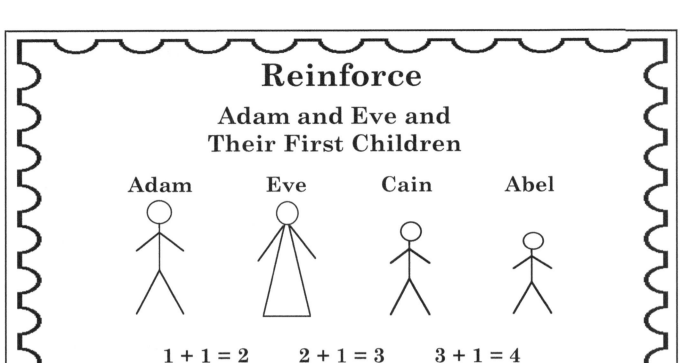

Adam	Eve	Cain	Abel

$$1 + 1 = 2 \qquad 2 + 1 = 3 \qquad 3 + 1 = 4$$

Learn These Terms

Addition (add) means to put together two or more numbers (addends) in one sum (total). The plus sign (+) is used in addition. Notice the picture above.

Adam + Eve = 2 people
2 people + Cain = 3 people
3 people + Abel = 4 people

"...And she [Eve] again bare his brother Abel...."
Genesis 4:2

Reflect

Each addition was leading toward One great Sacrifice.
The addition sign forms the <u>cross</u>. It reminds us:

"Let this mind be in you, which was also in Christ Jesus:

"Who, being in the form of God,

thought it not robbery to be equal with God:

"But made himself of no reputation,

and took upon him the form of a servant,

and was made in the likeness of men:

"And being found in fashion as a man,

he humbled himself, and became obedient unto death,

even the death of the cross." (+)

Philippians 2:5-8

Servant

God (Jesus Christ) came from heaven (↓) to become a man (↑).
Whenever we do an addition problem we can be reminded
of the sacrifice of the <u>Deliverer</u>.

The divine nature
and the human
nature combined
(addition +)
to give sinful man
a Saviour.

Divine

Human ⟶

+

*embodiment—taking on sinful flesh

When we desire a <u>deep</u>
<u>problem</u> <u>to</u> <u>study</u>, let our minds
fix on the most marvelous thing
that ever took place in earth or
heaven—the incarnation* of the
Son of God. God gave His Son
to die a death of dishonor and
shame for sinful human beings.
Christ who was highest in the
heavenly courts laid aside
His royal robe and kingly
crown, and clothing His
divinity with humanity,
came to this world to be
a pattern for man. He
humbly came to suffer
with the human race.

Remember These Definitions

Plus means to be added to or increased by.

Addends are the numbers that are to be added to another number, or numbers.

Sum means the whole, or total amount.

Remember, **addition** means to put together two or more numbers in one sum. The plus sign (+) is used in addition.

Remember to keep each set of numbers in their <u>proper</u> <u>place</u>.

```
  1 Addend
+ 1 Addend
  2 Sum
```

Earth's Family Increases
Looking for the Deliverer

"This is the book of the generations of Adam."
Genesis 5:1

As time went on more and more children were born and lived on this earth.

```
hundreds  tens  ones
      3      2     1
+     1      1     1
                   2
```

**Add the rest of the columns above
keeping each set of numbers
in their <u>proper</u> <u>place</u>.**

Some synonyms for the word addition are increase, enlargement, extension, expansion, and accession.

① ⊙ ◖ Zero - 0 0 ○ 0

Research
Zero

"But made himself of no reputation,
and took upon him the form of a servant,
and was made in the likeness of men."
Philippians 2:7

The word zero has many synonyms. Some are: "nothing," "naught," "empty," and "cipher." Christ came to this world "at the very crisis, when Satan seemed about to triumph...."* Satan (Lucifer) in heaven had said, *"I will exalt my throne above the stars of God...I will be like the Most High* (Isaiah 14:13-14). But Christ *"being in the form of God, thought it not robbery, to be equal with God. But made himself of <u>no reputation</u>* [as nothing] *and took upon him the form of a servant and was made in the likeness of men."* Because Christ became <u>nothing</u> He gives you value, for without Him you are <u>nothingness</u>. "The soul is of infinite value. Its worth can be estimated only by the price paid to ransom it. Calvary! Calvary! Calvary! will explain the true value of the soul."**

*The Desire of Ages 37 **Gospel Workers 1892 93
***to make less ****Matthew 25:33
*****Conflict and Courage 367

In arithmetic when zero (0) stands by itself, it expresses nothing, but increases or diminishes*** the value of other figures, according to their position. In whole numbers, when placed at the <u>right</u>**** hand of a figure, it increases its value ten fold (10), but in decimal fractions, placed at the <u>left</u>**** hand of a figure, it diminishes*** the value of that figure ten fold (.01). So it is with you, as you accept Christ's sacrifice your value increases many fold. If you reject the sacrifice you become a cipher. Christ is what gives you value.

We are told: "...Many a one who otherwise would be but a cipher in the world, perhaps only a helpless burden, will be able to say with the apostle Paul, *'I can do all things through Christ which strengtheneth me'* (Philippians 4:13)."*****

Addition 1 – Student – Page 19

Cipher

"Hereafter
I will not talk much
with you: for the prince of this world
cometh, and hath <u>nothing</u> in me."
John 14:30

Zero means empty or <u>nothing</u>. In mathematics zero acts as a place holder, and does not change the value of the number when added. When *"the fullness of the time"* was come, Jesus made Himself as <u>nothing</u> *"and took upon him the form of a servant, and was made in the likeness of men"* (Philippians 2:7). He came to witness about the Father. He could not make the Father greater than He already was, but came to reveal how great He was. When Satan came to tempt Christ he found <u>nothing</u> (no sin) in Him. *"...The prince of this world cometh, and hath <u>nothing</u> in me"* (John 14:30). With His powerful help, self will be completely subdued and it will become as <u>naught</u> and will be a witness for Him! Think on these thoughts as you do the following problems.

Remember when a zero is placed to the right of a single digit number, it increases the value of that number tenfold. For example, one with a zero to the right of it equals 10. It can remind us of how we only have value when we, who are <u>nothing</u> (0), line up on the right side of the Lord (1).

Reinforce

Another Word for Zero
is "_ _ _ _ _"

"For if a man think himself to be something, when he is <u>nothing</u>, he deceiveth himself."
Galatians 6:3

Remarkable Fact:
What is *googol*?
It is the number one followed by 100 zeros.

Review
Place I - II

Examples of Using Zero

1.
$$\begin{array}{r} 2 \\ + 0 \\ \hline 2 \end{array} \leftarrow$$

2.
$$\begin{array}{r} 67 \\ + 20 \\ \hline 87 \end{array} \leftarrow$$

3.
$$\begin{array}{r} 205 \\ + 140 \\ \hline 345 \end{array} \begin{array}{l} \leftarrow \\ \leftarrow \end{array}$$

1. **Place I—When adding zero in the ones' column, does the number increase?** _____

1	2	3	4	5	6
+ 0	+ 0	+ 0	+ 0	+ 0	+ 0

7	8	9	10	11	12
+ 0	+ 0	+ 0	+ 0	+ 0	+ 0

2. **Place II—When adding zero in the tens' column does the number increase?** _____

132	245	321	463	531	625
+ 205	+ 104	+ 301	+ 502	+ 206	+ 103

Jesus was not adding to God.
(God is all in all and cannot be added to.)
He was only expressing what was there!

3. **Place II—Add the following digits that have zero in them.**

N.	40	50	70	60	90	80
	+ 93	+ 72	+ 81	+ 48	+ 35	+ 97

O.	80	34	50	29	90	76
	+ 96	+ 40	+ 43	+ 70	+ 44	+ 60

T.	700	214	600	672	500	811
	+ 325	+ 400	+ 562	+ 900	+ 731	+ 800

H.	340 + 351	620 + 542	369 + 430	860 + 639	728 + 550	960 + 237
I.	242 + 305	408 + 341	566 + 603	808 + 751	506 + 632	634 + 704
N.	306 + 560	630 + 405	708 + 830	940 + 503	601 + 760	452 + 807
G.	504 + 592	760 + 609	330 + 960	820 + 673	559 + 740	408 + 661

Reflect

"He made himself of <u>no</u> reputation."

Philippians 2:7

When Jesus came
to earth
He emptied Himself
and took our place,
becoming as <u>nothing</u>.
He said of Himself
as a man,

"I can of mine own self
do nothing."

John 5:30

Review
Place III

Generation after generation came and went. God always had faithful, **alert** men who <u>witnessed</u> for Him until Jesus came, the perfect <u>Witness</u>. *"Behold, I have given him for a <u>witness</u> to the people"* (Isaiah 55:4).

Jesus came from heaven to earth. When we have a perfect man to look to, it gives us a perfect <u>witness</u> to copy. Jesus was that Man!

Jesus' life on earth can remind us of horizontal addition—one day (number) after another day (number), of living a perfect life added up to an example for men to copy. When we keep records we often use horizontal addition. One way to do horizontal addition is to work by 10s. See the example.

Reflect

"BEHOLD, I HAVE GIVEN HIM FOR A WITNESS TO THE PEOPLE"

Example

Problem $8 + 6 + 5 + 9 =$

Think $8 + (2 + 4) + 5 + (6 + 3) =$

Regroup $(8 + 2) + (4 + 6) + (5 + 3) =$

Solve $10 + 10 + 8 = 28$

This works best when most addends are a little above or below ten.

Example

Problem $9 + 8 + 12 + 7 + 13 =$

Think $9 + (7 + 1) + (10 + 2) + 7 + (10 + 3) =$

Regroup $(9 + 1) + (7 + 3) + 10 + (2 + 7) =$

Solve $10 + 10 + 10 + 9 = 39$

---

1. Regroup these problems in tens then find the sum.

W. $8 + 3 + 7 + 4 =$

I. $8 + 9 + 3 + 6 =$

T. $13 + 7 + 9 + 1 + 10 =$

N. $12 + 11 + 9 + 8 =$

E. $3 + 5 + 7 + 7 + 2 + 6 =$

S. $9 + 5 + 14 + 12 + 6 =$

S. $8 + 2 + 8 + 10 + 12 =$

Reflect
Deliverer

"...There shall come out of Sion the <u>Deliverer</u>, and shall turn away ungodliness from Jacob" (Romans 11:26).

"The Lord is my rock, and my fortress, and my <u>deliverer</u>..." (Psalm 18:2).

Example
Finding An Average

Problem: Find the average of the following numbers: 23, 24, 28, 30, 21, and 18. (There are 6 numbers)

Solution:

	23
	24
	28
	30
Add the	21
numbers.	$+\ 18$
	144

Divide by 6. $\qquad 144 \div 6 = \mathbf{24}$

Reinforce

1. Read the stories, "Witnessing for Christ or Selfishly Keeping for Ourselves."

2. Find zero shapes in nature and in the kitchen. (Examples: nature = some rocks; kitchen = some tomatoes)

3. What has a delivery man brought to your home? Why was Jesus called a Deliverer?

"Coming of a <u>Deliverer</u> from sin" (PK 697)
"Long-hoped for <u>Deliverer</u>" (DA 216)
"Long-looked for <u>Deliverer</u>" (DA 377)
"Promised <u>Deliverer</u>" (DA 216)

Witnessing for Christ or Selfishly Keeping for Ourselves

"No, I think not." Marie shrugged indifferently as she refused the request of her hostess to sing for the several friends who had chanced to drop in to spend the evening. "If I sing here and there and everywhere, my voice will become common and won't be properly appreciated," she explained.

We sincerely admired her musical ability and urged her to give us "just one song," but she was firm—we wouldn't call her stubborn, of course—and her decision stood.

Her brother used all his persuasive powers, but in vain. "You're selfish!" he finally declared frankly. "Just plain selfish!"

So we gathered around the piano and had a "community sing," which may not have been much as to technique, but which was good exercise and good fun. Marie was audience. She was "saving" her voice for a *real* occasion.

A solo for the church service? for Sabbath school? Not Marie!

And then the family moved away from our town, and years passed before I saw the sweet singer again. Somehow her hopes to become an outstanding artist have not materialized, though the way has been opened for her to study with teachers who are among the best in North America. She is disappointed, and just a little bitter about her failure.

I wonder—can it be that she has wrapped her talent in the napkin of selfish ambition and buried it deep beneath selfish pride, so that it is bringing no satisfaction to her, no blessing to witnessing to others through song?

One of the most popular concert artists many years ago dropped into a little Italian restaurant. "Signor!" cried the waiter, almost in tears, "I have saved my tips to hear you, and the manager, he would not let me off. I am sad, my friend, so very sad, because I may not hear you sing."

"You shall hear it now," said the famous singer with a smile, and standing there in that humble place, without accompaniment, he sang. When he had finished, he had only witnessed to the waiter, the manager, two taxi drivers, and an Italian importer.

One who has known him long says, "he has a great gift, and he gives it freely. All through his life, he has spilled song as wastefully as if it were water splashing in the sun." And the fountain, far from drying up, has increased in volume and beauty.

As a four-year-old he sat beside his mother at the parlor organ and discovered that he could sing, and that singing was a joy. As he grew into boyhood, the family and the neighbors remarked upon the child's voice, but there was no money for lessons. At twelve he sang a solo at the annual music festival at Trinton, New Jersey. The audience was blessed by his song.

An opportunity came for him to sing in church one Sabbath, and he and the organist became fast friends. She knew the mysteries of notes and helped him in the evenings. But soon his voice began to change; he dropped all thought of singing and devoted himself to growing up.

Then came the World War days. He was in the air service, and as he learned to fly, his voice came back. He tested it out, and lo, the soprano of his boyhood had completely vanished, but in its place there was a golden tenor!

To his great disappointment he was not permitted to go overseas, and suddenly he found himself on the ground again and out of the service. A job was an imperative necessity, and he found one in an ice plant. But while he worked he sang, and sang, and sang witnessing to those around him! Also he saved every cent possible, and when he had what he thought was enough, he went to New York to study music.

It was then that he discovered to his dismay that good voice teachers in "the big city" charge a lot of money for a half-hour lesson, and his savings were soon gone. But he found another job—this time in an insurance office—and married the organist who had helped him in the long ago. Once more she brought into his life inspiration and encouragement.

A large New York church announced an audition for a new tenor soloist, and this man took the test. He was forty-seventh on the list, and many followed him, but he got the place—which added twenty-five dollars in cash to his weekly income.

Then calls began to come for his service in many different places some high, some low. For some he received payment, for some he did not, but he never refused. Finally the New York Symphony Orchestra offered him an engagement, and on the great stage of Carnegie Hall he gave a concert that overwhelmed his audience. He was just twenty-two!

Several years of study in Europe followed, and before he returned home, he was a master tenor and was singing incessantly with or without contracts. Taxi drivers and waiters heard his voice in restaurants and cafes for nothing. Hospitals welcomed him for the concerts he loved to give—without a cent of remuneration. He enjoyed witnessing to others with the gift God had given him.

When he made his debut at the Metropolitan in New York in 1933, he received thirty-seven curtain calls, and stopped the performance for fifty minutes until the applause could be subdued.

For several years, from among the thousands of his "fan letters" Mr. Crooks picked a special one every few weeks. He had never seen Nancy Council, but she always wrote suggestions and criticisms which were extraordinarily helpful.

And he always sent a note in reply.

When he went to Berkeley, California, to sing in a concert, he visited his pen friend, and found that she was an invalid, strapped to a board. She could not attend the concert, for her doctor had forbidden it. This great singer telephoned to a piano dealer to send a grand piano to Nancy's home at once. His wife accompanied him, and he sang for her his entire program.

The time came for his appearance downtown, but when his manager at last located him, he did not interrupt the concert by the bedside of Nancy Council. Instead he returned to the hall and announced that Richard Crooks, the greatest tenor in the world, was singing to a sick child. When he arrived at last, *two hours late,* the patient crowd stood up and cheered him.

Are you being generous witnessing with the talents God has given you? Or are you wrapping them in the napkin of selfish ambition and hiding them where they will be a blessing to no one—not even yourself? Think it over!

Christ is the Giver of gifts and talents. He gave all His talents when He came to earth and finally gave His life for you! Are you witnessing for Him today?

Reflect
Nothing

"We have nothing, we are nothing, unless we receive virtue* from Jesus Christ." (*That I May Know Him* 109)

"I am become a fool in glorying; ye have compelled me: for I ought to have been commended of you: for in nothing am I behind the very chiefest apostles, though I be nothing" (II Corinthians 12:11).

"But of these who seemed to be somewhat, (whatsoever they were, it maketh no matter to me: God accepteth no man's person:) for they who seemed to be somewhat in conference added nothing to me" (Galatians 2:6).

"Whoso boasteth himself of a false gift is like clouds and wind without rain" (Proverbs 25:14).

"Seest thou a man wise in his own conceit? there is more hope of a fool than of him" (Proverbs 26:12).

"For I say, through the grace given unto me, to every man that is among you, not to think of himself more highly than he ought to think; but to think soberly, according as God hath dealt to every man the measure of faith." "Be of the same mind one toward another. Mind not high things, but condescend to men of low estate. Be not wise in your own conceits" (Romans 12:3, 16).

"For now ye are nothing; ye see my casting down, and are afraid" (Job 6:21).

*moral excellence: knowing what is right and acting in a right way.

Remind

1. When you write or read an "o" or "0" *"think on these things"* (Philippians 4:8): "This is how you can walk with Christ and increase your value—1, 10, 100, 1,000, 10,000, 100,000, 1,000,000,000...."

2. As you look at a picture book be aware of the "zero" shapes.

3. Seeing crosses tells me of Christ's great sacrifice for me!

Review
Place I - II - III

Write several paragraphs describing what zero means spiritually.

"And though I have
the gift of prophecy,
and understand all mysteries,
and all knowledge;
and though I have all faith,
so that I could remove mountains,
and have not charity, I am <u>nothing</u>."
I Corinthians 13:2

1 1 1 1 Ones - 1 1 1 11

Research
The Number One

"In that day shall there be one Lord, and his name one."

Zechariah 14:9

The number one in the Bible reminds us of beginning, and of the Divine unity. *"Hear* [or be **alert**], *O Israel: The Lord our God is one Lord"* (Deuteronomy 6:4). God desires unity with His people and unity in families. He planned to send His Son into a family on earth so the family of earth could learn how to be one with the family in heaven.

"The cause of division and discord in families and in the church is separation from Christ. To come near to Christ is to come near to one another. The secret of true unity in the church and in the family is not diplomacy, not management, not a superhuman effort to overcome difficulties— though there will be much of this to do—but union with Christ.

"Picture a large circle, from the edge of which are many lines all running to the center. The nearer these lines approach the center, the nearer they are to one another."*

*The Adventist Home 179

Reinforce
Color then read the meaning of the number one. Learn to say one in these languages.

French – un (unh)

Japanese – ichi (ee chee)

Spanish – uno (OO noh)

Swahili – moja (MOH jah)

```
  1 addend
+ 1 addend
  2 sum
```

ONE - 1 =
BEGINNING
AND
DIVINE
UNITY

1

"Thus it is in the Christian life. The closer we come to Christ, the nearer we shall be to one another. God is glorified as His people unite in harmonious action."*

<table>
<tr><td>"<u>ONE</u> who will always understand" (1 SAT 398)</td><td>Reflect
ONE</td><td>"<u>ONE</u> whom none can evade" (7 MR 232)</td></tr>
</table>

"<u>ONE</u> able to open the door" (7 MR 125)

"<u>ONE</u> above all question and above all law" (DA 285)

"<u>ONE</u> against whom the gates of hell could not prevail" (DA 413)

"<u>ONE</u> altogether lovely" (2 SAT 216)

"<u>ONE</u> appointed by God to carry our griefs and sorrows" (11 MR 356)

"<u>ONE</u> equal with God" (8 MR 355)

"<u>ONE</u> exalted above all other gods" (8 MR 100)

"<u>ONE</u> full of grace and truth" (15 MR 86)

"<u>ONE</u> greater than Moses" (DA 52)

"<u>ONE</u> greater than the temple" (DA 285)

"<u>ONE</u> wiser than Solomon" (DA 508)

"<u>ONE</u> like the Son of man" (9 MR 122)

"<u>ONE</u> like the sons of men" (MB 15)

"<u>ONE</u> mightier than angels" (AA 29)

"<u>ONE</u> mightier than Satan" (AA 576)

"<u>ONE</u> mighty to save and mighty to destroy" (3 MR 42; 4 MR 71)

"<u>ONE</u> of authority" (8 MR 33-34)

"<u>ONE</u> of whom Moses had written" (DA 52)

"ONE that can take away sin" (14 MR 129)

"ONE that saves us from all sin" (8 MR 223, 228)

"ONE to abide in the soul temple" (DA 556)

"ONE who commands and executes all things" (DA 606)

"ONE who could read the thoughts" (DA 198)

"ONE who has appointed to every man his work" (10 MR 222)

"ONE who held all nature under His control" (DA 246)

"ONE who is above all rulers" (10 MR 307)

"ONE who is interested in us" (7 MR 192)

"ONE with the Creator of the universe" (DA 210)

"ONE who is merciful to pardon" (TDG 176)

"ONE who uplifts" (6 MR 7; 1 SAT 112)

"ONE who is mighty in counsel" (1888 1619)

"ONE who is perfect in character" (6 BC 1098)

"ONE who is too wise to err" (7 MR 141)

"ONE who never finds fault with you" (7 MR 271)

"ONE who never makes a mistake" (1888 1619)

"ONE who provides efficiency for growth" (6 MR 17)

"ONE who sees and knows" (7 MR 404)

"ONE so dear to us" (HL 301)

"ONE who stands higher" (DA 464)

"ONE who was more than a prophet" (DA 567)

"ONE who was the foundation of the whole Jewish economy" (DA 52)

Bible Search

Ones

We start with God (<u>One</u>). The first verse in the Bible says, *"In the beginning God created the heavens and the earth"* (Genesis 1:1). The Scriptures go on to say: *"Seek ye <u>first</u> the kingdom of God, and his righteousness; and all these things shall be added unto you"* (Matthew 6:33).

Man's ways and thoughts are opposite of God's ways and thoughts. God says to seek Him and man says "take care of number one." Often man is "number one," in his own eyes and his great aim seems to be independent of God. Therefore, the first lesson to be learned is our dependence upon God.

1. Read the following verses and write any words that refer to one in the blanks:

Isaiah 44:6 _____

Isaiah 48:12-13 _____

Isaiah 43:10-11 _____

Revelation 1:11, 17 _____

Revelation 2:8 _____

Revelation 22:13 _____

2. What is the first book in the Bible?

Note: This book establishes God as Creator, and Redeemer. This book contains all the other books in embryo, it is "the seed plot of the Bible."

3. What was created on the first day of creation? (Genesis 1:3)

4. What is the first commandment? (Exodus 20:3)

5. What are the "ones" in Ephesians 4:4-6?

> **Remarkable Math**
>
> 1 x 1 x 1 = 1 (Divine Unity)
>
> 111,111,111 x 111,111,111
> = (equals)
> 12,345,678,987,654,321

6. Where is the word "one" first used in the Bible? Use a concordance to find the answer.

7. How was Eve created? (Genesis 2:21)

8. How many languages were there in the beginning of this earth's history? (Genesis 11:1)

9. There are many ones in the Bible. Go to the concordance and choose 3 or more verses you especially enjoy in the New Testament. Copy them on the blanks below.

More Bible Search—Other Bible Firsts

- What were the first recorded words spoken to man? (Genesis 1:28)

- What was the first lie? (Genesis 3:4)

- Who was the first murderer? (Genesis 4:8)

- What was the first city built? (Genesis 4:17)

- Who was the first recorded tentmaker? (Genesis 4:20)

- Who was the first recorded musician (Genesis 4:21)

- Who was the first mentioned worker in iron and brass? (Genesis 4:22)

- Who was the first recorded man to die a natural death? (Genesis 5:5)

- What was the first mountain mentioned? (Genesis 8:4)

- What was the first Biblical mention of weeping (Genesis 21:16)

- Who were the first recorded twins? (Genesis 25:23-26)

- Who was the first judge mentioned? (Exodus 18:13)

- Who were the first high priests mentioned in the Bible? (Exodus 28:1)

- Who was the first king of Israel? (I Samuel 11:15)

Reinforce

The First Family

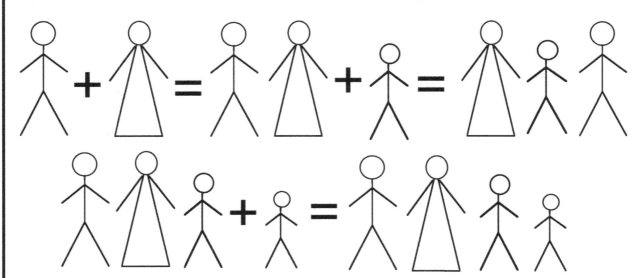

1 (Adam, first man) **+ 1** (Eve, first woman) **= 2**
(A family to help one another to be **alert** to Satan's temptations.)
2 + 1 (first son, Cain) **= 3 + 1** (second son, Abel) **= 4**
2 (Adam and Eve or family) **+ 1** (Jesus) **= 3** (Unity)

Remember

Store these facts in your mind.

$$\begin{array}{c} 1 \\ + 1 \\ \hline 2 \end{array} \qquad \begin{array}{c} 1 \\ + 2 \\ \hline 3 \end{array} \qquad \begin{array}{c} 1 \\ + 3 \\ \hline 4 \end{array} \qquad \begin{array}{c} 1 \\ + 4 \\ \hline 5 \end{array} \qquad \begin{array}{c} 1 \\ + 5 \\ \hline 6 \end{array} \qquad \begin{array}{c} 1 \\ + 6 \\ \hline 7 \end{array}$$

$$\begin{array}{c} 1 \\ + 7 \\ \hline 8 \end{array} \qquad \begin{array}{c} 1 \\ + 8 \\ \hline 9 \end{array} \qquad \begin{array}{c} 1 \\ + 9 \\ \hline 10 \end{array} \qquad \begin{array}{c} 1 \\ + 10 \\ \hline 11 \end{array} \qquad \begin{array}{c} 1 \\ + 11 \\ \hline 12 \end{array} \qquad \begin{array}{c} 1 \\ + 12 \\ \hline 13 \end{array}$$

Seth

"And Adam lived a hundred and thirty years, and begat a son in his own likeness, after his image; and called his name Seth."
Genesis 5:3

Cain became jealous of Abel, his brother, and slew him. How sad all of heaven must have been, to witness the first death of one of God's children.

God gave another son to the first family. *"For God, said she, hath appointed me another seed instead of Abel, whom Cain slew.*

"And to Seth, to him also there was born a son; and he called his name Enos: then began men to call upon the name of the Lord" (Genesis 4:25-26).

Seth had children, who had children, who had more children. "The descendants of Seth had separated themselves from the wicked descendants of Cain. They cherished the knowledge of God's will, while the ungodly race of Cain had no respect for God and His sacred commandments."* Seth and his family were **alert** to the promises of God. They knew that someday God would send forth His Son.

III Spiritual Gifts 60

Reflect

Abel worshiped God in the way God asked to be worshiped. Cain made up his own way to worship God.

Because of his false worship, "the Lord set a mark upon Cain."
Genesis 4:15

In the end, any man who chooses his own way to worship God will receive "...the mark of the beast...." and "...God shall add unto him the plagues...."
Revelation 16:2; 22:18

Example of Place Value

Seth lived 912 years.

hundreds	tens	ones
9	1	2

"And all the days of Seth were nine hundred and twelve years: and he died."
Genesis 5:8

Reflect
Children Added

As you do the problems remember what the plus sign means,
and all the children who were added to the family
of both Seth and Cain.

God's Children
Seth
Enos
Cainan
Mahalaleel
Enoch
Methuselah
Lamech
Noah

Satan's Children
Cain
Enoch
Irad
Mehujael
Methusael
Lamech
Jabal
Tubalcain

Review
Place I

1. Find the sum of these addition problems.
Let these sums remind you of children added to God's family.

$$\begin{array}{cccccc} 1 & 1 & 1 & 1 & 1 & 1 \\ +\,1 & +\,2 & +\,3 & +\,4 & +\,5 & +\,6 \end{array}$$

$$\begin{array}{cccccc} 1 & 1 & 1 & 1 & 1 & 1 \\ +\,7 & +\,8 & +\,9 & +\,10 & +\,11 & +\,12 \end{array}$$

1   Learn to spell the number one. Write it several times.

_____

Many children were born to Adam and Eve,
but they were not the <u>Deliverer</u>.

"...The Lord shall add to me another son."
Genesis 30:24

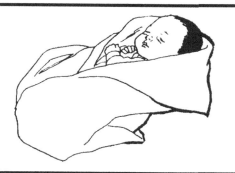

2. Find the sum of these addition problems.

1	1	1	1	1	1
+ 9	+ 5	+ 2	+ 6	+ 11	+ 3

1	1	1	1	1	1
+ 1	+ 8	+ 12	+ 4	+ 7	+ 10

3. What number comes after:

1 ___   7 ___   4 ___   3 ___   9 ___

7 ___   3 ___   5 ___   6 ___   8 ___

5 ___   4 ___   8 ___   2 ___   6 ___

Fill in the blanks to show how long
Adam lived before Seth was born.

____ ____ ____

What place is each number in?

_____ _____ _____

4. Find the sum. Think of the answers as being children born to godly parents.

1	1	1	1	1	1
+ 6	+ 9	+ 11	+ 3	+ 5	+ 12

1	1	1	1	1	1
+ 8	+ 2	+ 10	+ 4	+ 7	+ 1

1	1	1	1	1	1
+ 4	+ 10	+ 1	+ 7	+ 5	+ 2

1	1	1	1	1	1
+ 11	+ 9	+ 6	+ 3	+ 12	+ 8

5. Be <u>alert</u> and find the answers to these problems.

1 + 1 = _____   1 + 2 = _____   1 + 3 = _____

1 + 4 = _____   1 + 5 = _____   1 + 6 = _____

1 + 5 = _____   1 + 6 = _____   1 + 7 = _____

1 + 8 = _____   1 + 8 = _____   1 + 9 = _____

1 + 10 = _____   1 + 11 = _____   1 + 12 = _____

"When the tempests of temptation gather, and the fierce lightnings flash, and the waves sweep over us, we battle with the storm alone, forgetting that there is <u>One</u> who can help us...."
The Desire of Ages 336

Review
Place II

1. What does the plus sign mean? _____

Find the sum for these problems. Let the sums remind you of children added to God's family.

Example
How to carry

$$^{1}19$$
$$+ 12$$
$$\overline{31}$$

Add 2 + 9 = 11. Think; 11 is 1 ten and 1 one. Carry the 1 to the tens' column and write the 1 in the ones' place. Add 1 + 1 + 1 = 3

22	21	26	24	25	23
+ 1	+ 6	+ 2	+ 5	+ 4	+ 3

29	27	26	28	30	32
+ 7	+ 9	+ 8	+ 10	+ 11	+ 12

31	34	36	32	35	37
+ 18	+ 13	+ 15	+ 17	+ 14	+ 16

38	40	41	43	39	42
+ 24	+ 20	+ 19	+ 23	+ 22	+ 21

44	47	45	48	46	49
+ 26	+ 28	+ 25	+ 27	+ 30	+ 29

```
    50         52         55         51         53         54
  + 31       + 34       + 36       + 33       + 35       + 32


    56         58         57         59         61         60
  + 40       + 37       + 42       + 38       + 39       + 41
```

2. Find the sum for these addition problems.

10 + 8 = _____   12 + 9 = _____   11 + 7 = _____

15 + 1 = _____   18 + 5 = _____   13 + 2 = _____

14 + 3 = _____   16 + 4 = _____   15 + 6 = _____

17 + 9 = _____   20 + 7 = _____   19 + 8 = _____

26 + 1 = _____   24 + 6 = _____   23 + 4 = _____

25 + 5 = _____   22 + 3 = _____   21 + 2 = _____

27 + 10 = _____   30 + 12 = _____   28 + 11 = _____

26 + 13 = _____   29 + 15 = _____   31 + 14 = _____

3. Count by tens and fill in the missing blanks.

_____ 20 _____ 40 _____ _____ _____ 80 _____ _____ _____

120 _____ _____ _____ 160 _____ _____ 190 _____

4. Add by twos to do this dot-to-dot.
  Make a new start on numbers 42, 74, 94, 118, 142, and 150.

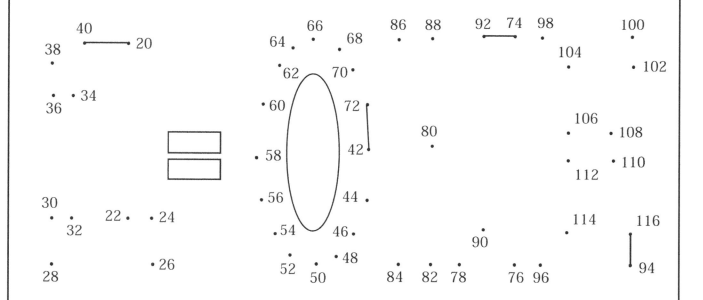

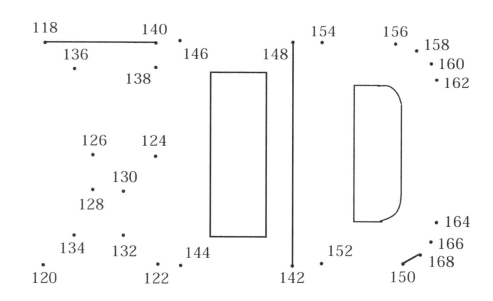

Color these words.

Review
Place III

"...And maketh him families
like a flock."
Psalm 107:41

When people are <u>added</u> together according to God's laws of addition they make a family. The family <u>group</u> is a sacred, social society, in which each member is to help one another. To have a happy family, we need to be **alert** to the needs of the other members of our family <u>group</u>. Many times it requires us to <u>regroup</u> when one member is out of order.

Example
Regrouping Addends

Problem: $1 + 7 + 5 + 3 + 4 + 6 + 2 =$
Think: $(1+7) + (5 + 3) + (6 + 2) + 4 =$
$8 + 8 + 8 + 4 = 28$
or
<u>Regroup</u> all pairs and multiply by the number of pairs.

$3 \times 8 = 24 + 4 = 28$

1. <u>Regroup</u> these problems in groups that equal 10.

F. $8 + 2 + 6 + 4 + 5 =$ **I.** $9 + 1 + 11 + 4 + 3 + 5 =$

A. $7 + 3 + 5 + 9 + 1 =$ **L.** $10 + 12 + 8 + 2 + 4 + 1 + 9 =$

M. $6 + 10 + 4 + 6 + 3 =$ **Y.** $5 + 11 + 9 + 8 + 7 + 1 + 3 + 6 + 5 =$

Fill in the letters in front of each problem in these blanks.

____ ____ ____ ____ ____ ____

2. <u>Regroup</u> these problems in your mind then write only the answer down.

A. $8 + 7 + 5 + 9 + 1 =$

L. $9 + 5 + 6 + 4 + 6 =$

E. $11 + 9 + 12 + 3 + 6 + 4 =$

R. $12 + 8 + 3 + 7 + 6 + 4 + 15 + 5 =$

T. $7 + 8 + 5 + 4 + 10 + 16 + 4 + 2 + 3 + 6 =$

"But made his own people
to go forth like sheep,
and guided them in the
wilderness like a flock."
Psalm 78:52

3. <u>Regroup</u> these pairs of numbers and find the sum.

S. $5 + 3 + 3 + 7 + 7 + 4 + 1 =$

E. $9 + 1 + 8 + 2 + 6 + 6 + 3 =$

T. $7 + 3 + 6 + 5 + 2 + 8 =$

H. $4 + 11 + 12 + + 3 + 6 + 2 =$

E. $7 + 6 + 3 + 5 + 2 + 8 =$

N. $2 + 5 + 4 + 1 + 6 + 3 =$

O. $5 + 3 + 4 + 7 + 3 + 2 =$

C. $2 + 9 + 7 + 4 + 5 + 6 + 3 + 1 + 8 =$

H. $5 + 7 + 9 + 3 + 6 + 1 + 7 + 2 + 5 =$

"Thus saith the Lord God,
Behold, I will lift up mine hand
to the Gentiles, and set up
my standard to the people:
and they shall bring thy sons
in their arms, and thy daughters
shall be carried
upon their shoulders."
Isaiah 49:22

Review
Word Problems
Place I

1. Fill in the blanks with the proper numbers.

Here is Adam. _____

Here are Adam's sons and son's sons. _____

There are _____ sons.
(Add Abel to the list of sons.)

1 son and 8 sons are _____ sons.

"To Adam was given another son,
to be the inheritor of the divine promise,
the heir of the spiritual birthright.
The name Seth, given to this son,
signified 'appointed,' or 'compensation...'"*

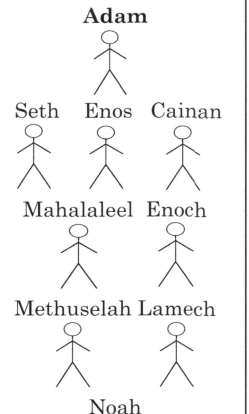

Adam

Seth   Enos   Cainan

Mahalaleel   Enoch

Methuselah   Lamech

Noah

2. Fill in the blanks.

Here is Noah. _____

Here are Noah's sons. _____

There are _____ sons. 1 son and 2

sons are _____ sons.

> "But the fulfillment
> of the promise tarried."**

*Patriarchs and Prophets 80 **The Desire of Ages 31*

Noah

Shem   Ham   Japheth

**Which of Noah's sons
became the family that
the promise came
through?**
(Genesis 11:10-26)

Addition 1 – Student – Page 44

Review
Word Problems
Place II

1. One family had 8 sons while another had 14 sons and 3 daughters. How many total sons were there in both families?

2. A family of 8 like Noah's plus 2 families totaling 16 people are how many in all?

3. Father, read for worship about the family of Adam, Noah, and Abraham. What is the sum of these three families?

4. *"Lo, children are an heritage of the Lord: and the fruit of the womb is his reward"* (Psalm 127:3). A family with brothers, sisters, cousins, aunts, and uncles, totaled 43 on the mother's side of the family. On the father's side there were 37. What was the sum of the family members on both sides?

Reinforce
SONS

List the eight members of Noah's family.

1. _____

2. _____

3. _____

4. _____

5. _____

6. _____

7. _____

8. _____

**Genesis 4:1-2;
Genesis 7:7;
Genesis 21:2-3**

Uncles, Aunts,
Brothers, Sisters,
Cousins

Review
Word Problems
Place III

1. How many members are there in each of your friends' families? Choose 7 families you know. List the numbers in each one.

___ + ___ + ___ + ___ + ___ +

___ + ___ =

Regroup and find the sum.

2. The following families had these members: 7, 3, 8, 2, 5, 5, and 4. How many members did all the families have together?

3. Adam had many sons. Three well known ones were __ __ __ __,

__ __ __ __, and __ __ __ __.

Then S__ __ __ had children who had children. Regroup these children.

1 + 6 +
9 + 12 +
9 + 14 +
8 =

Reinforce
FRIENDS

List your friends below:
1. _____
2. _____
3. _____
4. _____
5. _____
6. _____
7. _____

Jesus said: "Ye are my friends, if ye do whatsoever I command you."
John 15:14

"The friendship of the world is enmity with God."
James 4:4

Reinforce
Alert Families

1. Each **alert** family member working together makes chores so much easier. This week assign each member to one part of the meal preparation.

"...Infinite Wisdom called him [Moses] who was to become the leader of his people to spend forty years in the **humble work** of a shepherd."*

Example

(1) Father and Mother – Menus
(2) Member – Cook
(3) Member – Set Table
(4) Member – Put Food on the Table
(5) All Members – + <u>Clean</u> <u>Up</u> = Unity

When each member does his chores on time, all can eat according to schedule.

Make the waffles or pancakes recipe.

Serve with fresh fruit and nut spread. A cashew cream or frozen banana ice cream is good on top!

Waffles or Pancakes

2 Cups Water
1/2 Cup Cashews
1/2 Cup Almonds
1/4 Cup Coconut
1/4 Cup Dates
1 Cup Barley Flour
1/4 Cup Corn Flour
1/2 tsp. Salt

Bake in a hot waffle iron or for pancakes in a non-stick fry pan.

In a blender, blend first 5 ingredients together. Pour into a bowl and add the rest of the ingredients. Add more water or flour as needed.

*Patriarchs and Prophets 247-248

2. From the days of Seth and Enoch the promise was spoken through patriarchs and prophets, keeping alive the hope of Christ's appearing, and yet He tarried.

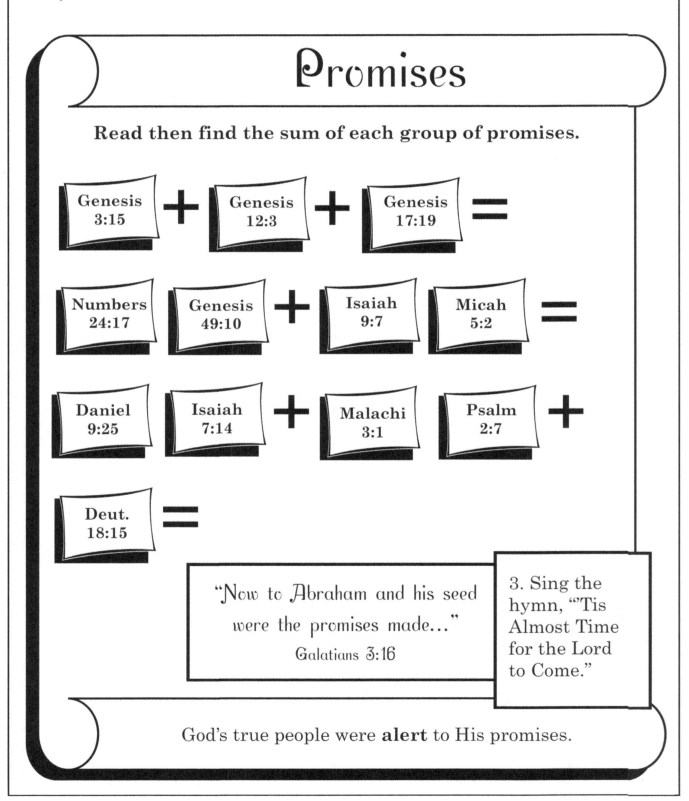

Promises

Read then find the sum of each group of promises.

Genesis 3:15 **+** Genesis 12:3 **+** Genesis 17:19 **=**

Numbers 24:17 Genesis 49:10 **+** Isaiah 9:7 Micah 5:2 **=**

Daniel 9:25 Isaiah 7:14 **+** Malachi 3:1 Psalm 2:7 **+**

Deut. 18:15 **=**

"Now to Abraham and his seed were the promises made…"
Galatians 3:16

3. Sing the hymn, "'Tis Almost Time for the Lord to Come."

God's true people were **alert** to His promises.

Remainder

J esus, O thers, Y ou

"And this is life eternal, that they might know thee the only true God, and Jesus Christ, whom thou hast sent."

John 17:3

How can you help bring unity to your home? The home is your first school, and "it is here that the foundation should be laid for a life of service. Its principles are to be taught not merely in theory. They are to shape the whole training.

"Very early the lesson of helpfulness should be taught the child. As soon as strength and reasoning power are sufficiently developed, he should be given duties to perform in the home. He should be encouraged in trying to help father and mother, encouraged to deny and to control himself, to put others' happiness and convenience before his own, to watch for opportunities to cheer and assist brothers and sisters and playmates, and to show kindness to the aged, the sick, and the unfortunate. The more fully the spirit of true ministry pervades the home, the more fully it will be developed in the lives of the children. They will learn to find joy in service and sacrifice for the good of others....

"Above any other agency, service for Christ's sake in the little things of everyday experience has power to mold the character and to direct the life into lines of unselfish ministry. To awaken this spirit, to encourge and rightly to direct it, is the parents' and teacher's work. No more important work could be committed to them. The spirit of ministry is the spirit of heaven, and with every effort to develop and encourage it angels will co-operate.

"Such an education must be based upon the word of God. Here only are its principles given in their fullness. The Bible should be made the foundation of study and of teaching. The essential knowledge is a knowledge of God and of Him whom He has sent."*

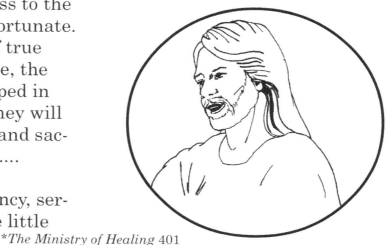

The Ministry of Healing 401

Reinforce
Others
1. Meditate on these thoughts.

"Every true,
self-sacrificing worker for God
is willing to spend and
be spent for the sake of others.
Christ says, 'He that
loveth his life shall lose it;
and he that hateth his life
in this world shall keep it
unto life eternal.'
By earnest, thoughtful efforts
to help where help is needed,
the true Christian shows his love
for God and for his fellow beings.
He may lose his life in service;
but when Christ comes
to gather His jewels to Himself,
he will find it again."

The Youth's Instructor, 9-10-1907

2. Read the stories on the next page.

Read these stories.

Other People Always First

I know a little boy who always puts himself first when speaking of himself in connection with anybody else. He always says, "Me and mama," or, "Me and papa," or, "Me and Freddie."

And it is the same when he wants to divide anything—he always helps himself first, and others afterward. What do you think of that way of doing? You don't like to hear other children speak that way, nor do you like to see them act that way. It is not the right way to do.

The Bible says we ought to esteem others better than ourselves. Then we ought to speak of others first, and serve them first, and put ourselves last.

The commandment says, *"Honour thy father and thy mother."* Then we surely ought to speak of them first, and wait on them first, and obey them first.
—*B. J. Farnsworth*

Unselfish Care for Others

A very poor and aged man, busied in planting and grafting an apple tree, was rudely interrupted by the interrogation, "Why do you plant trees, who cannot hope to eat the fruit of them?" He raised himself up, and leaning upon his spade, replied, "Some one planted trees before I was born, and I have eaten the fruit; I now plant for others, that the memorial of my gratitude may exist when I am dead and gone."

Others

The Romans had a law that no person should approach the Emperor's tent in the night upon the pain of death; but it once happened that a soldier was found in that situation, with a petition in his hand, waiting for an opportunity of presenting it. He was apprehended, and going to be immediately executed; but the Emperor, having overheard the matter in his pavilion, cried aloud, saying, "If the petition be for himself, let him die; it for another, spare his life." Upon inquiry, it was found that the generous soldier prayed for the lives of his two comrades who had been taken asleep on the watch. The Emperor nobly forgave them all. —*Arvine*

Thoughtfulness for Others

An engineer in the South West, on a locomotive, once saw a train coming with which he must collide. He resolved to stand at his post and slow up the train until the last minute, for there were passengers behind in the cars. The engineer said to the fireman, "Jump! One man is enough on this engine. Jump!" The fireman jumped, and was saved. The crash came. The engineer died at his post.
—*Talmage*

3. Review zero by reading these thoughts and meditating upon them.

"Nothing is apparently more helpless, yet really more invincible, than the soul that feels its nothingness and relies wholly on the merits of the Saviour. By prayer, by the study of His word, by faith in His word, by faith in His abiding presence, the weakest of human beings may live in contact with the living Christ, and He will hold them by a hand that will never let go.

"These precious words every soul that abides in Christ may make his own. He may say:

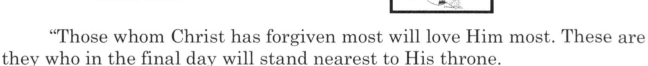

> '...I will look upon the Lord;
> I will wait for the God of my salvation:
> My God will hear me.
> Rejoice not against me, O mine enemy:
> When I fall, I shall arise;
> When I sit in darkness,
> The Lord shall be a light unto me.'
> Micah 7:7-8...

God has promised:

> 'I will make a man more precious than fine gold;
> Even a man than the golden wedge of Ophir.'
> Isaiah 13:12

> 'Though ye have lain among the pots,
> Yet shall ye be as the wings of a dove
> covered with silver,
> And her feathers with yellow gold.'
> Psalm 68:13

"Those whom Christ has forgiven most will love Him most. These are they who in the final day will stand nearest to His throne.

> "They shall see his face; and his name shall be in their foreheads.'
> Revelation 22:4."*

*The Ministry of Healing 182

2 2 2 Twos - 2 2 2 2

Research
The Number Two

"It is also written in your law, that the testimony of two men is true. I am one that bear witness of myself, and the Father that sent me beareth witness of me."
John 8:17-18

The number two, in the Bible, reminds us of difference. The difference that the number two represents can be a good difference, (or an evil difference) as when two are different in personality, yet are one in testimony and friendship. Two can remind us how Jesus took on a second nature, the human form, for our <u>deliverance</u>. Thus two reminds us of the incarnation. *"The second man is the Lord from heaven"* (I Corinthians 15:47). He came to <u>deliver</u> us from the ruin brought on mankind through the first man, Adam and the first woman, Eve.

The number two also reminds us of the fullness of testimony.

Reinforce
Color then read the meaning of the number two. Learn to say two in these languages.

French – deux (dŏo)

Japanese – ni (nee)

Spanish – dos (dohs)

Swahili – mbili (mm BEE lee)

$$\begin{array}{r} 2 \text{ addend} \\ + 2 \text{ addend} \\ \hline 4 \text{ sum} \end{array}$$

TWO - 2 = DIFFERENCE, FULLNESS OF TESTIMONY

2

The divine nature and the human nature combined (addition +) to give sinful man a Saviour.

Divine

Human →

+

"...At the mouth of two witnesses, or at the mouth of three witnesses, shall the matter be established."
Deuteronomy 19:15

God needs other witnesses to join Jesus' witness of Himself.

"Ye are my witnesses."
Isaiah 43:10

The time had come for Christ to bear <u>witness</u> of the Father in heaven. Jesus would be a perfect <u>witness</u> as a baby, as a child, as a youth, and as an adult. The Father and the Holy Spirit would bear <u>witness</u> of Jesus as a baby, as a child, as a youth, and as an adult. Would the people on the earth be **alert** to do the same?

Even nature bears <u>witness</u> about God. Everything in it has laws by which it is governed and these laws determine how many petals on a flower or legs on an insect. The Begonia Family (Begoniaceae) has 900 species. Mostly perennial herbs and shrubs, with staminate and pistillate flowers on the same plant. The staminate flowers have 2 petallike sepals, 2 petals, and many stamens. The pristillate flowers have 2 or more tepals and a compound pistil.

Reflect

Witness comes from a word which means, "to know."

1. Testimony

2. That which furnishes evidence or proof

3. A person who knows or sees any thing; one personally present. (See I Peter 5:1.)

4. One who sees the execution of an instrument, and subscribes it for the purpose of confirming its authenticity by his testimony.

5. One who gives testimony; as, the witnesses in court agreed in all essential facts.

Stones of Witness

"Like the people of Israel, let us set up our <u>stones of witness</u>, and inscribe upon them the precious story of what God has wrought for us. And as we review His dealings with us in our pilgrimage, let us, out of hearts melted with gratitude, declare, *'What shall I render unto the Lord for all his benefits toward me? I will take the cup of salvation, and call upon the name of the Lord. I will pay my vows unto the Lord now in the presence of all his people'* (Psalm 116:12-14)."*

*The Desire of Ages 348

 # Bible Search

Twos

The number one excludes all differences, and tells us there is a Sovereign. However, two affirms that there is a difference—there is another.

It is the first number by which we can divide another. We therefore may trace this fundamental idea of division or difference.

Two also can teach us contrast—light and darkness; day and night; good and evil; happiness and sadness; and **alertness** and unawareness.

1. What was the first and second statement in the Bible? (Genesis 1:1-2)

Note: The first thought speaks of perfection and of order. The second of ruin and desolation.

2. What is the second book in the Bible?

Note: The first book of the Bible speaks of man's beginnings and how sin came into the world and only a few who chose to serve God. The second book teaches of God's marvelous intervention on behalf of His people to deliver them from the slavery of sin. It recounts the stories of how He did this.

3. What is the first verse in the Bible that uses the word two? Use a concordance to find the answer.

4. Who was the first man who married two wives? (Genesis 4:19)

5. How did the unclean animals go into the ark? (Genesis 6:19-20)

6. Where did two angels visit? (Genesis 19:1)

7. Who had two daughters? (Genesis 29:16)

8. What did God give Moses on Mount Sinai? (Exodus 31:18)

9. How did Jesus describe the law? (Matthew 22:36-40)

10. What are some parables that have two in them? (Matthew 21:28-32; Matthew 25:14-30; Luke 7:41-43)

11. What is the last verse in the Bible that uses the word two? Use a concordance to find the answer.

12. There are many twos in the Bible—look up the list in the *Strong's Concordance.*

Reinforce

Place I

What parable is this?

_____

**Who is the other man
that is not
in the picture?**

_____

_____

**Color
this picture.**

Reinforce
The Father's Witness of Jesus as a:

 Baby The Father sent the wise men to Jerusalem.

12 **Child** The Father sent the Holy Spirit to impress the teachers at Jerusalem when Jesus was 12.

Youth The Father spoke, and also sent the Holy Spirit in the form of the dove when Jesus was baptized at the Jordan.

2 **Adult** The Father sent Elijah and Moses.

1 (Witness) + 1 (Witness) = 2 (Word Established)
2 (Witnesses) + 2 (Witnesses) = 4 (Word Established)

Remember
Store these facts in your mind.

$$\begin{array}{cc} 2 \\ +1 \\ \hline 3 \end{array} \qquad \begin{array}{cc} 2 \\ +2 \\ \hline 4 \end{array} \qquad \begin{array}{cc} 2 \\ +3 \\ \hline 5 \end{array} \qquad \begin{array}{cc} 2 \\ +4 \\ \hline 6 \end{array} \qquad \begin{array}{cc} 2 \\ +5 \\ \hline 7 \end{array} \qquad \begin{array}{cc} 2 \\ +6 \\ \hline 8 \end{array}$$

$$\begin{array}{cc} 2 \\ +7 \\ \hline 9 \end{array} \qquad \begin{array}{cc} 2 \\ +8 \\ \hline 10 \end{array} \qquad \begin{array}{cc} 2 \\ +9 \\ \hline 11 \end{array} \qquad \begin{array}{cc} 2 \\ +10 \\ \hline 12 \end{array} \qquad \begin{array}{cc} 2 \\ +11 \\ \hline 13 \end{array} \qquad \begin{array}{cc} 2 \\ +12 \\ \hline 14 \end{array}$$

The Speaking Word

"And the Word was made flesh,
and dwelt among us,
(and we beheld his glory, the glory as
of the only begotten of the Father,)
full of grace and truth."

John 1:14

Israel had many Scripture promises that pointed to Jesus' coming. They were not **alert**! They were asleep in their sins. Jesus would come and try to wake them up by giving them an example of how to be delivered from sin by faith in God's all-powerful, creative, speaking Word.

Review

Place I

1. Find the sum for these problems.

$$
\begin{array}{cccccc}
2 & 2 & 2 & 2 & 2 & 2 \\
+\,1 & +\,2 & +\,3 & +\,4 & +\,5 & +\,6 \\
\end{array}
$$

$$
\begin{array}{cccccc}
2 & 2 & 2 & 2 & 2 & 2 \\
+\,7 & +\,8 & +\,9 & +\,10 & +\,11 & +\,12 \\
\end{array}
$$

Learn to spell the number two. Write it several times.

2 _____ 2

2. Find the sum for these problems.

2	2	2	2	2	2
+ 4	+ 10	+ 6	+ 2	+ 8	+ 11

2	2	2	2	2	2
+ 5	+ 9	+ 1	+ 12	+ 7	+ 3

2	2	2	2	2	2
+ 5	+ 8	+ 12	+ 1	+ 4	+ 2

2	2	2	2	2	2
+ 10	+ 7	+ 3	+ 9	+ 11	+ 6

3. Promises About the Deliverer

Promises about the <u>Deliverer</u>, like people, increased as God added more and more messages through the prophets about the coming Saviour. There are seven (7) continents on the earth. People began to increase upon the face of the earth.

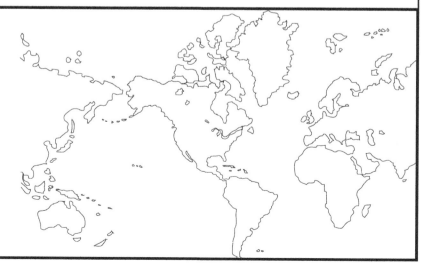

"And it came to pass, when men began to multiply on the face of the earth, and daughters were born unto them…"
Genesis 6:1

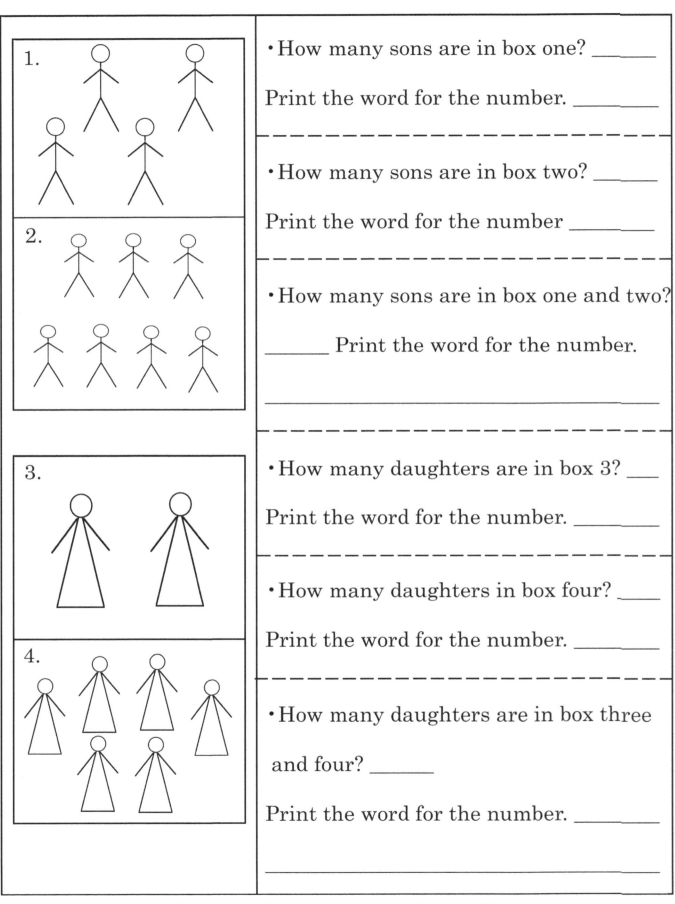

1.

2.

- How many sons are in box one? _____

Print the word for the number. _____

- How many sons are in box two? _____

Print the word for the number _____

- How many sons are in box one and two?

_____ Print the word for the number.

_____

3.

4.

- How many daughters are in box 3? ____

Print the word for the number. _____

- How many daughters in box four? _____

Print the word for the number. _____

- How many daughters are in box three

and four? _____

Print the word for the number. _____

_____

Research
Result of Witnessing Evil

"Because that, when they knew God, they glorified him not as God, neither were thankful; but became vain in their imaginations, and their foolish heart was darkened."

Romans 1:21

"For some time the two classes remained separate. The race of Cain, spreading from the place of their first settlement, dispersed over the plains and valleys where the children of Seth had dwelt; and the latter, in order to escape from their contaminating influence, withdrew to the mountains, and there made their home. So long as this separation continued, they maintained the worship of God in its purity. But in the lapse of time they ventured, little by little, to mingle with the inhabitants of the valleys. This association was productive of the worst results. *The sons of God saw the daughters of men that they were fair.'* The children of Seth, attracted by the beauty of the daughters of Cain's descendants, displeased the Lord by intermarrying with them. Many of the worshipers of God were beguiled into sin by the allurements that were now constantly before them, and they lost their peculiar, holy character. Mingling with the depraved, they became like them in spirit and in deeds; the restrictions of the seventh commandment were disregarded, *'and they took them wives of all which they chose.'* The children of Seth went *'in the way of*

Patriarchs and Prophets 81-82

Cain' (Jude 11); they fixed their minds upon worldly prosperity and enjoyment and neglected the commandments of the Lord. Men *'did not like to retain God in their knowledge,'* they *'became vain in their imaginations, and their foolish heart was darkened'* (Romans 1:21). Therefore *'God gave them over to a reprobate, mind'* (Verse 28). Sin spread abroad in the earth like deadly leprosy."*

If only God's people would have stayed in their mountain home.

Reflect

Children

God's   **Satan's**

God's children
and Satan's children married.
God says,

"Wherefore come out
from among them,
and be ye separate, saith the Lord,
and touch not the unclean thing;
and I will receive you,

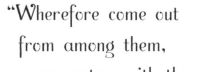

"And will be a Father unto you,
and ye shall be my sons
and daughters,
saith the Lord Almighty."
II Corinthians 6:17-18

Men "neglected the commandments of the Lord."

"Evil unchecked grows,
evil tolerated poisons the whole system."
Jawaharlal Nehru

"Woe unto them that call evil good,
and good evil; that put darkness
for light, and light for darkness;
that put bitter for sweet,
and sweet for bitter!"
Isaiah 5:20

"Be not overcome
of evil, but
overcome evil
with good."
Romans 12:21

**The
Earth Was Filled
With Sin**

Review
Ones and Twos
Place I

1. Find the sum for these problems.

1 + 8	1 + 10	1 + 5	2 + 9	1 + 3	2 + 11
2 + 7	2 + 1	1 + 6	1 + 12	2 + 4	1 + 2
2 + 5	2 + 8	1 + 9	2 + 12	2 + 2	2 + 6
2 + 10	1 + 4	1 + 7	1 + 1	1 + 11	2 + 3

Word Problems

2. There were many sons born to Adam and Eve. But just one (1) in each generation was chosen to be the ancestor from whom Jesus descended. There were nine (9) chosen sons up until the time of the Flood. What would the sum be counting Adam (1) plus nine (9) more generations?

3. Adam and Eve had two (2) sons. One (1) (Abel) was killed and the other (Cain) was wicked. Another son came to their home (Seth). How many sons is that?

> "Be always vigilant; there are many snares for the good."
> —Accius, c 100 B.C.

Review
Word Problems
Place II

"Hereafter I will not talk much with you:

for the prince of this world cometh,

and hath nothing in me."

John 14:30

Down Words

much
will
the
cometh
nothing
prince
this

Across Words

me
you
with
world
hereafter
in
hath

"...But was in all points
tempted like
as we are,
yet without sin."
Hebrews 4:15

"Who did no sin,
neither was guile found in his mouth."
1 Peter 2:22

"Ye are my Witnesses."

Isaiah 43:10

Review
Word Problems
Place III

1. One group sent out Health Study interest cards to one large community. Below is a calendar showing the daily responses in the mail. Add in your mind and write down each week's total. (See example on how to find an average on page 24.)

October

					④ 1	2
④ 3	⑩ 4	⑫ 5	⑭ 6	⑧ 7	⑦ 8	9
③ 10	⑬ 11	⑭ 12	⑫ 13	⑩ 14	⑨ 15	16
⑩ 17	⑭ 18	⑫ 19	⑪ 20	⑫ 21	⑫ 22	23
24 / 31	⑥ 25	④ 26	③ 27	① 28	② 29	④ 30

=
=
=
=
=

Total for 4 weeks and 1 day _____

What was the average number of interest cards that came in each day?

_____

2. The following are homes the follow-up team visited after receiving the health interest cards. They broke them into six different areas of the city. Add all the totals in your mind and write in the answers.

Area	Day 1	Day 2	Day 3	Day 4	Day 5	Day 6	Total
1	8	6	4	3	2	4	
2	6	7	3	11	6	2	
3	12	6	5	6	10	2	
4	13	4	2	1	4	4	
5	9	5	3	7	8	3	
6	8	3	7	6	5	5	

Total of Homes Visited _____

How many homes were not visited? _____

Alertness!

Remind

1. When one member of the family does a chore and does it well, that is a <u>witness</u> to God. When all members of the family do their chores well that is even a greater <u>witness</u>. People will notice!

2. As you do the dishes, be **alert** to wash them well and rinse them thoroughly.

Reflect
Witnessing

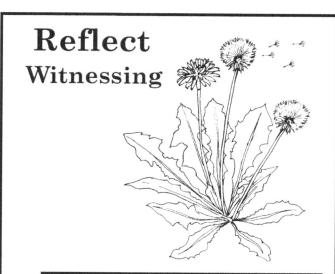

What does this house witness about the family living there?

"It became the most sacred duty of a new convert [among the early Christians] to diffuse among his friends and relations the inestimable blessing which he had received, and to warn them against a refusal that would be severely punished as a criminal disobedience to the will of a benevolent but all-powerful Deity."
—*Gibbon*

"I went by the field
of the slothful,
and by the vineyard
of the man
void of understanding;

"And, lo, it was
all grown over with thorns,
and nettles had covered
the face thereof,
and the stone wall thereof
was broken down.

"Then I saw,
and considered it well:
I looked upon it,
and received instruction."
Proverbs 24:30-32

Reinforce
Place I - II - III

Holy, **alert** men in each generation looked for and encouraged the people to prepare for the coming <u>Deliverer</u>.

Fill in the blanks below of some that we have learned about in this lesson.

A __ __ __

S __ __ __

E __ __ __ __

N __ __ __

"Seeing many things,
but thou <u>observest</u> <u>not</u>;
opening the ears,
but he heareth not."
Isaiah 42:20

Sing the chorus of the hymn, "Waiting and Watching."

Reinforce
Watchfulness or <u>Alertness</u>

Read these stories about watchfulness or alertness.

Watchfulness and Temptation

A countryman was riding with an unknown traveller (whom he thought was honest) over a dangerous place. "This place," said he, "is famous for robbery; but, for my own part, though often riding over it early and late, I never saw anything worse than myself." "In good time," replied the other, and thereupon demanded his purse and robbed him. Thus it is that in no place, no company, no age, no person, is temptation free. Be watchful!

Duty of Watchfulness

A believer's watchfulness is like that of a soldier. A sentinel posted on the walls, when he discerns a hostile party advancing, does not attempt to make head against them himself, but informs his commanding officer of the enemy's approach, and leaves him to take the proper measures against the foe. So the Christian does not attempt to fight temptation in his own strength; he is **alert** in observing its approach, and in telling God of it by prayer.
—*Mason*

Watching Ought to be Perpetual

Dr. Johnson, giving advice to an intimate friend, said, "Above all, accustom your children constantly to tell the truth, without varying in any circumstance." A lady present emphatically exclaimed, "Nay, this is too much; for a little variation in narrative must happen a thousand times a day if one is not perpetually watching." "Well, Madam," replied the Doctor, "and you ought to be perpetually watching. It is more from carelessness about truth than from intentional lying that there is so much falsehood in the world."

Are you watchful or <u>alert</u>?

Watchfulness Illustrated

A native hunter passed a whole night within a few paces of a wounded tiger. The man's bare knees were pressed upon the hard gravel, but he dared not shift, even by a hair's-breath, his uneasy position. A bush was between him and the wild beast; ever and anon the tiger, as he lay with glaring eye fixed upon it, uttered his hoarse growl of anger; his hot breath absolutely blew upon the cheek of the wretched man, and still he moved not. The pain of the cramped position increased every moment—suspense became almost intolerable; but the motion of a limb, the rustling of a leaf, would have been death. He heard the gong of the village strike each hour of that fearful night, that seemed to him an eternity, and yet he lived. The tormenting mosquitoes swarmed around his face, but he dared not brush them off. That fiend-like eye met his whenever he ventured a glance toward the horrid spell that bound him; and a hoarse growl grated on the stillness of the night, as a passing breeze stirred the leaves that sheltered him. Hours rolled on, and his powers of endurance were well-nigh exhausted, when at length the welcome streaks of light shot up from the eastern horizon. On the approach of day the tiger rose, and stalked away with a sulky face to a thicket at some distance, and the stiff and wearied watcher felt that he was safe.

—*C. J. Vaughan*

Faithfulness in Watchfulness

Vigilance is the price of everything good and great in earth or heaven. It was for his faithful vigilance that the memory of the Pompeian sentinel is embalmed in poetry and recorded in history. Nothing but unceasing **alertness** can keep the heart in harmony with God's heart.

A native hunter passed a whole night within a few paces of a wounded tiger. What did he do?

Color this picture.

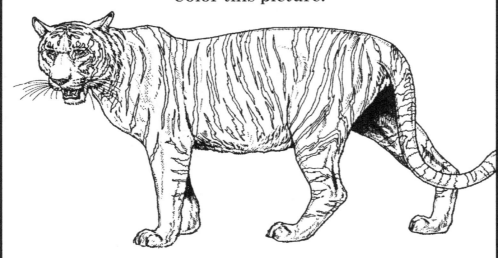

3 3 3 Threes - 3 3 3 3

Research
Three in Heaven

"For there are three that bear record in heaven, the Father, the Word, and the Holy Ghost: and these three are one."
1 John 5:7

Three in the Bible reminds us of reality, completeness, and entireness. It tells us of Divine perfection. God has had an **alert** family in every generation that served Him. The families on earth were to witness for the One (Three-3) in heaven and bear witness for God.

What is a witness?_____

_____

_____

_____

Jesus was to bear witness about the Father in heaven. (See John 5:19-47.) The Holy Spirit bears witness about both of Them.

Reinforce

Color then read the meaning of the number three. Learn to say three in these languages.

French – trois (trwah)

Japanese – san (sahn)

Spanish – tres (trehs)

Swahili – tatu (TAH too)

```
  3 addend
+ 3 addend
  6 sum
```

THREE - 3 = DIVINE PERFECTION

The divine nature and the human nature combined (addition +) to give sinful man a Saviour.

3

Divine

Human →

+

1. God refers to Himself as plural in many verses in the Bible.

Genesis 1:26 – *" And God said, Let <u>us</u> make man in <u>our</u> image, after <u>our</u> likeness...."*

Genesis 11:7 – *"Go to, let <u>us</u> go down, and there confound their language...."*

Note: "Elohim" is one of the Old Testament words for God. This Hebrew word is plural.

2. In some places God is the speaker, and He mentions both the Messiah and the Spirit, or at times the Messiah is the speaker who mentions both God and the Spirit.

Isaiah 48:16 – *"Come ye near unto me, hear ye this; I have not spoken in secret from the beginning; from the time that it was, there am I: and now the Lord God, and his Spirit, hath sent me."*

See Isaiah 61:1; 63:9-10.

Note: In the Old Testament, the Redeemer and Saviour is sometimes called Jehovah. See Job 19:25; Psalm 19:14; 78:35; 106:21; Isaiah 41:14; 43:3, 11, 14; 47:4; 49:7, 26; 60:16.

3. References that tell us the Father, Christ, and the Holy Spirit are individuals.

Matthew 3:16-17 – *"And <u>Jesus</u>, when he was baptized, went up straightway out of the water: and, lo, the heavens were opened unto him, and he saw the <u>Spirit of God</u> descending like a dove, and lighting upon him:*

"And lo <u>a voice</u> [the Father] *from heaven, saying, This is my beloved Son, in whom I am well pleased."*

Matthew 28:19 – *"Go ye therefore, and teach all nations, baptizing them in the name of the <u>Father</u>, and of the <u>Son</u>, and of the <u>Holy Ghost</u>."*

See I Corinthians 12:4-6; II Corinthians 13:14; and I Peter 1:2.

Sing the hymn, "Praise God From Whom All Blessings Flow."

4. There never was a time when Christ did not exist.

Isaiah 9:6 — *"For unto us a child is born, unto us a son is given: and the government shall be upon his shoulder: and his name shall be called Wonderful, Counsellor, The mighty God, The <u>everlasting</u> Father, The Prince of Peace."*

See John 1:1-2; Revelation 1:8; 22:13.

Note: In our Bible lesson we learn how Christ came to this earth and was born as a baby. However, He had always existed in all eternity.

(If you would like more information on this subject contact SonLight.)

1 + 1 + 1 = 3   **Reflect**   One in Purpose
Father, Son, and Holy Spirit

"In the name of <u>the Father, the Son, and the Holy Spirit</u>, man is laid in his watery grave, buried with Christ in baptism, and raised from the water to live the new life of loyalty to God. The <u>three great powers</u> in heaven are witnesses; they are invisible but present." *6 Bible Commentary* 1074

"The <u>eternal heavenly dignitaries—God, and Christ, and the Holy Spirit</u>—arming them [the disciples] with more than mortal energy...would advance with them to the work and convince the world of sin." *Evangelism* 616

"<u>The Father, the Son, and the Holy Spirit</u>, the <u>three holy dignitaries</u> of heaven, have declared that they will strengthen men to overcome the powers of darkness...." *5 Bible Commentary* 1110

"We are to co-operate with the <u>three highest powers</u> in heaven—<u>the Father, the Son, and the Holy Ghost</u>—and <u>these powers</u> will work through us, making us workers together with God." *Evangelism* 617

"<u>The three persons</u>" *6 Bible Commentary* 1074

"The <u>Godhead</u> was stirred with pity for the race, and <u>the Father, the Son, and the Holy Spirit</u> gave <u>Themselves</u> to the working out of the plan of redemption." *Counsels on Health* 222

"<u>Three dignitaries and powers</u> of heaven" *6 Bible Commentary* 1075

"There are <u>three living persons</u> of the <u>heavenly trio</u>; in the name of <u>these three great powers—the Father, the Son, and the Holy Spirit</u>—those who receive Christ by living faith are baptized, and <u>these powers</u> will co-operate with the obedient subjects of heaven...." *Evangelism* 615

See *6 Bible Commentary* 1075; *Great Controversy* 493; *5 Bible Commentary* 1148; and *Evangelism* 616-617

Note: The Father, the Son, and the Holy Spirit are three distinct, divine Personages. Yet they work in such perfect unity that their objectives and activities are as one.

 # Bible Search
Threes

What should three bring to our minds? The Father, One in sovereignty, highest in power or authority—ruler; the Son, the second person, incarnation (taking on a human body) and salvation, delivering from every enemy; and the Holy Spirit, the third person revealing in us and to us Divine things.

Three is the first of four perfect numbers:
    Three denotes devine perfection,
    Seven denotes spiritual perfection,
    Ten denotes ordinal perfection, and
    Twelve denotes govermental perfection.

Three, therefore stands for that which is solid, real, substantial, complete, and entire.

1. What did God create on the third day? (Genesis 1:9-13)

Note: The third day was the day on which the earth was caused to rise up out of the waters, symbolical of that resurrection life which we have in Christ and shown through baptism.

2. Why does three tell us of resurrection? (Matthew 12:39-40; Luke 11:29; Luke 13:32; Jonah 1:17)

3. When was Christ crucified? (Mark 15:25)

Note: Notice the threes in the above verses.

4. What is the third book in the Bible?

Note: In this book we learn what is true worship. We see Jehovah calling His people near unto Himself, explaining every detail of their worship. (Read John 4:23-24.) "Thus in Genesis we have sovereignty in giving life—the Father, the beginning of all things; in Exodus we have the oppressor and the Deliverer—the Son redeeming His people; while in Leviticus we have the Spirit prescribing, and ordering, and enpowering them for Divine worship."*

5. What do the Seraphim and the four beasts cry three times—one for each of the three Persons in the Godhead? (Isaiah 6:3; Revelation 4:8)

6. Who were the three men that appeared unto Abraham? (Genesis 18:2, 33, and 19:1)

7. What did Abraham bring to his guests? (Genesis 18:6)

8. What was brought as a meal offering in the Sanctuary? (Numbers 15:9)

9. For what else was the meal offering used? (Leviticus 14:10)

10. What parable did Jesus tell concerning the meal? (Matthew 13:33)

Note: Read *Christ's Object Lessons* 95-102.

11. What three major feasts did Israel celebrate each year? (Exodus 23:14-16)

Note: Read "The Annual Feasts," pages 537-542 from *Patriarchs and Prophets*. These three feasts reflect insight into the work of the heavenly Trio—Passover speaks of Christ; Pentecost pictures the work of the Holy Spirit; and the Feast of Tabernacles tells of the Father when all will once again be in harmony with His will.

12. How far into the wilderness marked a complete separation from Egypt? (Exodus 5:3)

13. What three things did the spies bring back from Canaan? (Numbers 13:23)

14. What words did Israel say three times at the giving of the Law? (Exodus 24:3, 7)

15. What was divided three times? (Joshua 4; II Kings 2:8, 14)

16. What parable speaks about seeking fruit from Israel for three years? (Luke 13:7)

17. What three people did Jesus raise from the dead? (Luke 7:11-15; Matthew 9:18; John 11)

18. What three things was Christ called? (Deuteronomy 17:15; 18:3-5; 18:15)

19. What three multitudes were miraculously fed? (II Kings 4:42-43; Matthew 15:34, 38; Mark 6:38, 44)

20. What was Abraham called three times? (II Chronicles 20:7; Isaiah 41:8; James 2:23)

21. What word, referring to God's people is found in the New Testament three times? (Acts 11:26; Acts 25:28; and I Peter 4:6)

Bees

Insects such as bees are known for the numbers 3 and 6.

- In three days the egg of the queen is hatched.
- It is fed for nine days (3 + 3 + 3 or 3 x 3).
- It reaches maturity in 15 days (5 + 5 + 5 or 5 x 3).
- The worker grub reaches maturity in 21 days (7 + 7 + 7 or 7 x 3)
- And it is at work three days after leaving its cell.
- The drone matures in 24 days (8 + 8 + 8 or 8 x 3)
- The bee is composed of three sections—head, thorax, and abdomen.
- The two eyes are made up of about 3,000 small eyes, each like the cells of the comb, having six sides (3 + 3 or 2 x 3)
- Underneath the body are six (2 + 2 + 2 or 2 x 3) wax scales with which the comb is made.
- It has six (2 + 2 + 2 or 2 x 3) legs. Each leg is composed of three sections.
- The foot is formed of three triangular sections.
- The antennae consist of nine (3 + 3 + 3 or 3 x 3) barbs on each side.

What wonderful witnesses the bees are about the Father, Son, and Holy Spirit!

22. In what three languages was the inscription written that was put on the cross? (Luke 23:38)

23. What was let down three times from heaven to Peter that he might understand the work for the Gentiles? (Acts 10:10-16)

24. What does I Corinthians 13:13 say?

25. There are many other threes in the Bible, check the *Strong's Concordance* to see what is listed.

Remarkable Facts
Three

All things that are spiritually complete are stamped with the number three.

 - -

• God's attibutes are three: omniscience, omnipresence, and omnipotence.

• There are three great divisions completing time—past, present, and future.

• Three kingdoms embrace our idea of matter—mineral, vegetable, and animal.

• The tent tabernacle was broken into three parts: the courtyard; the holy place; and the most holy place.

• In this number we come to the first geometrical figure. Two straight lines cannot possibly enclose any space or form a plane figure; neither can two plane surfaces form a solid. Hence three lines can enclose a geometric figure.

Reinforce

An Alert Family in Every Generation

God   **Man**

Father + Son + Holy Spirit + Godly Family

 = **6**

Godly Family   Godly Family

 = **6** (Man)

Is your family a witness in this generation?

Remember

Store these facts in your mind.

3	3	3	3	3	3
+1	+2	+3	+4	+5	+6
4	5	6	7	8	9

3	3	3	3	3	3
+7	+8	+9	+10	+11	+12
10	11	12	13	14	15

Abraham

"...They shall prosper
that love thee."
Psalm 122:6

Many years after the flood of Noah's time, a child was born into the family of Shem.

"These are the generations of Shem...and Terah lived seventy years, and begat Abram [Abraham], Nahor, and Haran..." (Genesis 11:10, 26).

Abraham grew to be a man, and was **alert** to God's call for him to leave the city and move to the country. There, he was to be an **alert** witness for the coming Deliverer.

"Now the Lord had said unto Abram, Get thee out of thy country, and from thy kindred, and from thy father's house, unto a land that I will shew thee:

"And I will make of thee a great nation, and I will bless thee, and make thy name great; and thou shalt be a blessing:

"And I will bless them that bless thee, and curse him that curseth thee: and in thee shall all families of the earth be blessed" (Genesis 12:1-3).

Noah
↓
Shem
↓
Terah
↓
Abram
Nahor
Haran

Review
Place I
Can you hear God's call to you like Abraham did?

1. Think of Abraham's many family members moving to the country as you find the sum for each problem.

3 + 1	3 + 2	3 + 3	3 + 4	3 + 5	3 + 6
3 + 7	3 + 8	3 + 9	3 + 10	3 + 11	3 + 12
3 + 2	3 + 5	3 + 10	3 + 7	3 + 1	3 + 8
3 + 3	3 + 6	3 + 9	3 + 12	3 + 4	3 + 11

Review
Place II

1. Write in the missing numbers and be reminded that not one generation has passed in the history of the world that God has not had <u>witnesses</u>.

$$
\begin{array}{r} 43 \\ + 34 \\ \hline \_\,7 \end{array}
\qquad
\begin{array}{r} \_\,1 \\ + 72 \\ \hline 83 \end{array}
\qquad
\begin{array}{r} 19 \\ + 2\_ \\ \hline 39 \end{array}
\qquad
\begin{array}{r} 25 \\ + \ 1\_ \\ \hline 46 \end{array}
\qquad
\begin{array}{r} 56 \\ + 41 \\ \hline 9\_ \end{array}
\qquad
\begin{array}{r} 3\_ \\ + 26 \\ \hline 57 \end{array}
$$

$$
\begin{array}{r} 26 \\ + \ \ 3 \\ \hline 99 \end{array}
\qquad
\begin{array}{r} 84 \\ + 15 \\ \hline 9\_ \end{array}
\qquad
\begin{array}{r} 72 \\ + 25 \\ \hline \_\,7 \end{array}
\qquad
\begin{array}{r} 42 \\ + \ 3 \\ \hline 95 \end{array}
\qquad
\begin{array}{r} 17 \\ + \ 2 \\ \hline 99 \end{array}
\qquad
\begin{array}{r} 83 \\ + \ 4 \\ \hline 97 \end{array}
$$

$$
\begin{array}{r} 16 \\ + 53 \\ \hline \_\,9 \end{array}
\qquad
\begin{array}{r} 23 \\ + \ 4 \\ \hline 77 \end{array}
\qquad
\begin{array}{r} 71 \\ + 22 \\ \hline 9\_ \end{array}
\qquad
\begin{array}{r} \_\,1 \\ + 66 \\ \hline 87 \end{array}
\qquad
\begin{array}{r} \_\,2 \\ + 84 \\ \hline 96 \end{array}
\qquad
\begin{array}{r} \_\,3 \\ + 16 \\ \hline 69 \end{array}
$$

$$
\begin{array}{r} 47 \\ + 1\_ \\ \hline 59 \end{array}
\qquad
\begin{array}{r} 19 \\ + \ 0 \\ \hline 99 \end{array}
\qquad
\begin{array}{r} 72 \\ + \ 3 \\ \hline 95 \end{array}
\qquad
\begin{array}{r} 38 \\ + 51 \\ \hline \_\,9 \end{array}
\qquad
\begin{array}{r} \_\,7 \\ + 42 \\ \hline 59 \end{array}
\qquad
\begin{array}{r} 51 \\ + 28 \\ \hline 7\_ \end{array}
$$

$$
\begin{array}{r} 64 \\ + \ 4 \\ \hline 98 \end{array}
\qquad
\begin{array}{r} \_\,7 \\ + 22 \\ \hline 69 \end{array}
\qquad
\begin{array}{r} \_\,4 \\ + 63 \\ \hline 97 \end{array}
\qquad
\begin{array}{r} \_\,1 \\ + 88 \\ \hline 99 \end{array}
\qquad
\begin{array}{r} 24 \\ + 7\_ \\ \hline 99 \end{array}
\qquad
\begin{array}{r} 53 \\ + \ 4 \\ \hline 97 \end{array}
$$

2. Write in the missing numbers.

$23 + 72 = 9\ \underline{\hphantom{0}}$ $14 + 3\ \underline{\hphantom{0}} = 49$

$\underline{\hphantom{0}}\ 1 + 41 = 92$ $82 + 17 = \underline{\hphantom{0}}\ 9$

$14 + 2\ \underline{\hphantom{0}} = 39$ $\underline{\hphantom{0}}\ 1 + 26 = 97$

$13 + 16 = \underline{\hphantom{0}}\ 9$ $3\ \underline{\hphantom{0}} + 27 = 58$

$47 + 52 = \underline{\hphantom{0}}\ 9$ $46 + \underline{\hphantom{0}}\ 3 = 99$

See Genesis 11:10-26.

Print in the name of each righteous generation starting with Noah and ending with Abram.

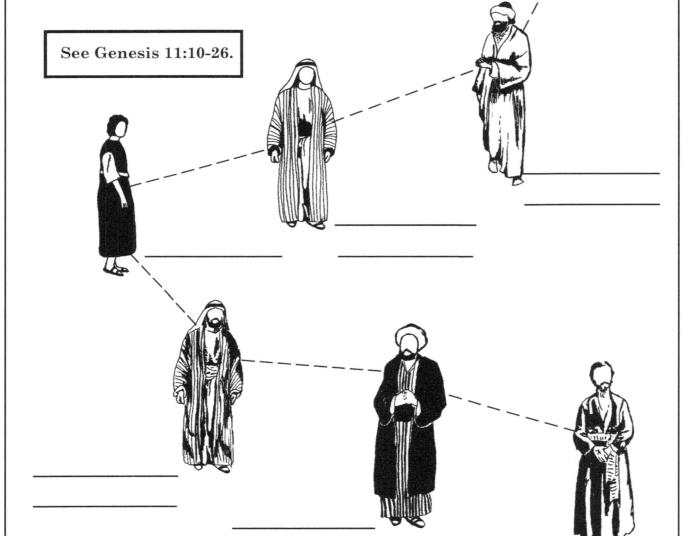

Addition 1 – Student – Page 82

Review
Place III

As you do the problems in this section, be reminded that three means divine perfection. Remember, how in each generation God has had witnesses.

It is easy to add two digits in your mind and that saves time from writing it on paper. Mental addition can be done by adding tens then ones. See the example below.

Problem	Example
24 + 12 = p	Think there are no ones to carry.
	20 + 10 = 30
p = 36	Then add the ones. (4 + 2 = 6)
	30 + 6 = 36

When carrying, first add the tens in your mind then think, "How many more makes another ten?"

Problem	Example
65 + 76 = m	Think 65 + 70 = 135
	5 more ones are needed to make 140.
m = 141	The other 1 makes the answer 141.
	(The 6 ones in 76 are thought of as
	5 + 1)

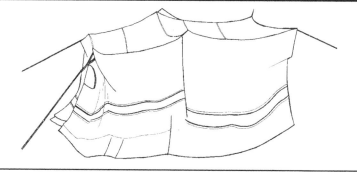

1. Do these addition problems in your mind then write down the answers. Check your answers by adding in reverse order.

P	53 + 10 = ___	18 + 30 = ___	29 + 50 = ___
E	26 + 70 = ___	82 + 31 = ___	32 = 70 = ___
R	56 + 43 = ___	82 + 90 = ___	49 + 82 = ___
F	73 + 50 = ___	56 + 77 = ___	65 + 38 = ___
E	42 + 79 = ___	87 + 88 = ___	87 + 35 = ___
C	12 + 18 = ___	34 + 55 = ___	20 + 25 = ___
T	15 + 26 = ___	46 + 27 = ___	28 + 36 = ___

- -

W	72 + 87 = c	63 + 18 = o	58 + 62 = m
I	25 + 35 = p	30 + 17 = l	28 + 32 = e
T	56 + 68 = t	74 + 46 = e	36 + 75 = n
N	85 + 48 = e	16 + 85 = s	40 + 78 = s
E	45 + 73 = e	47 + 71 = n	66 + 33 = t
S	51 + 34 = i	53 + 98 = r	46 + 82 = e
S	25 + 44 = n	43 + 52 = e	23 + 45 = s

**Fill in these blanks using the letters
at the end of each problem going across.**

Three reminds us of

_ _ _ _ _ _ _ _ _ _ _ _ _

and _ _ _ _ _ _ _ _ _ _s.

Research
No Haste, No Delay

"My deliverer, make no <u>tarrying</u>,
O my God."
Psalm 40:17

"But be not thou far from me,
O Lord: O my strength,
<u>haste</u> thee to help me."
Psalm 22:19

The promise of a Deliverer was shared from one patriarch to another. Prophets were sent to warn the people. The prophet Daniel told the time of Christ's advent (Daniel 9:25). But many people misunderstood the message. Century (100 years) after century passed. Israel had many trials, and many must have cried out: *"The days are prolonged, and every vision faileth"* (Ezekiel 12:22).

God had not forgotten, but His "purposes know no haste and no delay."*

The Desire of Ages 32

Reinforce

100 YEARS +
100 YEARS +
100 YEARS +
100 YEARS =
___ YEARS

**What is
100 years called?**

_____

Read about "Haste and Delay"
on the next page.

Reflect

"<u>Haste</u> manages
all things badly."
Latin Proverb

"Who pours water <u>hastily</u>
into a bottle
spills more than goes in."
Spanish Proverb

<u>Haste</u> Makes Waste!

Haste and Delay

God is our director to know when to hurry and when to wait.
These stories and thoughts of the past illustrate <u>haste</u> and <u>delay</u>.

Walking along the street one day we were startled by a carriage dashing by furiously. The driver leaned forward to give loose rein to a noble horse that needed no lash to accelerate his dangerous speed. People in the street and teams made way quickly for the rushing riders. A glance at the sadly suggestive word in large capitals AMBULANCE, told the story of their haste. The telegraph had called! Somebody was crushed by falling timbers. Faster! Faster! for that spouting artery must be tied, and the mutilated limb bound up. The surgeons sat quietly waiting with their tools at hand, and the stretcher was adjusted, ready for the sufferer if able to be moved. The unlawful speed they made through crowded streets was only tolerated because of the fact that they were rushing to save a life.

David's words to Abimelech, *"The king's business requires haste,"* though wrongly used by him, convey a universal truth. God's business does require haste. The ambulance surgeon is always within hearing of his telegraphic signal. Often the message is *"Run, speak to that young man!" "Go quickly and tell them I am risen."* Yes, man of God, make haste! A human life depends on your coming. Men may deride your zeal, and say you violate the rules of orderly propriety, but let your answer be, "I am on the King's business, and it requires haste." — *Adapted From Thwing*

Delay can be dangerous. A captain says that on a dark and tempestuous evening he heard the firing of minute-guns, as signals of distress. He bore down in the direction of the sounds, and saw a large steamer, with her flag at half-mask. He put his trumpet to his mouth and hailed, "What's the matter?" The reply was, "I am in a sinking condition." "Send all your passengers on board my ship." The answer was, "No; lie by me till morning." Again he urged him to send his passengers on board, and again the answer was, "Lie by me till morning." Then he requested him to set his lights, which he did; but in an hour and a half no lights could be seen. It was the ill-fated "Central America," and she had gone down.

Delay can be fatal. How many loose the battle of life because either they do not start early enough, or they make fatal mistakes after they have been started. For these two reasons Napoleon lost Waterloo. History tells us, that the night before the memorable June 18, 1815, there was a great deluge of rain, and the ground was so soaked that Napoleon could not move his artillery, and he had to wait until the ground was somewhat settled; so that, instead of opening the battle as he had expected at six o'clock in the morning, he opened it at nearly twelve at noon. Of course, that gave time for Blucher to come up with his reinforcements.

"<u>Delay</u> is preferable to error."
    —*Thomas Jefferson*

"<u>Procrastination</u> is the thief of time."
    —*Edward Young*

"Too <u>swift</u> arrives as tardy as too <u>slow</u>."
    —*Shakespeare*

Reinforce

Notice these sons of Noah and their descendants.

"These are the three sons of Noah:

and of them was the whole earth overspread."

Genesis 9:19

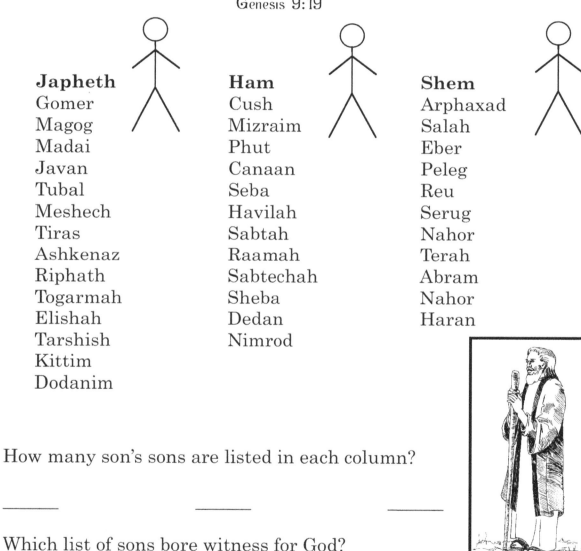

Japheth
Gomer
Magog
Madai
Javan
Tubal
Meshech
Tiras
Ashkenaz
Riphath
Togarmah
Elishah
Tarshish
Kittim
Dodanim

Ham
Cush
Mizraim
Phut
Canaan
Seba
Havilah
Sabtah
Raamah
Sabtechah
Sheba
Dedan
Nimrod

Shem
Arphaxad
Salah
Eber
Peleg
Reu
Serug
Nahor
Terah
Abram
Nahor
Haran

How many son's sons are listed in each column?

_____   _____   _____

Which list of sons bore witness for God?

_____

Circle Abraham (Abram) with a green crayon.
Green reminds us how Abraham was a man of __ __ __ __ __. (tifha)
Unscramble.

Review
Place I
Noah's Sons

1. Finish each problem.

Noah   Japheth   Ham   **Shem**

 + + +   = _____

Japheth

   = _____

Ham

   = _____

Shem   Arphaxad

 + = _____

Through whose children would the Deliverer come?

____ ____ ____ ____

The Stars Teach

2. Read the following information; then do the addition problems below.

Like the stars in the large circuit in their appointed paths, God's purposes know no <u>rush</u> (haste) and no <u>hinderances</u> (delay). God had shared with Abraham that his children would be like the stars of the heaven in number. The promised Deliverer would come through his children.

Abraham married Sarah = _____

Abraham and Sarah had a child named Isaac = _____

Abraham, Sarah, Isaac, and Rebekah = _____

Isaac and Rebekah had twin boys, Jacob and Esau = _____

Jacob married four wives and had twelve sons = _____

Is it God's will for a man to have more than one wife?
What Bible verse gives the answer?

Like the Stars

3. Do these problems; then put star stickers where there is an asterisk (*).

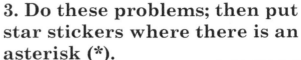

Abraham *   Sarah *

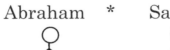 + 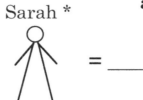 = _____

Abraham *   Sarah *   Isaac *

  + = _____

Abraham *   Sarah *   Isaac *   Rebekah *

   + = _____

Abraham *   Sarah *   Isaac *   Rebekah *   Esau * Jacob *

    + 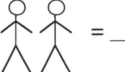 = _____

Isaac's Family   Leah *   Rachel *   Zilpah *   Bilhah *

 +   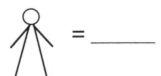 = _____

Jacob's Family   Jacob's Sons

 +   12   = _____

*   *   *   *   *   *   *   *   *   *   *   *

4. Find the sum for these problems. Think of the answers as being godly families, alert and waiting for the <u>Deliverer</u>.

1 + 10	1 + 6	1 + 2	1 + 9	1 + 4	1 + 12
1 + 7	1 + 1	1 + 8	1 + 11	1 + 3	1 + 5
2 + 3	2 + 11	2 + 6	2 + 8	2 + 1	2 + 4
2 + 12	2 + 7	2 + 2	2 + 5	2 + 9	2 + 10
3 + 4	3 + 9	3 + 12	3 + 7	3 + 5	3 + 10
3 + 2	3 + 8	3 + 6	3 + 3	3 + 11	3 + 1

Learn to spell the number three. Write it several times.

3   _____ _____ _____   3

Father   Son Holy Spirit

3

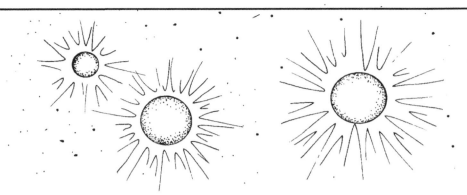

2 + 6 = _____	1 + 11 = _____	1 + 5 = _____
3 + 5 = _____	1 + 7 = _____	3 + 9 = _____
3 + 2 = _____	2 + 1 = _____	3 + 12 = _____
1 + 3 = _____	3 + 6 = _____	1 + 9 = _____
2 + 10 = _____	3 + 3 = _____	2 + 2 = _____
1 + 10 = _____	2 + 3 = _____	1 + 1 = _____
1 + 8 = _____	3 + 8 = _____	2 + 8 = _____
2 + 12 = _____	3 + 12 = _____	2 + 9 = _____
3 + 1 = _____	2 + 5 = _____	3 + 4 = _____
1 + 12 = _____	2 + 11 = _____	1 + 4 = _____
2 + 7 = _____	1 + 2 = _____	3 + 9 = _____
1 + 6 = _____	3 + 7 = _____	2 + 4 = _____
3 + 8 = _____	3 + 10 = _____	2 + 8 = _____
1 + 12 = _____	3 + 5 = _____	3 + 12 = _____

5. Review the Ones, Twos, and Threes. 1 - 2 - 3

1 + 12	2 + 6	3 + 3	3 + 10	1 + 3	2 + 8
3 + 6	2 + 3	2 + 11	1 + 6	1 + 9	3 + 1
3 + 4	2 + 9	1 + 11	2 + 5	1 + 4	2 + 7
1 + 10	1 + 1	3 + 7	2 + 2	3 + 12	1 + 7
1 + 8	2 + 10	1 + 5	3 + 2	3 + 8	2 + 12
1 + 2	3 + 5	2 +1	3 + 11	3 + 9	2 + 4
1 + 2	2 + 1	1 + 3	3 + 1	2 + 3	3 + 2

1 + 2 = _____   1 + 3 = _____   2 + 3 = _____

2 + 1 = _____   3 + 1 = _____   3 + 2 = _____

 # Review
Place II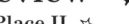

1. Find the sum for these addition problems. As you do them, be reminded of all the stars that will be in the crowns of God's true witnesses. Write the plus sign in the proper place in each problem. What does the addition sign mean?

41	14	10	12	18	34
17	11	21	36	20	22
31	33	64	21	41	43

76	11	24	10	12	13
13	23	51	46	32	14
10	42	13	43	55	22

40	24	55	45	35	25
42	51	22	31	14	12
17	14	21	13	20	50

15	23	35	42	16	65
32	45	31	15	32	24
51	21	33	43	51	12

2. Write the sums for these problems.

22 + 14 + 53 = _____   11 + 25 + 45 = _____   10 + 36 + 24 = _____

33 + 13 + 15 = _____   12 + 12 + 70 = _____   13 + 62 + 10 = _____

53 + 14 + 20 = _____   70 + 10 + 18 = _____   65 + 21 + 16 = _____

3. Write your own problem. The answer must be 59.

_____ + _____ + _____ = 59

Review
Place III

In this lesson you will learn another way
to <u>quickly</u> add in your mind.

Example

Problem

$56 + 37 = w$
$w = 93$

Think $56 + 30 = 86$
$86 + 7 = 93$

In adding three numbers, add the first two and then add
the third number to that total. Check by adding in reverse order.

Example

Problem

$24 + 47 + 34 = e$

$e = 105$

Think $24 + 40 = 64$
$64 + 7 = 71$
$71 + 30 = 101$
$101 + 4 = 105$

Slow and Quick

Color these pictures
that show <u>plodding</u> and
<u>swift</u>.

1. Do these addition problems in your mind then check by adding in reverse order.

D. $13 + 33 = t$ $85 + 17 = h$ $52 + 78 = e$

E. $84 + 44 = d$ $72 + 76 = a$ $25 + 34 = y$

L. $12 + 18 = s$ $45 + 73 = a$ $58 + 80 = r$

I. $42 + 46 + 40 = e$ $35 + 32 + 30 = p$

V. $47 + 33 + 12 = r$ $63 + 27 + 47 = o$

E. $33 + 52 + 45 = l$ $58 + 13 + 41 = o$

R. $37 + 22 + 61 = n$ $82 + 55 + 37 = g$

E. $75 + 28 + 13 = e$ $75 + 41 + 57 = d$

R. $32 + 15 + 33 = a$ $72 + 42 + 87 = n$

W. $97 + 48 + 35 = d$ $96 + 63 + 79 = e$

I. $42 + 36 + 55 = v$ $81 + 64 + 87 = e$

L. $35 + 14 + 43 = r$ $62 + 42 + 92 = y$

L. $48 + 60 + 23 = v$ $35 + 71 + 28 = i$

C. $49 + 70 + 36 = s$ $46 + 82 + 39 = i$

O. $50 + 60 + 47 = o$ $57 + 93 + 40 = n$

M. $23 + 58 + 35 = f$ $34 + 69 + 46 = a$

E. $57 + 38 + 17 = i$ $37 + 46 + 27 = l$

What statement did some make as they waited for the **Deliverer**? Copy all the letters after each problem reading from left to right in the spaces below.

Witness

" _ _ _   _ _ _ _   _ _ _

_ _ _ _ _ _ _ _ _ _,

_ _ _   _ _ _ _ _ _ _

_ _ _ _ _ _ _   _ _ _ _ eth."

Research
Numberless

"...Look now toward heaven,
and tell the stars,
if thou be able to number them...
So shall thy seed be."
Genesis 15:5

"To Abraham was given the promise that of his line [through his family] the Saviour of the world should come: *In thy seed shall all the nations of the earth be blessed.*' *He saith not, And to seeds, as of many; but as of one, And to thy seed, which is Christ*' (Genesis 22:18; Galatians 3:16)."*

As you look up in the silent night, you can read God's promise to Abraham of a seed numberless as the stars. You can also read about the redeemed of all ages (numberless as the stars), saved because of Christ's great sacrifice (+).

"*And they sung a new song, saying, Thou art worthy to take the book, and to open the seals thereof: for thou wast slain, and hast redeemed us to God by thy blood out of every kindred, and tongue, and people, and nation*" (Revelation 5:9).

*The Acts of the Apostles 222

Infinite Numbers

God uses stars, seeds, and sand to illustrate infinite numbers.

What are some synonymn's for numberless?

_____

_____

_____

_____

_____

_____

Review
Word Problems
Place I

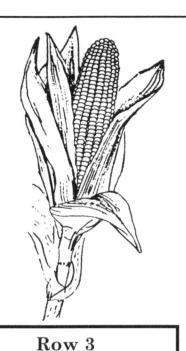

1. Find the answer to the word problem below.
A seed can represent a person.
A star can represent a person.
A grain of sand can represent a person. •
The Abraham family planted a garden.
They made three (3) short rows of corn.
In each row they planted six (6) kernels of corn.
Draw the seeds in each row below.

Row 1	Row 2	Row 3

2. There are about 100 kernels of corn on an ear.
About two (2) or three (3) ears grow on each stalk of corn.
Six (6) seeds were planted in a row.
Three (3) rows were planted.
How many ears of corn would there be?
There are two possible answers.
Draw your answer below.

Work Area

3. *"And Abraham called
the name of his son
that was born unto him,
whom Sarah bare to him, Isaac."*
(Genesis 21:3)

Abraham had only one (1) son
who could be the ancestor of Christ.
What was that son's name?

_____

4. As the Isaac family looked up into the heavens they saw the stars. They especially noticed three (3) bright stars in the belt of Orion. There were four (4) more in the cup of the Big Dipper that shone brightly. How many stars did they especially notice in the sky?

Draw below in the square the Orion constellation. How many main stars are there in it?

_____

Draw below in the square the Big Dipper. How many main stars are there in it?

_____

Orion	Big Dipper

Review
Word Problems
Place II

Think of God's people as stars shining in the night sky as you do these problems.

1. The Lyre has 4 main stars, the Archer has 23, and the Scorpion 22. Write out a problem telling how many shining stars are in these three constellations that shine for God.

2. Canis Major and Canis Minor have 16 stars, while the Big Dipper and the Little Dipper have 14, and the Pleiades has 7. Write out an addition problem using the total of all these constellations.

3. Some other stars are the Lion with 9 shining stars, the Herdsman with 10 which together with the Twins totals how many stars?

Twins

Lyre

Canis Major

Lion

Review
Word Problems
Place III

As one views the bright stars in the heavens, we are reminded of great lights of the past shining and **alert** for Jesus, like: Abraham, Isaac, Jacob, and many others. Solve the following problems. Be sure to do them in your mind as the previous examples explained.

1. Some of the brightest stars seen from Earth are Vega which is 26 light years away, Capella, 47 light years away, and Arcturus which is 41 light years away. What is the total distance in light years of these bright stars?

2. Other bright stars are Canopus, about 650 light years from Earth, and Rigel which is about 540 light years away. Canopus is in the constellation Carina. Do you know what constellation Rigel is found in? How many total light years away are these two bright stars?

3. Procyon is in the constellation Canis Minor and 10 light years from the Earth. Achernar is in the constellation Eridanus and 66 light years away. Beta Centauri is in the constellation Centaurus, 300 light years away. The light of these distant stars shines brightly as they *"declare the glory of God"* (Psalm 19:1). Give the total light years that Procyon, Achernar, Beta Centauri, and Vega are from planet Earth.

 Work Area

> 1 light year = the distance light would travel in one year (at its speed of about 186,000 miles per second).

Remind
One in
Every Generation

1. A true <u>witness</u> will complete a job he begins. When given a pile of wood to cut or stack (or clothes to fold), add up how many pieces you handled. Take a stick, and after you have counted for awhile, mark the number in the dirt (or on a piece of paper). When you are through working, total up the numbers. How many sticks of wood did you cut or stack (pieces of laundry folded)?

Each stick of wood can remind you how God has had an **alert**, faithful, <u>witness</u> in every generation.

As you are **alert** and do this job well, being aware of each piece, you are preparing for greater responsibilities. God tests us with small duties to see if He can trust us with greater responsibilities.

2. When drying the dishes, as you put them away, write down in separate columns how many forks there were, then spoons, plates, and serving dishes. Then add all the numbers together. Be reminded of how a faithful witness is to be used by God to serve spiritual food to others—sort of like we would use a plate to offer a person physical food. And, as with a plate, the more empty a person is of self, the more they can hold. (When *"the fulness of the time"* has come to set the table, consider how you seek only the empty, clean plates and think of the Master choosing His witnesses from within His church just as you look within the cabinet or drawer for table service that is ready and waiting for immediate use.)

Reinforce

1. When doing a project do it thorough and do it well. Read the story, "Only Your Best Is Good Enough."

2. Sing the hymn, "Ready to Do His Will."

**Witnessing for Christ
by how well I do my work.**

Remainder
Tested

"And he said, Take now thy son, thine only son Isaac, whom thou lovest, and...offer him there for a burnt offering...."

Genesis 22:2

Abraham was tested. He was even asked to give up the promised son, Isaac. You can read about this in Genesis 22:1-19. He was **alert** to God and His will so when the time of test came He passed it.

"And said, By myself have I sworn, saith the Lord, for because thou hast done this thing, and hast not withheld thy son, thine only son:

"That in blessing I will bless thee, and in multiplying I will multiply thy seed as the stars of the heaven, and as the sand which is upon the sea shore; and thy seed shall possess the gate of his enemies;

"And in thy seed shall <u>all the nations of the earth be blessed;</u> because thou hast obeyed my voice" (Genesis 22:16-18).

Abraham had become like God who also was willing to give His only Son. And, because God the Father gave Jesus to us, <u>all the nations of the earth</u> were <u>blessed</u> *"when the fulness of the time was come...."*

Only Your Best Is Good Enough

Every job we do in life should witness about God's character.

It is said that when Daniel Webster, as a fledgling lawyer, was starting his practice in Portsmouth, New Hampshire, he found it hard to get a foothold. For months he scraped along with barely enough money to pay his weekly board bill and keep himself clothed in the somber black garments suitable to his profession. Indeed, clients were so few and far between that he was highly gratified one day when the local blacksmith sought his advice. The case which he laid before the young lawyer had to do with a tract of land, regarding which he and a neighbor had conflicting claims.

Webster listened to the smith's story. It involved a question which he could not answer offhand; so he said he would look into the matter and report in three or four days. The client left with no hint that the young lawyer was puzzled, but the instant the office door closed behind him, Webster began an eager search through his small law library. However, he could find nothing that seemed applicable.

The average attorney would have made a makeshift plea and trusted to luck to win the case. But Daniel Webster was not that kind of lawyer. He decided that he would go to the very bottom of things for his own satisfaction; also he had a very high standard of honor toward even the humblest client.

Therefore, even though he could ill afford it, he took the stage to Boston and spent a whole day in the law libraries there. To his dismay he discovered that the point at issue had never been decided in just the form in which it had come to him. Nevertheless, he found some similar cases, and pursued the subject back to the statute and common law of England. Then he developed an argument which he felt was consistent with decisions rendered in these like cases, made copious (many) notes, purchased out of his lean purse the books which contained the references he needed, and took the stage back to Portsmouth.

At the appointed time the blacksmith called for his opinion. "It is not an easy case," Webster explained, "but obviously your side is the right one, and I think that I can secure a verdict for you."

And when he went before the local court, it was to present a case prepared with as much research and thought and care as if he had been making his appeal to the Supreme Court of the United States. And he won.

After court, the blacksmith inquired: "How much do I owe you Mr. Webster?"

"Oh," answered the lawyer, who was always careless about money matters, "pay me whatever you think you can afford."

"Well," returned the smith, "you seemed to run it off pretty easily; so I guess a dollar will be about right."

Considerably taken aback, Webster pocketed the dollar and walked thoughtfully to his office. In his record book he made notation of the fact that his journey to Boston and books he had purchased had cost him fifty dollars, and that he had received a fee of one dollar. Then he promptly forgot all about it.

Twenty-five years later, when he was head of the American Bar Association and a statesman of outstanding ability, the president of a large railway corporation telegraphed him, asking for an appointment. The two men met in the famous lawyer's office in Boston behind closed doors, and the railroad man said earnestly and anxiously: "Mr. Webster, I wish to lay before you a question that has lately arisen, and that vitally affects the interests of my road. The very eminent counsel whom I have consulted tell me that they believe my contention to be correct, but that they are quite unable to find any decision which bears upon the subject. The case is to be tried in a very short time, and yet my side is wholly unprepared. If I lose, then my opponents will seriously cripple the corporation of which I am president."

"Please state your case fully," was Webster's response. The man did so, and also produced notes and papers and all the data which was to be had bearing on the question. The lawyer glanced through the material briefly, and then, it is said, an **alert** gleam lighted up his eyes. In principle the case was precisely the same as that of the blacksmith who had come to him during those hard beginning days back in Portsmouth. But he merely said: "This involves a very knotty problem. I will undertake to act for you if you will give me the necessary authority. I shall not need the assistance of other counsel."

The railroad man felt the first thrill of hope, rose, shook Webster's hand warmly, and then sat down again and wrote a check for five thousand dollars as a retaining fee.

When the client had gone his way, the lawyer started a search among his files. Finally he found a little package of notes which he had set down long years before. The paper was now yellow with age. In an hour or two of concentrated study he was able to adapt the arguments he had used in the blacksmith's case to that of the railroad company, for his memory was remarkable, and it brought back to him the decisions and precedents upon which he had built the former case.

On the appointed day he appeared before the highest court of the State of Massachusetts—and won the verdict. In fact, without so much as leaving their seats for consultation, the judges were all convinced, and when later they handed down a written opinion, it was in reality merely a restatement of Webster's plea.

The railroad president was, of course, delighted to have won such a sweeping victory, when he had been almost certain of defeat. He sent the lawyer a check for ten thousand dollars, with a letter of appreciation from himself and from the directors of the company.

And the teller of this experience in the life of one of the outstanding statesmen in the early days of the United States of America, adds that as Webster pocketed the ten-thousand-dollar check and mentally added to it the five thousand dollars he had received as a retaining fee, he smiled rather grimly to himself, and said pensively, "I have now received the blacksmith's fee—with compound interest!"

This story proves and emphasizes the truth of the old adage, **"What is worth doing at all is worth doing well."**

Witnessing by our Work

4 4 4 Fours - 4 4 4 4

Research
The Number Four

"And God made two great lights; the greater light to rule the day, and the lesser light to rule the night: he made the stars also."

Genesis 1:16

Four in the Bible reminds us of the fourth day of creation. It is also the fourth commandment that **alerts** us that God is our Creator and desires to recreate us in His image. This lesson teaches about the creation of the people of Israel. *"Thou art worthy, O Lord, to receive glory and honour and power: for thou hast created all things, and <u>for thy pleasure they are and were created</u>"* (Revelation 4:11).

It all began when *"...Abraham said unto his eldest servant of his house, that ruled over all that he had, Put, I pray thee, thy hand under my thigh: And I will make thee swear by the Lord, the God of heaven, and the God of the earth, that thou shalt not take a wife unto my son of the daughters of the Canaanites, among whom I dwell: But thou shalt go unto my country,*

Reinforce
Color then read the meaning of the number four. Learn to say four in these languages.

French – quatre (KAH truh)

Japanese – shi (shee)

Spanish – cuatro (KWAH troh)

Swahili – nne (NN neh)

```
  4 addend
+ 4 addend
  8 sum
```

FOUR - 4 = CREATION

The divine nature and the human nature combined (addition +) to give sinful man a Saviour.

4

Divine
Human ⟶
+

and to my kindred, and take a wife unto my son Isaac" (Genesis 24:2-4).

"In ancient times marriage engagements were generally made by the parents, and this was the custom among those who worshiped God. None were required to marry those whom they could not love; but in the bestowal of their affections the youth were guided by the judgment of their experienced, God-fearing parents. It was regarded as a dishonor to parents, and even a crime, to pursue a course contrary to this.

"Isaac, trusting to his father's wisdom and affection, was satisfied to commit the matter to him, believing also that God Himself would direct in the choice made. The patriarch's thoughts turned to his father's kindred in the land of Mesopotamia. Though not free from idolatry, they cherished the knowledge and the worship of the true God. Isaac must not leave Canaan to go to them, but it might be that among them could be found one who would leave her home and unite with him in maintaining the pure worship of the living God. Abraham

"Isaac, trusted in his father's wisdom and love...."

committed the important matter to *'his eldest servant,'* a man of piety, experience, and sound judgment, who had rendered him long and faithful service. He required this servant to make a solemn oath before the Lord, that he would not take a wife for Isaac of the Canaanites, but would choose a maiden from the family of Nahor in Mesopotamia. He charged him not to take Isaac thither. If a damsel could not be found who would leave her kindred, then the messenger would be released from his oath. The patriarch encouraged him in his difficult and delicate undertaking with the assurance that God would crown his mission with success. *The Lord God of heaven,'* he said, *'which took me from my father's house, and from the land of my kindred...He shall send his angel before thee.'* " *

"And these are the generations of Isaac, Abraham's son: Abraham begat Isaac:

"And Isaac was forty years old when he took Rebekah to wife, the daughter of Bethuel the Syrian of Padanaram, the sister to Laban the Syrian.

Patriarchs and Prophets 171-172

"And Isaac entreated the Lord for his wife, because she was barren: and the Lord was entreated of him, and Rebekah his wife conceived.

"And the children struggled together within her; and she said, If it be so, why am I thus? And she went to inquire of the Lord.

Groom

Marriage brings about the creation of children. Isaac and Rebekah had twins.

Bride

Those who serve God are like the stars shining in the sky for a dark, sinful world. Remember the number four means

_ _ _ _ _ _ _ _.

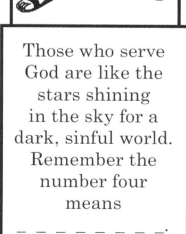

"And the Lord said unto her, Two nations are in thy womb, and two manner of people shall be separated from thy bowels; and the one people shall be stronger than the other people; and the elder shall serve the younger.

"And when her days to be delivered were fulfilled, behold, there were twins in her womb."

"And the boys grew: and Esau was a cunning hunter, a man of the field; and Jacob was a plain man, dwelling in tents" (Genesis 25:19-24, 27).

Jacob then married and he and his wives had twelve sons. From these twelve sons came the children of Israel and finally the Messiah who became the light of the world.

Reflect

Which son was the son who was **alert** to spiritual things?

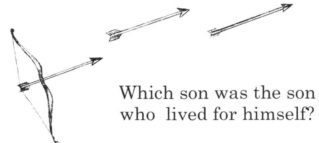

Which son was the son who lived for himself?

Esau the Hunter a Man of the Field

Jacob, a Plain Man Dwelling in Tents

Bible Search

Fours

Four is the number of material completeness. Hence it is the world number, the home God created for us, and especially, the "city"—the heavenly home as described in Revelation 21 as the city foursquare. On each side of this city/cube were 3 gates. 3 = Godhead + 4 = material creation = 7 (a perfect place to live). Those who are recreated will live there one day.

1. What was spoken into existence on the fourth day of creation? (Genesis 1:14-19)

Note: The fourth day saw the material creation finished (for on the 5th and 6th day it was only the furnishing and peopling of the earth with living creatures). The sun, and moon, completed the work, they were to give light upon the earth which had been created, and to rule over the day and over the night. The stars though created earlier, are here mentioned, in passing, by Moses, inasmuch as he is discussing the luminaries of the heavens.

2. What kept watch at the tree of life after man sinned? (Genesis 3:24)

3. Read the description of these beings in Ezekiel 10.

4. What is the fourth book in the Bible?

Note: This book relates to the earth, which is a wilderness compared with heaven; and to our pilgrimage through it. It tells of striving, and records the history of the murmurings, rebellions, and wanderings of Israel.

5. What is the fourth commandment? (Exodus 20:8-11)

6. Who were the four prophetesses of the Old Testament? (Exodus 15:20; Judges 4:4; II Kings 22:14; Nehemiah 6:14—3 were good and 1 was bad.)

7. Who were the four Hebrew children in Daniel 1?

8. Who were the four that were in the fiery furnace? (Daniel 3)

9. There were four kings in the book of Daniel which are:_____ . (1-4; 5-6)

10. What were Satan's four names in Revelation 20:2?

11. What were the four-fold witnesses to show nature's inability to find wisdom? (Job 28:7-8)

12. What were the four things *"little and wise?"* (Proverbs 30:24-28)

13. In the parable of the sower (Matthew 13) what were the four kinds of soil?

14. What four things was the lost son given when he was welcomed home by his father? (Luke 15)

15. *"The Seventy"* went forth to do their missionary work with what four-fold prohibition? (Luke 10:4)

16. What is God's four-fold witness in the earth? (Hebrews 2:4)

17. Who is mentioned in the Bible by name four times? (Genesis 3:20; Genesis 4:1; II Corinthians 11:3; and I Timothy 2:13)

18. What is the four-fold suffering in II Corinthians 4:8-9?

19. There are many fours in the Bible—look up the list in the *Strong's Concordance*.

The term *Bible* (Greek, *biblia*) means "little books."

What are the first five books of the Bible?

Remarkable Fact:
Slugs have four noses.

Remarkable Facts
Four

• Four is the number of the great elements—earth, air, fire, and water.

• Four are the regions of the earth—north, south, east, and west.

• Four are the divisions of the day—evening, midnight, morning, and noon. From evening to evening is how God reckons time.

• Four are the seasons of the year—spring, summer, autumn, and winter.

• Four are the great variations of the lunar phases.

• Four marks division. It is the first number which is not a "prime," the first which can be divided. It is the first square number also, and therefore it marks a king of completeness as well, which is called material completeness.

• Four and the things that deal with it:

—Of the four great offerings, three were connected with blood and life; while one was meal.

—The meal offering (Leviticus 2) was either baked in three ways (oven, flat-plate, or frying-pan); or not at all.

—The sin offering (Leviticus 4) was offered for three classes of individuals—the Priest that is anointed (3); the Ruler (22); and the Common person (27).

—The materials of the Tabernacle were four, three-being metals (gold, silver, brass); and one non-metal (wood).

—The coverings of the Tabernacle were four—three animal (goats' hair, rams' skin, and badger skins); and one vegetable (fine linen).

—The ornamentations of the curtains were four, three being colors (blue, purple, and scarlet); while one was a pattern (the cherubim).

—The Priests and Levites were of four orders or persons; one was Aaron and his sons (Aaronites); the three were the sons of Gershon, Kohath, and Merari (Levites).

—The manna (Exodus 16:14, 31) has a four-fold description, three referring to sight or appearance (small, white, round); and one to taste (sweet).

—Of the four prohibited or unclean animals, three chewed the cud, but did not divide the hoof (camel, hare, and coney); while one divided the hoof, but did not chew the cud (the swine); and thus the swine stands out in marked contrast to the other three.

—Of the four Houses of God (erected by the Divine plan) on the earth, three were or will be, material, the Tabernacle, the Temple (Solomon's, and Ezekiel's); while the one is a Spiritual house (I Peter 2:5).

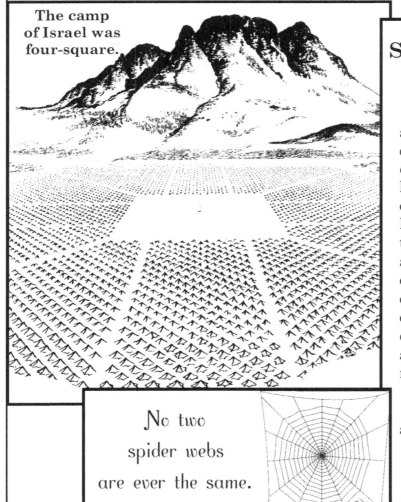

The camp of Israel was four-square.

No two spider webs are ever the same.

Spiders and the Number Four and Eight

Many people think spiders are insects. However, scientists classify spiders as arachnids. How do these differ from insects? Spiders have 2 parts to their bodies (cephalothorax and abdomen); four pairs of legs (2 x 4); four legs on each side of the cephalothorax; and no wings or antennae. Most species have eight eyes arranged in two rows of four each, others have six, four, or two eyes. Other arachnids include daddy longlegs, scorpions, mites, and ticks. The spider's special number is four and eight.

You will want to study more about the spiders.

Reinforce
Israel

Isaac   Rebekah

$$1 + 1 = 2$$

Esau   Jacob

$$1 + 1 = 2$$

Isaac   Rebekah   +   Esau   Jacob   =   4

$$2 \quad + \quad 2 \quad = \quad 4$$

There were four members in Isaac's family.

Remember
Store these facts in your mind.

$\begin{array}{r}4\\+\,1\\\hline 5\end{array}$	$\begin{array}{r}4\\+\,2\\\hline 6\end{array}$	$\begin{array}{r}4\\+\,3\\\hline 7\end{array}$	$\begin{array}{r}4\\+\,4\\\hline 8\end{array}$	$\begin{array}{r}4\\+\,5\\\hline 9\end{array}$	$\begin{array}{r}4\\+\,6\\\hline 10\end{array}$
$\begin{array}{r}4\\+\,7\\\hline 11\end{array}$	$\begin{array}{r}4\\+\,8\\\hline 12\end{array}$	$\begin{array}{r}4\\+\,9\\\hline 13\end{array}$	$\begin{array}{r}4\\+\,10\\\hline 14\end{array}$	$\begin{array}{r}4\\+\,11\\\hline 15\end{array}$	$\begin{array}{r}4\\+\,12\\\hline 16\end{array}$

 **Mercy**

"The Lord is merciful and gracious,
slow to anger, and plenteous
in mercy…

"He hath not dealt with us
after our sins; nor rewarded us
according to our iniquities.

"For as the heaven
is high above the earth,
so great is his mercy toward them
that fear him."
Psalm 103:8, 10-11

We remember the lesson of how Jacob stole the birthright. God forgave Jacob for his sin and blessed him. His descendants became like the stars of heaven or the dust of the earth in number.

"And thy seed shall be as the dust of the earth, and thou shalt spread abroad to the west, and to the east, and to the north, and to the south: and in thee and in thy seed shall all the families of the earth be blessed" (Genesis 28:14).

God's mercy to Jacob was as great as the stars are high.

Reinforce

1. The story of Jacob can be read in the Scriptures in Genesis 27-33.

2. Read this poem about our merciful God.

Merciful God

The Lord Jehovah gracious is,
    And He is merciful,
Long-suffering and slow to wrath,
    In kindness plentiful.

He will not chide continually,
    Nor keep His anger still.
With us He dealt not as we sinned,
    Nor did requite our ill.

For as the heaven in its height
    The earth surmounteth far;
So great to those that do Him fear
    His tender mercies are:

As far as east is distant from
    The west, so far hath He
From us removed, in tender love,
    All our iniquity.

—*W. B. Bradbury*

Review
Place I

1. Find the sum for these problems. Think of the sum as Abraham's children covering the earth as the dust or the sky as the stars.

4	4	4	4	4	4
+ 1	+ 2	+ 3	+ 4	+ 5	+ 6

4	4	4	4	4	4
+ 7	+ 8	+ 9	+ 10	+ 11	+ 12

4	4	4	4	4	4
+ 10	+ 8	+ 6	+ 1	+ 5	+ 11

4	4	4	4	4	4
+ 7	+ 2	+ 4	+ 9	+ 3	+ 12

4	4	4	4	4	4
+ 6	+ 3	+ 12	+ 8	+ 5	+ 2

4	4	4	4	4	4
+ 10	+ 9	+ 7	+ 1	+ 11	+ 4

4

4

Learn to spell the number four. Write it four times.

_____ _____ _____ _____

4

2. Draw Abraham and his descendants in the boxes below.

Abraham

Sarah

Isaac

= _____

Isaac's Sons

Esau

Jacob

= _____

Jacob's Sons by Leah

Reuben

Simeon

Levi

Judah

Issachar

Zebulun

= _____

Jacob's Sons by Leah's Handmaid—Zilpah

Gad

Asher

= _____

See Genesis 35:23-26.

Jacob's Sons by Rachel

Joseph

Benjamin

= _____

Jacob's Sons by Rachel's Handmaid—Bilhah

Dan

Naphtali

= _____

3. Write the numbers 0 - 21.
Abraham and Sarah, Isaac and Rebekah,
Jacob and Leah, Rachel, Bilhah, Zilpah,
and Jacob's twelve sons equal 21 people.

____ ____ ____ ____ ____ ____ ____ ____

____ ____ ____ ____ ____ ____ ____ ____

____ ____ ____ ____ ____

Remarkable Fact:
In a year,
the average person
walks four miles
making his
or her bed.

Example

Jacob had four wives.
This was not God's plan.
Four women were married to Jacob.
God wants a man to have only one wife.

$$\begin{array}{r} 4 \\ +1 \\ \hline 5 \end{array} \quad \textbf{or} \quad \begin{array}{r} 1 \\ +4 \\ \hline 5 \end{array} \qquad 1 + 4 = 5 \quad \textbf{or} \quad 4 + 1 = 5$$

4. Fill in the missing numbers for these problems. Notice the example on the previous page.

$$\begin{array}{r} 4 \\ + 1 \\ \hline \end{array} \qquad \begin{array}{r} 1 \\ + \underline{} \\ \hline 5 \end{array} \qquad \begin{array}{r} 4 \\ + 2 \\ \hline \end{array} \qquad \begin{array}{r} 2 \\ + \underline{} \\ \hline 6 \end{array} \qquad \begin{array}{r} 4 \\ + 3 \\ \hline \end{array} \qquad \begin{array}{r} 3 \\ + \underline{} \\ \hline 7 \end{array}$$

4 + 1 = _____   4 + 2 = _____   4 + 3 = _____

1 + 4 = _____   2 + 4 = _____   3 + 4 = _____

5. Find the sum for these addition problems.

$$\begin{array}{r} 4 \\ + 3 \\ \hline \end{array} \qquad \begin{array}{r} 4 \\ + 10 \\ \hline \end{array} \qquad \begin{array}{r} 4 \\ + 9 \\ \hline \end{array} \qquad \begin{array}{r} 4 \\ + 6 \\ \hline \end{array} \qquad \begin{array}{r} 4 \\ + 1 \\ \hline \end{array} \qquad \begin{array}{r} 4 \\ + 11 \\ \hline \end{array}$$

$$\begin{array}{r} 4 \\ + 8 \\ \hline \end{array} \qquad \begin{array}{r} 4 \\ + 4 \\ \hline \end{array} \qquad \begin{array}{r} 4 \\ + 7 \\ \hline \end{array} \qquad \begin{array}{r} 4 \\ + 12 \\ \hline \end{array} \qquad \begin{array}{r} 4 \\ + 2 \\ \hline \end{array} \qquad \begin{array}{r} 4 \\ + 5 \\ \hline \end{array}$$

$$\begin{array}{r} 4 \\ + 11 \\ \hline \end{array} \qquad \begin{array}{r} 4 \\ + 4 \\ \hline \end{array} \qquad \begin{array}{r} 4 \\ + 2 \\ \hline \end{array} \qquad \begin{array}{r} 4 \\ + 9 \\ \hline \end{array} \qquad \begin{array}{r} 4 \\ + 5 \\ \hline \end{array} \qquad \begin{array}{r} 4 \\ + 10 \\ \hline \end{array}$$

$$\begin{array}{r} 4 \\ + 6 \\ \hline \end{array} \qquad \begin{array}{r} 4 \\ + 1 \\ \hline \end{array} \qquad \begin{array}{r} 4 \\ + 8 \\ \hline \end{array} \qquad \begin{array}{r} 4 \\ + 12 \\ \hline \end{array} \qquad \begin{array}{r} 4 \\ + 3 \\ \hline \end{array} \qquad \begin{array}{r} 4 \\ + 7 \\ \hline \end{array}$$

"We must be as courteous to a man as we are to a picture, which we are willing to give the advantage of a good light."
—Emerson (1860)
Share your light with others!

6. Find the sum for these addition problems.

4 + 6 = _____   4 + 2 = _____   4 + 3 = _____

4 + 9 = _____   4 + 8 = _____   4 + 10 = _____

4 + 7 = _____   4 + 5 = _____   4 + 8 = _____

4 + 11 = _____   4 + 4 = _____   4 + 9 = _____

4 + 1 = _____   4 + 7 = _____   4 + 12 = _____

7. Write the numbers zero to twelve.

_____

_____   _____   _____   _____

_____   _____   _____   _____

_____   _____   _____   _____

The 12 Sons of Jacob = The Nation of Israel

8. Review your ones, twos, threes, and fours.

2 + 2	4 + 8	3 + 1	2 + 10	2 + 6	3 + 9
1 + 3	4 + 4	1 + 11	3 + 5	1 + 7	4 + 12
3 + 10	4 + 1	1 + 12	1 + 4	4 + 9	2 + 3
2 + 11	1 + 8	3 + 2	2 + 7	4 + 5	3 + 6
4 + 6	3 + 3	1 + 9	3 + 12	3 + 7	1 + 1
4 + 10	2 + 8	4 + 2	1 + 5	3 + 11	2 + 4
1 + 6	2 + 9	1 + 10	2 + 1	3 + 8	2 + 5
4 + 7	4 + 11	3 + 4	2 + 12	1 + 2	4 + 3

Review
Place II

What does the word unit mean? A unit is a definite quantity such as an inch (millimeter) or a foot (meter). In place value, the ones' place are small units; and the tens' place are larger units. We do not add unlike units. We cannot add feet (meters) and inches (millimeters) in the same column. Even so, in place value, tens are added in the tens' column and ones in the ones' column. Each unit has a place. Each person in Bible history also had a definite place.

In Revelation 21:15-17, where it speaks of the city foursquare, it says, *"And he that talked with me had a golden reed to measure the city, and the gates thereof, and the wall thereof."* It tells of measuring in furlongs and cubits. A furlong equals about 607 English feet (606 feet 6 inches), and 12,000 furlongs are about 1,378.4 miles. Read these verses and determine the size of the City!

Example for Adding Like Units and Converting Smaller Units to Larger Ones.

12 feet + 9 feet 13 inches

1. 12 feet   0 inches
+ 9 feet 13 inches
21 feet 13 inches
(unconverted answer)

2. 1 foot r 1 inch
12 inches) 13 inches
12
1 remaining inch

3. 12 feet 0 inches
+ 9 feet 13 inches
21 feet ~~13~~ inches
+ 1 foot   1 inch
22 feet   1 inch

(converted answer)

Note:

**(22 feet 1 inch) is the same as (21 feet 13 inches)
22 feet 1 inch is the converted answer.
Your child may convert his answers if capable.**

1. Write out, then add, to find the sum of these problems. Convert your answers (if capable).

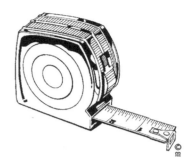

D.   316 pounds and 400 pounds

E.   229 yards 165 inches and 53 yards 356 inches

F.   133 weeks 85 days and 96 weeks 45 days

2. Add these problems and find the sum. Then convert if possible.

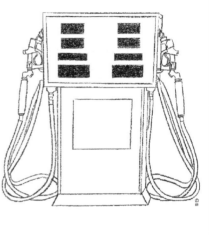

I.   6 years 9 months   4 days 12 hours
      + 3 years 4 months   + 9 days   7 hours

N.   18 gallons 6 quarts   17 feet 8 inches
      + 3 gallons 4 quarts   + 9 feet 6 inches

I.   47 pounds   6 ounces   9 gallons 10 quarts
     + 18 pounds 12 ounces   + 7 gallons   6 quarts

T.   22 feet 18 inches   19 yards 8 feet
      + 17 feet   5 inches   + 13 yards 4 feet

E.   21 yards 5 feet   11 hours 25 minutes
      + 18 yards 3 feet   + 9 hours 16 minutes

3. Write out six of your own problems using the above units.

Review
Place III

When adding numbers with more than three sets of digits, they need to be written in column form. You can use the methods you have learned for mental addition. These methods will be like shortcuts in adding very long columns.

1. As you do the following problems, be reminded of how the children of Israel were created as a nation to be like shining stars to the world. Place the + sign where appropriate.

C	27	51	38	57	86	58
	48	23	72	22	21	16
	76	30	44	65	60	16
	13	84	18	52	37	73

R	82	320	708	238	646	352
	32	42	54	34	43	724
	43	322	40	240	66	86
		63	528	27	346	14

E	215	602	373	190	837	736
	22	782	560	426	346	750
	37	317	366	343	630	281
	32	236	613	388	342	880

"No one is a light unto himself, not even the sun."
Antonio Porchia (1968)

A	463	437	425	704	324	603
	773	337	907	334	717	224
	377	842	28	43	443	134
	228	34	262	73	528	52
		450	98	822	75	500

T	151	847	344	681	269	885
	14	673	74	341	594	40
	123	58	608	302	89	287
	274					

I	734	836	725	810	920	932
	208	410	309	146	257	368
	341	563	452	300	400	51
	712	904	803	510	621	732
	406	628	517	68	179	280
	653	875	764	443	556	667
		927	816	334	465	576

O Set these numbers up as three problems on a separate piece of paper. 588, 601, 276, 211, 666, 114, 442/ 699, 712, 387, 322, 777, 205, 153, 708/ 824, 498, 437, 768, 306, 264

N Set these numbers up as four problems on a separate piece of paper. 640, 507, 185, 458, 103, 523, 816/ 755, 618, 296, 559, 117, 634, 908/ 862, 709, 397, 679, 226, 745, 908/ 536, 367, 131, 328, 681, 224, 744 (Fill in the blanks below using the letters in front of each set of problems.)

— — — — — — — —

Review
Word Problems
Place I - II - III

"Honour thy father

and thy mother."

Exodus 20:12

The family of Israel was to teach us many lessons. God recorded those stories in the Bible for that purpose.

Help your parents balance the check book by adding up the checks. If you do not have a check book, count out and add up the amounts of money to go into each envelope for its designated purpose. Let each check remind you of one of God's promises that can be "cashed in" by claiming them prayerfully if you have met the conditions of answered prayer. Jacob sinned, but he repented. Thus, he was able to receive (cash in on) the spiritual birthright promise.

Remember also, that as the family chooses and trusts one **alert** member to keep the household books, so Isaac trusted his father to choose a wife for him.

Remainder
Abraham and Sarah's Family

"I will make of thee a great nation."

Genesis 12:2

From Abraham and Sarah came one son, Isaac. From Isaac and Rebekah came two sons, but only one received the birthright. From Jacob and his wives came twelve sons. These sons multiplied, and the children of Israel became a nation. Through Israel, the <u>Deliverer</u> was born. He would save His people from their sins.

In English, "four" is the only number that has the same number of letters as its value.

Color this picture.

Reinforce
"Ye are...

an holy nation."

1 Peter 2:9

Read the stories on the next page about lights. Remember that the sun and moon were created on the fourth day.

Sing the hymn, "Like a Little Candle."

Reinforce – Lights

Are you a light shining for Jesus like Abraham? How can you shine for Him?

The Light of the World

Out West a friend of mine was walking along one of the streets one dark night, and saw approaching him a man with a lantern. As he came up close to him he noticed by the bright light that the man seemed as if he had no eyes. He went past, but the thought struck him, "Surely that man is blind." He turned round and said, "My friend, are you not blind?" "Yes," "Then what have you got the lantern for?" "I carry the lantern that people may not stumble over me, of course," said the blind man. Let us take a lesson from that blind man, and hold up our light, burning with the clear radiance of heaven, that men may not stumble over us. —*Moody*

Reflected Light

There is one kind of diamond which, after it has been exposed for some minutes to the light of the sun, when taken into a dark room will light for some time. The marvellous property of retaining light, and thereby becoming the source of light on a small scale, shows how analogous to light its very nature must be. Those who touched the Saviour became sources of virtue to others. As Moses' face shone when he came from the mount, so converse with spiritual things makes Christians the light which shines in the dark places of the earth. *"Let your light so shine before men."* —*Weekly Pulpit*

Sufficient Light

"How can I know," said a young man, "that even if I do begin a religious life I shall continue faithful, and finally reach heaven?" He wanted to see the whole way there before taking the first step. While in this state of indecision he sought the house of his favorite professor—for he was a college student at the time—and they talked for several hours upon the all-absorbing topic. When he was about to go home the professor accompanied him to the door, and observing how dark the night was, prepared a lantern, and handing it to his friend, said, "George, this little light will not show you the whole way home, but only one step at a time; but take that step, and you will reach home in safety." It proved the word in season. As George walked securely along, brightened by the little lantern, the truth flashed through his mind, "Why can I not trust my Heavenly Father," he said to himself, "even if I can't see my way clear to the end, if He gives me light to take one step? I will trust Him; I do trust Him."

Light in Darkness

I was in a darkened room, that I might observe the effect produced by the use of what is appropriately called "luminous paint." A neat card, on which the words "Trust in the Lord" were printed, rested upon the bookcase, and shone out clearly in the darkness. The effect fairly startled me. It was the first time that I had seen this simple but interesting effect. How remarkable that, if from any cause the light of sun or day failed to rest upon the card, its luminousness gradually declined, but returned when the sun's action infused fresh light! Truly, we also, if hidden from the face of our Lord, cease to shine. *"Are ye light in the Lord: walk as children of the light."*
—*Henry Varley*

Reinforce
Spiders—Four

Place I - II - III
1. Color these pictures of spiders.

Desert
Tarantula

Black Orb

Black Widow

Place III

2. Do more research on one
of the spiders on this page.
OR
Do research about spiders that
live in water.

Place I - II - III

3. Use a field guide for insects
and spiders and learn to iden-
tify spiders in your area.

4. Search in your home to find
spiders that live there.

Research
The Number Five

"For this cause I bow my knees unto the Father of our Lord Jesus Christ,

"Of whom the whole family in heaven and earth is named."
Ephesians 3:14-15

Five, in the Bible, reminds us of grace, and how favor is shown to us who are unworthy and weak.

From the twelve (12) sons of Jacob, weak and unworthy, came the favored Israelites. This was the family that Jesus was born into when He came from heaven to live on earth.

Would the family of Israel be **alert** to know Jesus and quick to understand His great sacrifice? Would they be aware of what was taking place around them so they could make the right response?

"It is the privilege of every family so to live that Satan can take no advantage of anything that they may say or do, to tear one another

Reinforce

Color then read the meaning of the number five. Learn to say five in these languages.

French – cinq (sank)

Japanese – go (goh)

Spanish – cinco (SEEN koh)

Swahili – tano (TAH noh)

```
  4 addend
+ 1 addend
  5 sum
```

FIVE - 5 = GRACE, FAVOR

The divine nature and the human nature combined (addition **+**) to give sinful man a Saviour.

5

down."* Israel, the family Jesus was born into on this earth, should have been such an **alert** family.

We are told: "It was God's plan for the members of the family to be associated in work and study, in worship and recreation, the father as priest of his household, and both father and mother as teachers and companions of their children. But the results of sin, having changed the conditions of life, to a great degree prevent this association. Often the father hardly sees the faces of his children throughout the week. He is almost wholly deprived of opportunity for companionship or instruction. But God's love has set a limit to the demands of toil. Over the Sabbath He places His merciful hand. In His own day He preserves for the family opportunity for communion with Him, with nature, and with one another."**

God needs these kinds of families today, as described in the above paragraph, as we prepare for His second coming. *"But by the grace of God I am what I am: and his grace which was bestowed upon me was not in vain; but I laboured more abundantly than they all: yet not I, but the grace of God which was with me"* (I Corinthians 15:10).

*1 Testimonies 309 **Education 250-251*

Grace—Exhaustless

Mountains have been exhausted of their gold, mines of their diamonds, and the depths of ocean of their pearly gems. The demand has emptied the supply. Over once busy scenes, silence and solitude now reign; the caverns ring no longer to the miner's hammer, nor is the song of the pearl-fisher heard upon the deep. But the riches of grace are inexhaustible. All that have gone before us have not made them less to those who follow us. When they have supplied the wants of unborn millions, the last of Adam's race, that lonely man, over whose head the sun is dying beneath whose feet the earth is reeling, shall stand by as full a fountain, as this day invites you to drink and live, to wash and be clean.

—Guthrie

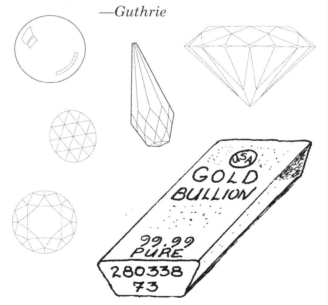

"Happy is said to be the family which can eat onions together. They are, for the time being separate from the world, and have a harmony of aspiration."
—Charles Dudley Warner (1871)

Bible Search

Fives

What is grace? Favor! What is favor? Favor shown to the miserable we call mercy; favor shown to the poor we call pity; favor shown to the suffering we call compassion; favor shown to the obstinate we call patience: but favor shown to the unworthy we call GRACE! Grace is the power God gives to a person to accomplish everything that He requires of them.

1. What was spoken into existence on the fifth day of creation? (Genesis 1:20-23)

2. What is the fifth book of the Bible?

Note: This book magnifies the grace (favor and power) of God, and it emphasizes the fact that not for the sake of the people, but for God's own Name's sake had He called, and chosen, and blessed them.

3. What were the 5 parts to the great image in Daniel 2?

4. When David went to meet the giants, he picked up what 5 things? (I Samuel 17:40)

5. What does Romans 8:31 mean? (Leviticus 26:8)

6. There are many fives in the Bible—look up the list in the *Strong's Concordance*.

5 5 5 5 5 5 5 5

Remarkable Facts: Most flower families have 5 sepals, 5 petals, and 5 stamens. However, 3, 4, and 6 are common among a few families. Try counting petals next time you see a flower.

Remarkable Facts
The Tabernacle—Five

Almond Blossoms

The tabernacle had five as its all-pervading number;
almost every measurement was a multiple of five.
How fitting that the number of grace would be one
of the special numbers of this house of worship.

• The Divine title of the book called Leviticus is in the Hebrew Cannon "He called." It is the book of worship especially dealing with the Sanctuary. *"And Jehovah spake"* an expression which occurs in the book 36 times (3^2 x 2^2). (3 = Divine perfection and 2 = there is a difference between good and evil—divided and 3 + 2 = 5 or grace.)

• The outer court was 100 cubits long and 50 cubits wide. On either side were 20 pillars, and along each end were 10 pillars, or 60 in all; that is 5 x 12, or grace in governmental display before the world, 12 being the number of the tribes.

• The pillars that held up the curtains were 5 cubits apart and 5 cubits high, and the whole of the outer curtain was divided into squares of 25 cubits (5 x 5). Each pair of pillars thus supported an area of 5^2 cubits of fine white linen, thus witnessing to the perfect grace by which alone God's people can witness for Him before the world.

• 5 x 5 was the measure of the brazen altar of burnt offering. This was the perfect answer of Christ to God's righteous requirements, and to what was required of man. The brazen altar was only 3 cubits high, but this tells us that the provision was Divine in its origin, that atonement emanates solely from God.

• The building itself was 10 cubits high, 10 cubits wide, and 30 cubits long. Its length was divided into two unequal parts, the Holy place being 20 cubits long; and the Holy of Holies 10 cubits, being therefore a perfect cube of 10 cubits.

• It was formed of forty-eight boards, twenty on either side, and eight at the end, the front being formed of a curtain hung on five pillars. These forty-eight boards (3 x 4^2) are significant of the nation as before God in the fulness of privilege on the earth (4 x 12). The twenty boards on each side were held together by five bars passing through rings which were attached to them.

• The curtains which covered the Tabernacle structure were four in number. The first was made of ten curtains of byssus in various colors adorned with embroidered cherubim. Each curtain was 28 (4 x 7) cubits long and four wide. They were hung five on each side, probably sewn together to form one large sheet (20 x 28); the two sheets coupled together by loops, and fifty (5 x 10) taches of gold. The second covering was formed of eleven curtains of goats' hair, each 30 cubits long and four wide, joined together in two sheets fastened by loops and taches of brass. The third was of rams' skins dyed red, and the fourth was of skins, of which the dimensions are not given.

• The entrance veils were three in number. The first was "the gate of the court," 20 cubits wide and 5 high, hung on 5 pillars. The second was "the door of the Tabernacle," 10 cubits wide and 10 high, hung like the gate of the court on 5 pillars. The third was the "beautiful veil," also 10 cubits square, which divided the Holy place from the Holy of Holies. One feature of these three veils is remarkable. The dimensions of the veil of the court and those of the Tabernacle were different, but yet the area was the same. The former was 20 cubits by 5 = 100 cubits; the latter were 10 cubits by 10, equalling 100 cubits also. Thus while there was only one gate, one door, one veil, they each typified Christ as the only door of entrance for all the blessings connected with salvation. But note that the "gate" which admitted to the benefits of atonement was wider and lower (20 cubits wide, and 5 cubits high); while the door which admitted to worship was both higher and narrower, being only 10 cubits wide, half the width, and twice the height (10 cubits high).

• The holy anointing oil (Exodus 30:23-25) was composed of five parts, for it was a revelation of pure grace. This five is marked by the numbers four and one. For four parts were spices, and one was oil.
   –Myrrh, 500 shekels (5 x 100)
   –Sweet cinnamon, 250 shekels (5 x 50)
   –Sweet calamus, 250 shekels (5 x 100)
   –Cassia, 500 shekels (5 x 100)

5 Parts

—Olive oil, one hin

This anointing oil was holy, for it separated to God; nothing else could separate. It was of God, and therefore of grace; and therefore the number of its ingredients was five, and their quantities were all multiples of five.

• The incense (Exodus 30:34) also was composed of five parts.
  Four were "sweet spices," and one was salt.
    —Stacte, a drop of aromatic gum
    —Onycha, the shell of a species of mussel which burnt with an odor of musk
    —Galbanum, a fragrant gum
    —Frankincense, a bright burning gum
    —Salt

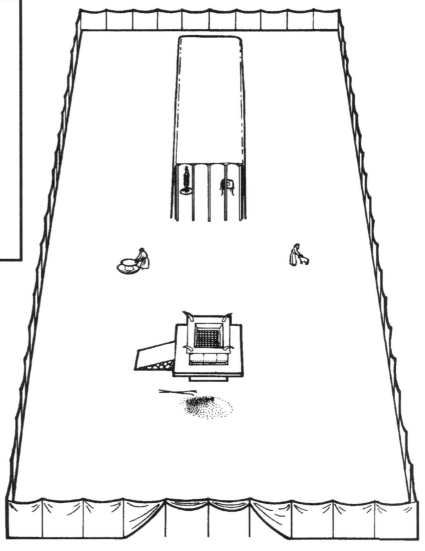

"Let my prayer
be set forth before thee
as incense;
and the lifting up
of my hands
as the evening sacrifice."
Psalm 141:2

"Its [incense]
fragrance enwraps
our tears and groans,
and clothes our deepest
yearnings with beauty.
When breathed from our
hearts our prayers soar up
to God as in a rising flame.
The radiance from the
seven-starred candelabrum
shining through
these perfumed clouds
formed rainbows dancing
in joy with new
covenant assurances."
—Leslie Hardinge

Reinforce

Jesus is Coming!

$$1 + 4 = 5$$

Is your family ready?

1 (God) **+ 4** (Creating Godly Families) **= 5** (A Favored Family Living in the Days of Christ's Second Advent.)

Remember

Store these facts in your mind.

5	5	5	5	5	5
+ 1	+ 2	+ 3	+ 4	+ 5	+ 6
6	7	8	9	10	11

5	5	5	5	5	5
+ 7	+ 8	+ 9	+ 10	+ 11	+ 12
12	13	14	15	16	17

Family

"I bow my knees unto the Father of the Lord Jesus Christ,
of whom the whole family in heaven and earth is named."

Ephesians 3:14-15

The word "family" is said to have originally signified servants. Each member can be **alert** to serving others. In the *Noah Webster's 1828 Dictionary,* we are told that the three most common definitions of "family" are:

1. The collective body of persons who live in one house under one head or manager; a household, including parents, children and servants, and as the case may be, lodgers or boarders.

2. Those who descend from one common progenitor; a tribe or race; kindred; lineage. (Thus the Israelites were a branch of the family of Abraham. The whole human race are the family of Adam, the human family.)

3. Course of descent; genealogy; line of ancestors.

"But I would have you know, that the head of every man is Christ; and the head of the woman is the man; and the head of Christ is God" (I Corinthians 11:3).

Christ should be the Head of every family! He came from heaven to earth to show us how He can be our Head.

"The only rock I know
that stays steady,
the only institution I know
that works, is the family."
—Lee Iacocca (1988)

A Family
Is A Group
Of Servants

Review
Place I

1. Find the sum for these problems. Think of these sums as families in the time of Jesus' first advent and today.

5	5	5	5	5	5
+ 1	+ 2	+ 3	+ 4	+ 5	+ 6

5	5	5	5	5	5
+ 7	+ 8	+ 9	+ 10	+ 11	+ 12

2. Do these addition problems.

5	5	5	5	5	5
+ 4	+ 9	+ 7	+ 2	+ 8	+ 3

5	5	5	5	5	5
+ 6	+ 11	+ 5	+ 12	+ 10	+ 8

5	5	5	5	5	5
+ 1	+ 8	+ 11	+ 2	+ 4	+ 7

5	5	5	5	5	5
+ 3	+ 6	+ 10	+ 5	+ 12	+ 9

3. Write in the answers for these problems.

5 + 8 = _____	5 + 5 = _____	5 + 10 = _____
5 + 13 = _____	5 + 11 = _____	5 + 1 = _____
5 + 6 = _____	5 + 4 = _____	5 + 9 = _____
5 + 8 = _____	5 + 9 = _____	5 + 8 = _____
5 + 12 = _____	5 + 4 = _____	5 + 5 = _____
5 + 3 = _____	5 + 2 = _____	5 + 7 = _____
5 + 9 = _____	5 + 6 = _____	5 + 11 = _____
5 + 10 = _____	5 + 3 = _____	5 + 1 = _____
5 + 7 = _____	5 + 2 = _____	5 + 4 = _____
5 + 11 = _____	5 + 9 = _____	5 + 10 = _____
5 + 6 = _____	5 + 12 = _____	5 + 7 = _____

The family altar
would alter
many a family.

4. Review of Ones - Fives

(1) What does one in the Bible remind you of? _____

(2) What does two in the Bible remind you of? _____

(3) What does three in the Bible remind you of? _____

(4) What does four in the Bible remind you of? _____

(5) What does five in the Bible remind you of? _____

5. Adding these ones through fives, think of <u>alert</u>, godly, families as the sums of these addition problems.

3 + 12	3 + 7	1 + 10	5 + 8	1 + 5	4 + 8
2 + 1	3 + 2	2 + 11	5 + 4	4 + 3	2 + 6
3 + 1	5 + 7	3 + 11	1 + 9	4 + 7	2 + 5
5 + 3	2 + 10	3 + 6	1 + 4	4 + 12	4 + 2
4 + 6	2 + 9	3 + 10	5 + 2	1 + 3	3 + 5

4 + 11	4 + 1	1 + 8	5 + 12	5 + 6	2 + 4
5 + 11	3 + 9	4 + 4	2 + 3	5 + 1	4 + 10
2 + 8	1 + 2	3 + 3	5 + 9	1 + 7	2 + 12
5 + 5	1 + 12	2 + 7	4 + 5	1 + 11	1 + 1
4 + 9	3 + 4	1 + 6	2 + 2	5 + 10	3 + 8

"And he is the head
of the body, the church:
who is the beginning,
the firstborn from the dead;
that in all things he might
have the preeminence."

Colossians 1:18

Addition 1 – Student – Page 142

5 + 1 = 6   6 is 1/2 of the 12 sons of Jacob

5 + 2 = 7   Seven (7), eight (8) and nine (9) are more
                   than half of the twelve (12) sons of Jacob.

5 + 3 = 8   When you add one more the answer is
                   always one more. Notice the problems on
                   the left.

6. Do the following addition problems.
Notice that all the answers are less than 12.

```
  5        1        5        2
+ 1      + 5      + 2      + 5


  5        3        5        4
+ 3      + 5      + 4      + 5


  4        1        4        2
+ 1      + 4      + 2      + 4


  4        3        4        4        3        1
+ 3      + 4      + 4      + 4      + 1      + 3


  3        2        3        3        3        4
+ 1      + 3      + 3      + 3      + 4      + 3
```

Review
Like Units
Place II
Remember only like units can be added.
Notice the example below.

Example

5 feet	14 inches
+ 2 feet	24 inches
7 feet	38 inches

<u>To Convert to Inches Only</u>

7 feet x 12 inches = 84 inches

84 inches
+ 38 inches
122 inches

<u>To Convert to Feet</u>
(As many inches to feet as possible)

38 inches ÷ 12 inches =

$$\begin{array}{r} 3 \text{ feet r 2 inches} \\ 12\overline{)38} \\ \underline{36} \\ 2 \text{ remaining inches} \end{array}$$

Therefore:

7 feet + 3 feet = 10 feet

<u>10 feet + 2 inches</u>

Note: 122 inches is the same as 10 feet 2 inches.

$$\begin{array}{r} 10 \text{ feet remainder 2 inches} \\ 12\overline{)122 \text{ inches}} \\ \underline{120} \\ 2 \text{ remaining inches} \end{array}$$

**See the chart in the teacher's section
of Mathematics lesson 2, *A Place*, pages 27-28 for conversions.**

1. Change these larger units to smaller units.

A.   1 foot = _____ inches   4 feet = _____ inches

L.   1 yard = _____ feet   8 yards = _____ feet

E.   1 gallon = _____ quarts   6 gallons = _____ quarts

R.   2 gallons = _____ pints   4 gallons = _____ pints

T.   1 pound = _____ ounces   6 pounds = _____ ounces

F.   1 ton = _____ pounds   4 tons = _____ pounds

A.   1 hour = _____ minutes   3 hours = _____ minutes

M.   1 year = _____ months   7 years = _____ months

I.   1 dozen = _____ items   5 dozen = _____ items

L.   6 feet 4 inches = _____ inches

I.   4 gallons 2 quarts = _____ quarts

E.   5 gallons 4 pints = _____ pints

S.   3 pounds 9 ounces = _____ ounces

     6 hours 25 minutes = _____ minutes

     5 years 6 months = _____ months

Review
Place III

1. Add and then check your answer
   by adding in the opposite direction.
   Think of these sums as godly families
   training their children to be ready
   for Jesus' second coming.

F.	41	97	48	41	59	54
	68	67	54	63	17	48
	16	32	92	37	79	13
	52	10	14	38	24	40

A.	91	73	19	39	28	74
	87	27	82	15	10	11
	31	29	36	49	51	25
	10	66	96	83	43	15

V.	64	33	11	89	37	85
	92	71	25	37	17	19
	12	32	10	72	45	29
	13	59	14	17	23	81

O.	54	29	16	54	13	21
	84	32	29	35	24	43
	82	36	45	46	56	32
	12	67	67	16	10	19
	41	87	63	23	60	38

R.	16	64	32	62	42	63
	97	21	53	35	27	51
	25	24	25	16	33	34
	54	75	42	51	40	35
	27	11	15	23	24	61

G.	707	800	312	543	649	441
	332	177	114	246	111	156
	525	767	455	302	819	900
	111	515	480	202	555	564
	462	818	678	700	647	427

R.	854	311	557	703	621	199
	900	904	320	317	131	967
	633	717	777	671	396	263
	238	110	617	110	124	621
	776	652	478	400	483	373

A.	5673	5143	2331	2119	1145
	8922	1321	1005	3657	4849
	2367	1075	2567	7652	1565
	7132	1509	1032	2113	2387
	1543	9132	2165	7219	3114

Godly
Families
Train
Their
Children

C.	1940	3797	1187	8735	8118
	5096	6113	9118	5804	1505
	3562	7294	7570	8659	7811
	8868	6745	3239	3089	1942
	3561	6579	2928	2912	5036

E.			
1128	6454	58038	37961
2942	2403	87326	94095
7284	7227	18245	50253
7732	3821	30345	63884
5062	3946	75793	35655
1942	8536	91692	61019

favor
grace
favor
grace

The <u>Sum</u> of It All ✚

✚   The boy that by <u>addition</u> grows,

━   And suffers no <u>subtraction</u>;

X   Who <u>multiplies</u> the thing he knows,

1/2   And <u>carries</u> every <u>fraction</u>

÷   Who well <u>divides</u> his precious time,

     The due proportions giving,

=   To sure success aloft will climb,

     Interest compound receiving.

          —Dr. Ray Palmer

Review
Word Problems
Place I

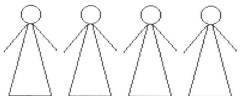

Remember, God does not want a man to have more than one wife. Jacob had married four wives. It was now important he care for them and his children.

1. Jacob had six (6) sons by his first wife and two (2) sons by his second wife.

How many sons did he have by them?

2. Jacob's other two (2) wives each had two (2) sons.

How many sons did he have by them?

3. What is the total of six (6) sons, two (2) sons and four (4) sons?

Review
Word Problems
Place II

1. The Bund family had 6 brothers and 2 sisters. The children grew up, married, and among them had 15 children. The Sorey family had 3 brothers and 4 sisters. When the children grew up and married there were 21 of them. The Koch family had 3 sisters and 3 brothers. When the children grew up they had 24 children. How many total children were there in these families?

2. Families need homes. Some country property was divided into 10 acre plots. The houses and garages built on this property had the following floor space, 2,400 square feet, 3,000 square feet, and 2,130 square feet. The plans could be altered to add an additional 230 square feet for each house and 175 square feet for each garage. How much square footage would be in the additional space added to each house including the garage?

Work Area

The best part of a family tree is underground.

Review – Word Problems
Place III

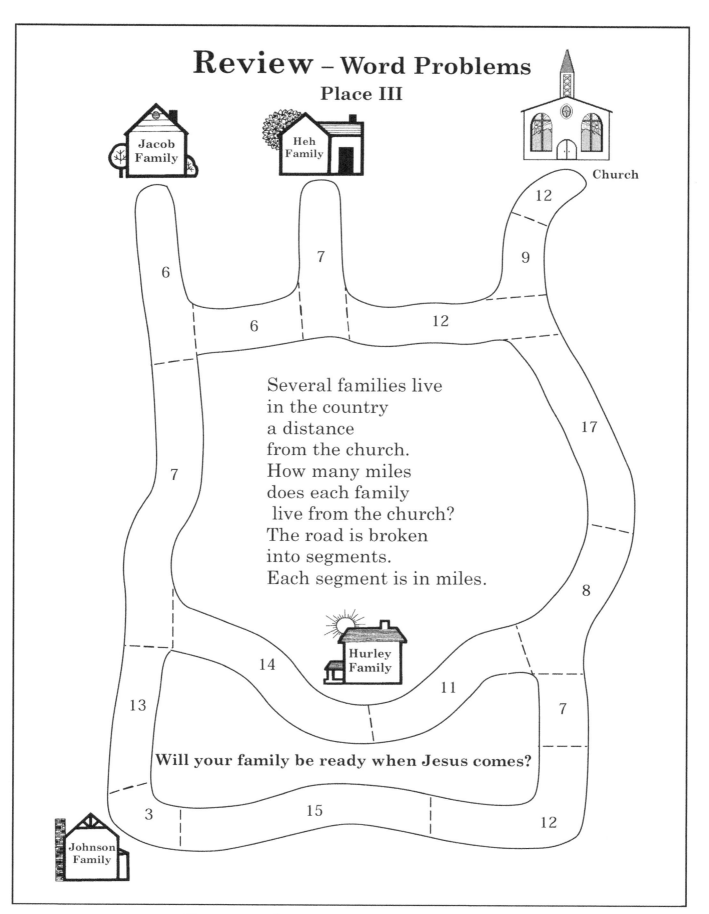

Jacob Family

Heh Family

Church

6

7

12

9

6

12

Several families live
in the country
a distance
from the church.
How many miles
does each family
live from the church?
The road is broken
into segments.
Each segment is in miles.

7

17

Hurley Family

14

8

11

13

7

Will your family be ready when Jesus comes?

Johnson Family

3

15

12

Review
Place I

Test On Ones Through Fives
God's time is always perfect. Everything in heaven
was in order and it was time for Jesus to be born.
Would God's people be **alert** and ready for His Son?

**1. Do you remember? Write the sum for these addition problems.
Think about the sums as people ready for Jesus' first advent.**

$$
\begin{array}{cccccc}
1 & 1 & 1 & 1 & 1 & 1 \\
+\,1 & +\,2 & +\,3 & +\,4 & +\,5 & +\,6 \\
\end{array}
$$

$$
\begin{array}{cccccc}
1 & 1 & 1 & 1 & 1 & 1 \\
+\,7 & +\,8 & +\,9 & +\,10 & +\,11 & +\,12 \\
\end{array}
$$

$$
\begin{array}{cccccc}
2 & 2 & 2 & 2 & 2 & 2 \\
+\,1 & +\,2 & +\,3 & +\,4 & +\,5 & +\,6 \\
\end{array}
$$

$$
\begin{array}{cccccc}
2 & 2 & 2 & 2 & 2 & 2 \\
+\,7 & +\,8 & +\,9 & +\,10 & +\,11 & +\,12 \\
\end{array}
$$

$$
\begin{array}{cccccc}
3 & 3 & 3 & 3 & 3 & 3 \\
+\,1 & +\,2 & +\,3 & +\,4 & +\,5 & +\,6 \\
\end{array}
$$

$$
\begin{array}{cccccc}
3 & 3 & 3 & 3 & 3 & 3 \\
+\,7 & +\,8 & +\,9 & +\,10 & +\,11 & +\,12 \\
\end{array}
$$

4	4	4	4	4	4
+ 1	+ 2	+ 3	+ 4	+ 5	+ 6

4	4	4	4	4	4
+ 7	+ 8	+ 9	+ 10	+ 11	+ 12

5	5	5	5	5	5
+ 1	+ 2	+ 3	+ 4	+ 5	+ 6

5	5	5	5	5	5
+ 7	+ 8	+ 9	+ 10	+ 11	+ 12

2. See how quickly you can add up these addition problems.

1	4	3	2	5	1
+ 10	+ 6	+ 12	+ 2	+ 1	+ 4

3	2	4	3	1	2
+ 9	+ 7	+ 4	+ 6	+ 8	+ 11

5	2	1	3	4	2
+ 6	+ 4	+ 2	+ 5	+ 9	+ 10

3	3	2	5	4	1
+ 1	+ 11	+ 8	+ 3	+ 12	+ 7

5	4	5	3	2	4
+ 12	+ 1	+ 8	+ 10	+ 5	+ 11

3	1	5	2	4	3
+ 3	+ 1	+ 4	+ 9	+ 7	+ 8

1	1	2	3	5	5
+ 6	+ 12	+ 3	+ 4	+ 2	+ 11

4	2	4	1	4	3
+ 5	+ 6	+ 2	+ 9	+ 10	+ 7

5	2	5	1	4	3
+ 7	+ 1	+ 10	+ 3	+ 8	+ 2

2	5	1	1	4	5
+ 12	+ 5	+ 5	+ 11	+ 3	+ 9

The most essential element in any home is God.

3. Alert to Our Place

Each patriarch had a place in history to fill
if all would be in order when Jesus came.
Adam · Seth · Enoch · Noah · Shem ·
Abraham · Isaac · Jacob · Judah ·
David · Solomon · and many others · Joseph·
Jesus Christ, the <u>Deliverer</u>!

Abraham to David = 14 generations
David to Babylon = 14 generations
From Babylon to Christ = 14 generations
(Matthew 1:1-17; Luke 3:23-28)

Matthew 1:1-17 gives Jesus' family record.
Count the names and fill in the blanks in each column.
Then write the name of the answer on the second line.

Abraham	Solomon	Jechonias
Isaac	Roboam	Salathiel
Jacob	Abia	Zorobabel
Judas	Asa	Abiud
Phares	Josaphat	Eliakim
Esrom	Joram	Azor
Aram	Ozias	Sadoc
Aminadab	Joatham	Achim
Naasson	Achaz	Eliud
Salmon	Ezekias	Eleazar
Boaz	Manasses	Matthan
Obed	Amon	Jacob
Jesse	Josias	Joseph
<u>David</u>	<u>Jehoiakim</u> (not listed)	<u>Jesus Christ</u>

_____   _____   _____

_____   _____   _____

4. Be alert to the place!

```
tens   ones
 1   | 4
 1   | 4
 1   | 4
 4     2
```

The genealogy of Jesus is divided up into sets of 14 generations.
Fourteen is 2 sets of 7 (7 + 7 or 2 x 7) and the number 2 reminds us of the incarnation (God becoming a human).

$$\begin{array}{r} 10 \\ + 4 \end{array} \qquad \begin{array}{r} 14 \\ + 14 \end{array} \qquad \begin{array}{r} 9 \\ + 14 \end{array} \qquad \begin{array}{r} 12 \\ + 14 \end{array} \qquad \begin{array}{r} 14 \\ 10 \\ + 4 \end{array} \qquad \begin{array}{r} 12 \\ 14 \\ + 16 \end{array} \qquad \begin{array}{r} 15 \\ 11 \\ + 16 \end{array}$$

5. From Abraham to Phares was how many generations?

_____

Esrom to Naasson is _____ generations.

Salmon to David is _____ generations.

How many generations is this? _____

Count the generations from Solomon to Ozias. _____

How many generations are there from Ozias to Achaz?___

What is the total? _____

6. There are five generations left in the second list. Add these to the last list of fourteen generations and what is the answer that you get? _____

The sum of   5   +   9   = _____

    + 9   +   + 19   = _____

_____   + _____ = _____

Six (6) sevens = _____
     (6 x 7)

7
7
7
7
7
7
42

---

6 = man

7 = spiritual   =   Jesus Christ
      perfection

     Remember, Five is the number of grace. Grace means favor. Favor shown to miserable people is called mercy; favor shown to the poor is called pity; favor shown to the suffering is called compassion; favor shown to the stubborn we call patience; but favor shown to the unworthy is called grace. *"Being justified freely* [without a cause] *by his grace"* (Romans 3:24).

**Learn to spell the number five.
Write it five times.**

_____
_____
_____
_____
_____

5

5

Review
Place II

God encouraged His **alert** people to stay together, and to choose a wife or husband from a godly family. People will become like those whom they are around. It is good to choose our associates or friends from families that love and serve God. When working with units we keep time with time, distance with distance, length with length, capacity with capacity, and weight with weight. You cannot mix pounds with days and get a correct answer. All must be kept within each "family." Years and months can be added together, ounces and pounds can be added. *"Be ye not unequally yoked together with unbelievers: for what fellowship hath righteousness with unrighteousness? and what communion hath light with darkness?"* (II Corinthians 6:14).

1. Add the following units in each family. You will need to "convert" or change some. See the example on page 144.

2 years + 9 months =   4 years + 6 months =

3 weeks + 5 days =   4 days + 18 days =

8 weeks + 10 weeks =   5 weeks + 4 days =

1 hour + 35 minutes =   3 hours + 20 minutes =

4 hours + 24 hours =   12 feet + 7 inches =

9 feet + 8 inches =   3 pounds + 14 ounces =

4 pounds + 6 ounces =   6 pounds + 9 pounds =

2.

4 gallons + 3 quarts	8 feet + 2 inches	5 years +6 months	4 pounds + 3 ounces
6 yards + 2 feet	9 years + 2 months	10 weeks + 2 days	8 feet + 4 inches
3 feet + 8 inches	2 hours + 11 minutes	3 yards +3 feet	9 gallons + 12 gallons
3 pounds + 9 ounces	12 yards + 8 feet	5 weeks +7 days	10 feet + 15 feet
7 years + 9 months	39 inches + 11 inches	5 hours +5 minutes	7 gallons + 3 quarts

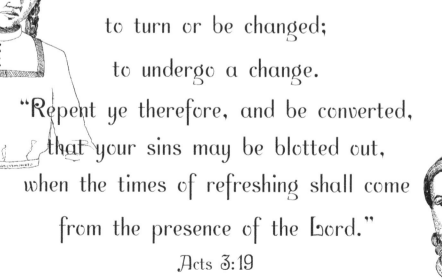

Convert means:

to turn or be changed;

to undergo a change.

"Repent ye therefore, and be converted,

that your sins may be blotted out,

when the times of refreshing shall come

from the presence of the Lord."

Acts 3:19

Review
Place III

1. Solve these problems and check them. Think of the sums as homes where godly parents and children live.

357	314	846	5934	9430
123	360	937	1391	7170
546	526	203	2753	8106
438	415	625	4616	4183

7901	26528624	87506
3549	28565251	52478
2431	15435676	49742
3665	43162823	10658
8262	66323650	8070

620	568	66761	81660
3861	6891	28244	261
345	7137	81523	71892
5092	8875	4561	63501
487	611	938	84362
8216	935	5288	4311
912	98962	65428	439276

600 students at one university were asked to vote on the most beautiful word in the English language. 422 wrote "Mother." 112 wrote "Home."

The ornament of a house is the friends who frequent it.

—Ralph Waldo Emerson

Reinforce

1. As a family, invite several families to enjoy a special meal with your family. Add up how many plates, silverware, napkins (serviettes), etc., you will need. Make sure you also have enough chairs.

In cooking the meal, be sure to increase the recipe as to allow for the extra people.

Teach your guests what the addition sign means.

2. Review what the addition sign means and read this poem.

What Does The Addition Sign Mean?

It can remind us of the cross.

What is the Cross?

But what is the cross?
Is it bars at right angles,
Or is it a tree on which
Jesus was slain?
Is it a symbol of gold,
Ornamented with spangles,
On the neck of that fair one,
Attached to a chain?

Ah! no—'tis the curb
Of our turbulent passions,
A rein on the powers
That lead us astray,
Which bind down the soul
To the world and its fashions,
And lure it from wisdom
And virtue away.

—Unknown

3. Each family member of Jesus has a special place.
Draw the members of your family below.
Add them up. How many are there?
What do those numbers mean in the Bible?

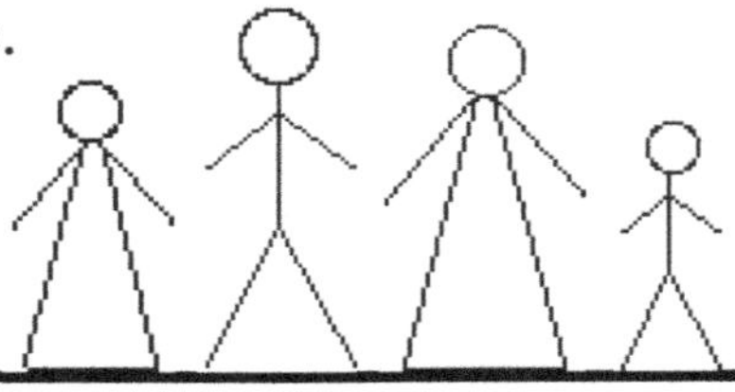

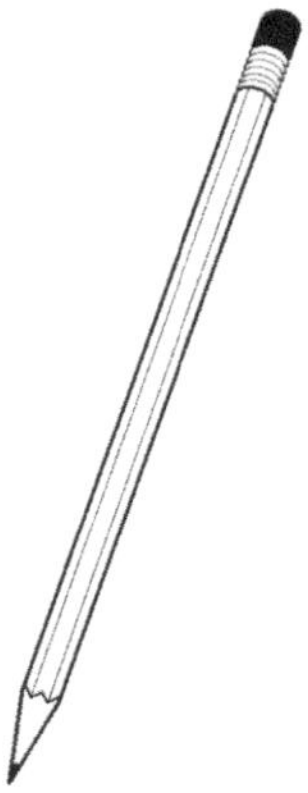

_____ means _____

_____

Remainder
The Home

"The family firm is a sacred, social society, in which each member is to act a part, each helping the other. The work of the household is to move smoothly, like the different parts of well-regulated machinery.

"Every member of the family should realize that a responsibility rests upon him individually to do his part in adding to the comfort, order, and regularity of the family. One should not work against another. All should unitedly engage in the good work of encouraging one another; they should exercise gentleness, forbearance, and patience; speak in low, calm tones, shunning confusion; and each doing his utmost to lighten the burdens of the mother....

"Each member of the family should understand just the part he is expected to act in union with the others. All, from the child six years old and upward, should understand that it is required of them to bear their share of life's burdens.

"I must grow in grace at home and wherever I may be, in order to give moral power to all my actions. At home I must guard my spirit, my actions, my words. I must give time to personal culture, to training and educating myself in right principles. I must be an example to others. I must meditate upon the word of God night and day and bring it into my practical life. The sword of the Spirit, which is the word of God, is the only sword which I can safely use."*

We need God's grace or power to live in our homes the way we should with our families. "The Lord saw our fallen condition; He saw our need of grace [five], and because He loved our souls, He has given us grace [five] and peace. Grace [five] means favor to one who is undeserving, to one who is lost. The fact that we are sinners, instead of shutting us away from the mercy and love of God, makes the exercise of His love to us a positive necessity in order that we may be saved."** He sent His Son to accomplish this task! Are you **alert** to the great sacrifice God has made for you?

Flowers are the poetry of children.

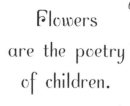

*The Adventist Home 179-180; **6 Bible Commentary 1117*

Sing
the hymn,
"Happy
the Home."

Reinforce

Color these pictures.

Buttercup

Columbine

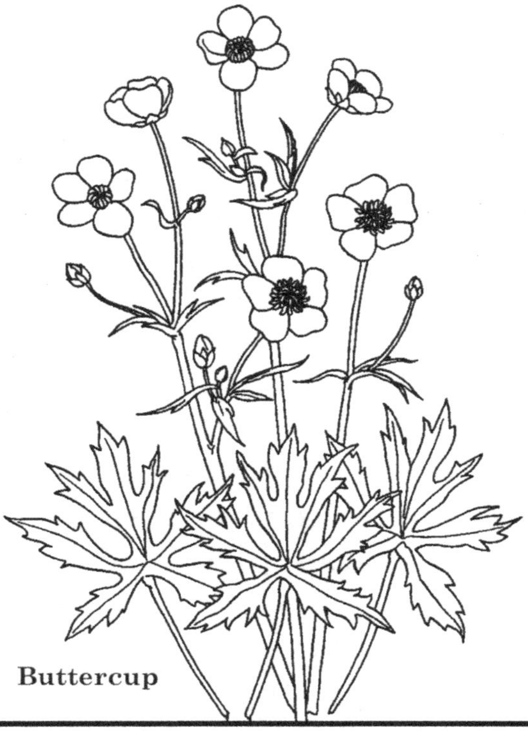

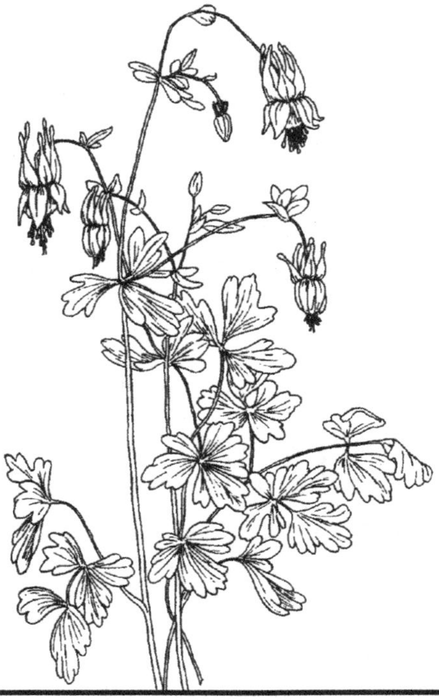

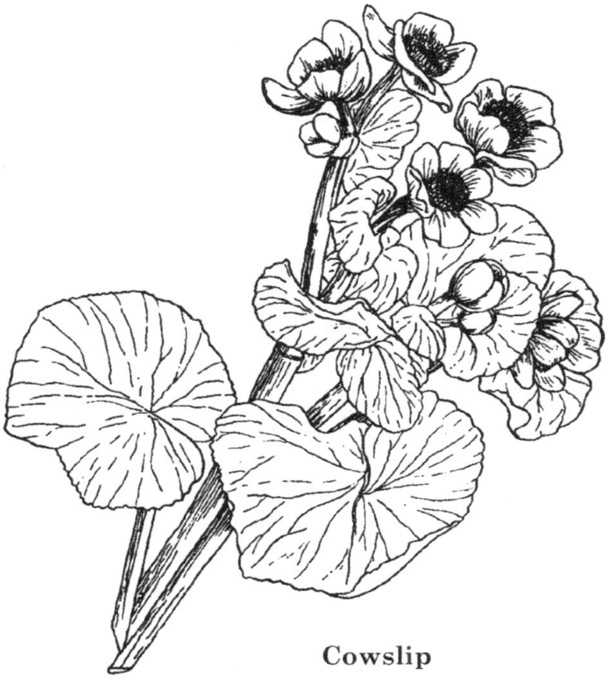

Cowslip

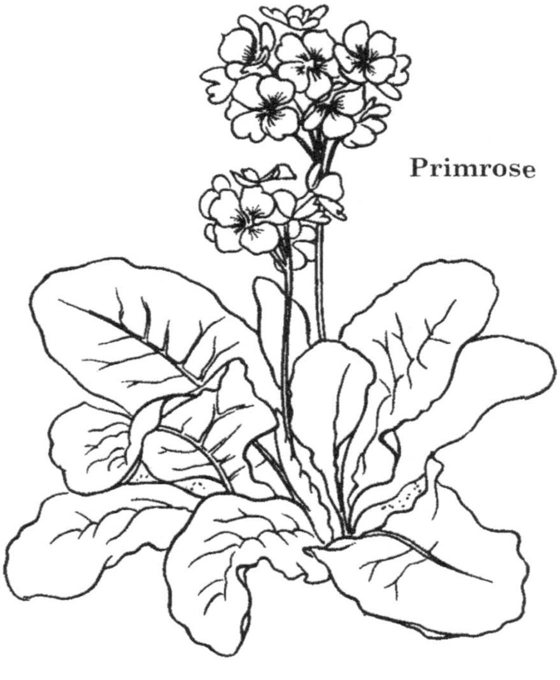

Primrose

G 66 Sixes - 6 6 6 6

Research
The Number Six

"Deck thyself now with majesty and excellency; and array thyself with glory and beauty."
Job 40:10

Six, in the Bible, reminds us of man. It is one less than seven which is a perfect number, therefore falling short of perfection. Sin is falling short of the character of God. *"The wages of sin is death"* (Romans 6:23). But Jesus became a man so He could suffer the death that was ours that we might receive the life that was His.

Jesus *"...made himself of no reputation, and took upon him the form of a servant, and was made in the likeness of men:*

"And being found in fashion as a man, he humbled himself, and became obedient unto death, even the death of the cross" (Philippians 2:7-8).

"Before Christ left heaven and came into the world to die, He was

Reinforce
Color then read the meaning of the number six. Learn to say six in these languages.

French – Six (sees)

Japanese – roku (roh koo)

Spanish – seis (sayss)

Swahili – sita (SEE tah)

```
  5 addend
+ 1 addend
  6 sum
```

SIX - 6 = MAN

The divine nature and the human nature combined (addition +) to give sinful man a Saviour.

Divine

Human

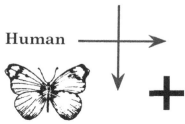

taller than any of the angels. He was majestic and lovely. But when his ministry commenced, He was but little taller than the common size of men then living upon the earth. Had He come among men with His noble, heavenly form, His outward appearance would have attracted the minds of the people to Himself, and He would have been received without the exercise of faith....

"The faith of men in Christ as the Messiah was not to rest on the evidences of sight, and they believe on Him because of His personal attractions, but because of the excellence of character found in Him, which never had been found, neither could be, in another."* *"Deck thyself now with majesty and excellency; and array thyself with glory and beauty."*

Christ's personal beauty was His excellence of character.

In the Promised Land Once More

"He brought them forth also with silver and gold: and there was not one feeble person among their tribes."
Psalm 105:37

Israel was in bondage in Egypt for 400 years, and *"afterward shall they come out with great substance"* (Genesis 15:14). Later, they were carried away captive into Babylon! Finally, they were living once more in the Promised Land (Canaan), where the <u>Deliverer</u> was to be born. The <u>time</u> between the last Old Testament book of Malachi to the first New Testament writer was about 400 years.

Illustration

Hundreds	Tens	Ones
1	0	0
1	0	0
1	0	0
+ 1	0	0
4	0	0

Sing The Hymn,
"'Tis Almost Time
For The Lord To Come."

7 Bible Commentary 904

It is Time!

Reasons

1 reason
+ 1 reason
2 reasons

1 reason
+ 2 reasons
3 reasons

1 reason
+ 3 reasons
4 reasons

Roman
Soldier

Heaven set the hour for the coming of Christ. When the great clock of time pointed to that moment, Jesus was born in the stable of Bethlehem.

Remember there were several reasons why this was the very best time for Jesus to be born. Then:

1. All nations were under one government.

2. One language was widely spoken.

3. Jews in other countries came to Jerusalem to the annual feasts from all lands.

4. People longed to know God.

The Romans had conquered most of the then-known world. The nations were under one government. As we have learned in our geography class, there are seven (7) continents. Parts of some of these continents were conquered by the Roman government. It was time for these nations to be **alert** to the coming Deliverer. Today,

1. Many nations are united through the United Nations. People are trying to have a one world government.

2. The English language is the universal language.

3. Travel is quick and easy throughout the world. Many countries are friendly with one another.

4. People are longing to know God.

Bible Search

Sixes

Six is 7 (spiritual perfection) minus (–) 1 (God), that is man coming short of spiritual perfection. It is the human number; the number of man as destitute of God.

1. What was made on the sixth day of creation week? (Genesis 1:24-28)

Note: The serpent was also created on the 6th day!

2. What six names are given to the serpent? (**1**–Genesis 3:1, Job 26:13; **2**– Psalm 140:3; **3**–Job 20:16, Isaiah 30:6, 59:5; **4-5**–Isaiah 11:8, 59:5; **6**–Numbers 21:8, Isaiah 14:29, 30:6)

3. What was man to do for six days? (Exodus 20:9)

Note: Six is the number of man's labor. Six seems to be stamped upon his measures which he uses in his labor, and on the time during which he labors. *"Come unto me all ye that labour and are heavy laden, and I will give you rest"* (Matthew 11:28).

4. What is the sixth commandment? (Exodus 20:13)

5. Whose throne had only six steps leading up to it, and his kingdom was soon divided? (I Kings 10:19)

6. Describe the loaves of the shewbread. (Leviticus 24:6)

Note: The twelve tribes were divided tribes.

7. Who interceded for a city 6 times? (Genesis 18)

8. What was Jesus charged with six times? (Mark 3:22; Matthew 12:24; John 7:20; John 8:48; John 8:52; John 10:20; and Luke 11:15)

9. What six groups asked our Lord for a sign? (Matthew 12:38, Mark 8:11; Matthew 16:1; Matthew 24:3, Mark 13:3-4; Luke 11:16; John 2:18; and John 6:30)

10. What six persons bore testimony to the Saviour's innocency at His trial and crucifixion? (Luke 23:13-14; Luke 23:15; Matthew 27:3; Matthew 27:19; Luke 23:41; and Luke 23:47)

Remarkable Facts
Six

11. There are many sixes in the Bible— look up the list in the *Strong's Concordance*.

• The number six is stamped upon the measurements of the Great Pyramid, the unit of which was the inch and its sexagesimal* multiples. The first multiple is the foot, 12 inches (2 x 6); and after this the rises are 18 (3 x 6), 24 (4 x 6), 30 (5 x 6), and 36 (6 x 6) of 6 = the yard.

• The base of the Great Pyramid shows that the unit-inch was obtained by a division of the original circuit, 36,000 inches or 1,000 yards.

• A day is measured by 24 hours (4 x 6), divided into the day and night of 12 hours (2 x 6). The multiples and subdivisions are also stamped by the number six. The months being 12; while the hour consists of 60 minutes (6 x 10), and the minutes of 60 seconds (6 x 10).

• Cain's descendants are given only as far as the sixth generation.

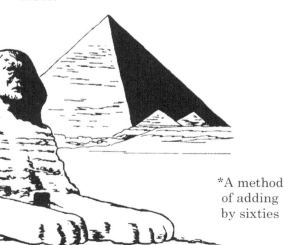

*A method of adding by sixties

Reinforce

7 Continents

Which continent
did Jesus come to?
Which country?
Place a
star sticker
on that spot
on the map.

$$\begin{array}{r} 6 \text{ Continents} \\ +\,1 \text{ That Jesus came to} = \\ \hline 7 \text{ Continents} \end{array}$$

1 + 1 + 1 + 1 + 1 + 1 + 1 (1 - Where Jesus came as a man) =
7 Continents

Remember

Store these facts in your mind.

6	6	6	6	6	6
+ 1	+ 2	+ 3	+ 4	+ 5	+ 6
7	8	9	10	11	12

6	6	6	6	6	6
+ 7	+ 8	+ 9	+ 10	+ 11	+ 12
13	14	15	16	17	18

Father the Priest

"Depart from evil, and do good; seek peace, and pursue it."
Psalm 34:14

God never planned for a few men to rule the whole world. Especially when they are evil, they will influence the whole world to be like themselves.

"Thou lovest evil more than good; and lying rather than to speak righteousness" (Psalm 52:3).

"Ye that love the Lord, hate evil: he preserveth the souls of his saints; he delivereth them out of the hand of the wicked" (Psalm 97:10).

God's plan has always been for each father to rule his own home, assisted by mother. Each child becomes an **alert**, loyal, subject of the home government.

Father, The Priest
Mother, The Assistant
Children, As Loyal Subjects
and the Church to encourage
the Family Government

Sisters

Mothers and Fathers

Brothers

Family

Paste your family's picture above.

Review
Place I

1. Think of these sums as being happy families while doing these problems.

6	6	6	6	6	6
+ 1	+ 2	+ 3	+ 4	+ 5	+ 6

6	6	6	6	6	6
+ 7	+ 8	+ 9	+ 10	+ 11	+ 12

2. Do these addition problems.

6	6	6	6	6	6
+ 8	+ 2	+ 6	+ 1	+ 2	+ 7

6	6	6	6	6	6
+ 5	+ 1	+ 3	+ 10	+ 9	+ 6

6	6	6	6	6	6
+ 4	+ 2	+ 11	+ 8	+ 12	+ 7

6	6	6	6	6	6
+ 3	+ 6	+ 10	+ 5	+ 12	+ 9

3. Write in the answers for these problems.

6 + 8 = _____   6 + 5 = _____   6 + 12 = _____

6 + 11 = _____   6 + 10 = _____   6 + 1 = _____

6 + 6 = _____   6 + 4 = _____   6 + 9 = _____

6 + 8 = _____   6 + 9 = _____   6 + 8 = _____

6 + 12 = _____   6 + 4 = _____   6 + 5 = _____

6 + 7 = _____   6 + 3 = _____   6 + 2 = _____

6 + 9 = _____   6 + 6 = _____   6 + 12 = _____

6 + 11 = _____   6 + 3 = _____   6 + 1 = _____

6 + 4 = _____   6 + 2 = _____   6 + 7 = _____

6 + 11 = _____   6 + 9 = _____   6 + 10 = _____

6 + 7 = _____   6 + 11 = _____   6 + 6 = _____

Learn to spell the word six. Write it six times.

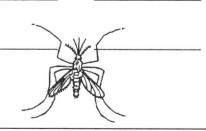

Review
Units
Place II

You have already learned that when there is more than one unit of <u>time</u> to add, you place like units under one another. The larger unit is placed on the left. Remember there are 60 seconds in 1 minute, and 60 minutes in 1 hour.

When there are more than 60 units in the smaller place they are carried to the larger place. See the example below.

Example

8 minutes 30 seconds	30 hours 42 minutes
+ 5 minutes 47 seconds	+ 2 hours 56 minutes
13 minutes 77 seconds	32 hours 98 minutes
+ 1 − 60	+ 1 − 60
14 minutes 17 seconds	33 hours 38 minutes

---

1. What were the reasons given in our lesson to explain why it was the best time for Jesus to come the first time?

1. _____

2. _____

3. _____

4. _____

2. Why is it almost time for Jesus to come again?

1. _____

2. _____

3. _____

4. _____

3. Add these problems then carry if needed. Think about the time Jesus came (carried) from heaven to this earth as you find the sums.

T.   3 minutes 13 seconds
          + 5 minutes 42 seconds

          4 hours 16 minutes
          + 3 hours 35 minutes

I.   5 hours 48 minutes
          +2 hours 53 minutes

          2 minutes 43 seconds
          + 6 minutes 56 seconds

M.   6 minutes 53 seconds
          + 4 minutes 41 seconds

          3 hours 39 minutes
          + 1 hour   51 minutes

E.   1 hour 19 minutes
          + 3 hours 45 minutes

          7 minutes 52 seconds
          + 6 minutes 17 seconds

C.   8 hours 41 minutes and 52 minutes and 7 hours

O.   15 minutes 55 seconds and 26 seconds 6 minutes.

M.   45 minutes 6 hours + 25 minutes 3 hours

E.   43 seconds 52 minutes + 23 minutes 44 seconds

Addition 1 – Student – Page 175

Review
Columns
Place III

Adding long columns is challenging, but necessary many times in our daily life. One has to be very **alert** to make no mistakes. Do you remember how generation after generation of **alert** witnesses added up until Jesus the perfect witness came? Think of this as you continue to practice column addition.

1. **Answer these questions:**

T.   When was Jesus born? _____

_____

_____

I.   Why was this the best time? _____

_____

_____

M.   Is it almost time for Jesus to come the second time? _____

_____

_____

E.   Why? _____

_____

_____

2. Add these columns then check your work.

J.

377	424	843	685	572	609
123	381	737	514	785	530
668	726	231	1023	416	726
238	615	605	864	281	890

E.

4667	1650	7522	7635	2879
339	1756	4141	8950	249
5886	943	5678	853	4982
9384	6632	181	2976	377
3793	3303	255	9999	5731
1876	472	7649	739	7215

S.

67979	88856	56761	49639	72716
80603	53193	28334	93655	79647
87787	36587	81520	63394	45979
99824	19077	35048	26794	52380

U.

3920	4455	6525	4324	9484
6496	8807	2763	4671	2816
8420	8179	2865	1703	8063
8992	8748	8646	9166	5836
5629	7749	6367	7586	2915

S.

96257	2282	78761	44923	54232
5939	68752	48225	8518	24670
409	132	69020	65014	8621
8116	5774	8894	2282	88748
4826	3452	3200	11923	6419

"Take care of the minutes, for the hours will take care of themselves."
—Lord Cesterfield

"Those who make the worst use of their time most complain of its shortness."
—La Bruyere

Review
Word Problems
Place I

1. Two (2) continents are Asia and Africa. Add to these North America, South America, and Antarctica. How many continents do you have?

2. Australia and Europe are two (2) more continents and when you add the other continents you have how many total continents?

God says about these continents:

"Go ye therefore, and teach all nations, baptizing them in the name of the Father, and of the Son, and of the Holy Ghost:

"Teaching them to observe all things whatsoever I have commanded you: and, lo, I am with you alway, even unto the end of the world" (Matthew 28:19-20).

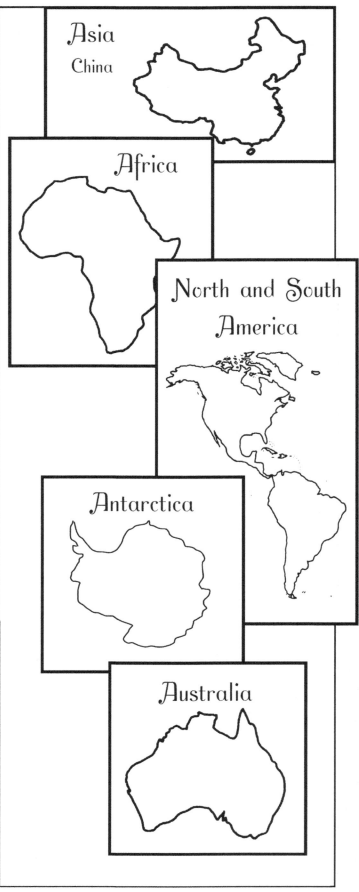

Asia
China

Africa

North and South America

Antarctica

Australia

Europe

Review
Word Problems
Place II

For families to keep **alert** to the times, daily worship is necessary. In every family there should be a fixed time for morning and evening worship. How fitting it is for parents to gather their children about them before breakfast, to thank the heavenly Father for His protection over them during the night, and to ask Him for His help and direction and watch care during the day! Then when evening comes, the parents and children can again come before Him and thank Him for the blessings of the day that is past!

Read the following about part of the Johnston family's daily schedule.

The Johnston family arises at 5:00 a.m. They care for their personal needs and each has their private devotions. After an hour and fifteen minutes father gathers them into the family room for family worship. There, they pray, sing, and read the Word of God.

After a delightful hour, final breakfast preparations are made which takes 15 minutes. Breakfast is one favorite family time with sharing about what God has taught

Johnston Family

"To every thing there is a season, and a time to every purpose under the heaven."
Ecclesiastes 3:1

them in their private devotions. They also go over plans for the new day, as they eat their juicy fruits, crunchy nuts, and chewy grains.

After breakfast is clean up time, which is done by the children, and other chores, which takes until 9:00 a.m. Then it is time for Mathematics class which lasts one hour. Nature class is next and is over at 11:30 a.m. The children take a half hour break then help mother fix lunch. All anticipate father joining them once more.

1. What time was family worship?

2. When was final breakfast preparation?

3. What time did breakfast start?

4. How long was breakfast and clean up time?

5. When did Nature class start?

6. When did the children start helping mother with lunch?

7. How long does it take your family to fix a meal?

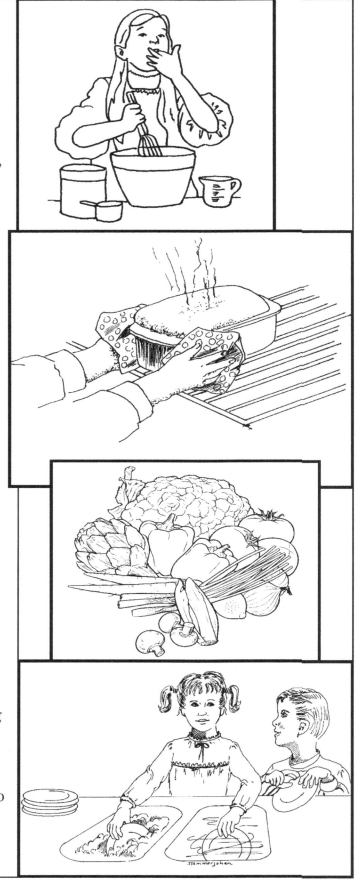

Review
Word Problems
Place III

What did it mean for Christ to become a man? He took on flesh and bones.

1. One man had his resting heart beat taken for one week. It read 90, 88, 92, 91, 94, 99, and 97. Add these daily readings up and find the average.

2. In an adult human's blood, there are 250,000 or more platelets, 5,400,000 or more red blood cells, 5,000 or more white blood cells, which is about _____ blood cells in the human body!

3. In the body of an adult human there are 8 bones around the brain, 14 in the face and jaw, and 6 in the ear. How many total bones is that?

The spinal column has 26, the thorax 25, how many bones is this?

The following are the other bones in the body: 1 hyoid; shoulders 4; arms and hands 60; pelvic and hips 2; and legs and feet 60. How many bones is that?

What is the total number of bones in an adult human?

Work Area

Example

To find an average:

(1) Add 1 – 1st addend
      2 – 2nd addend
      5 – 3rd addend
      9 – 4th addend
      3 – 5th addend
    20 – sum

(there is a total of 5 addends)

(2) Then divide the total number of addends into the sum.

$$\begin{array}{r} 4 \text{ average} \\ 5)\overline{20} \\ \underline{20} \\ 0 \text{ remainder} \end{array}$$

4 is the average

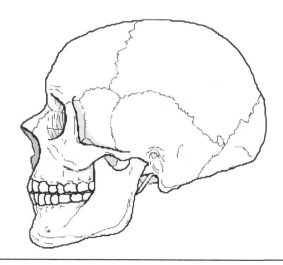

Remind

1. As you put batteries in a clock and reset it to the correct time, or set a timer to **alert** you when the bread is baked, remember your lesson.

2. As you write the number six, be **alert** to how it looks. Did you notice that it looks "bottom-heavy"? The number eight is a lot like the number six with another circle added to the top of the six. (See the diagram.) The number eight looks more <u>balanced</u> than the number six. Jesus' number is eight. He has a perfectly <u>balanced</u> character. Man's character, represented by the number six, is unbalanced. His <u>lower</u> nature (the flesh) tends to rule him just like the <u>lower</u> circle tends to predominate in the figure of number six. But, when the divine nature is <u>added</u> to man's nature, a higher nature rules (is on top of) his <u>lower</u> nature. Then man becomes truly <u>balanced</u> in character.

1. After doing your mathematics lesson, make a "Mark Your Bible" about addition. +

+ +

Balance

"Ye are complete in Him, which is the head [upper circle]..."
Colossians 2:10

Reinforce

2. Write below the numbers six and eight.

_____

_____

Wasting Time

"Moab hath been <u>at ease</u> from his youth, and he hath <u>settled</u> <u>on</u> <u>his</u> <u>lees</u>, and hath not been emptied from vessel to vessel, neither hath he gone into captivity: therefore his taste remained in him, and his scent is not changed" (Jeremiah 48:11).

Remainder
Son

"For he shall grow up before him as a tender plant, and as a root out of a dry ground:
He hath no form nor comeliness; and when we shall see him, there is no beauty that we should desire him.

"He is despised and rejected of men; a man of sorrows, and acquainted with grief: and we hid as it were our faces from him; he was despised, and we esteemed him not."

Isaiah 53:2-3

The Son of God coming to this earth in human flesh is a marvelous thought to often ponder. He who was the leader in the heavenly courts laid aside His kingly robe and royal crown, and clothing His divinity with humanity, came to this world.

The whole world belonged to Christ, but so completely did He empty Himself that during His ministry He said, *"Foxes have holes, and the birds of the air have nests; but the Son of man hath not where to lay his head"* (Matthew 8:20).

Are you **alert** to the great sacrifice made for you?

Reinforce
Time is Valuable
Time

Christ came to this world at just the right time. He never wasted a moment but used it wisely while He lived on earth. Are you **alert** to how you use your time?

Read these stories.

Time and Eternity

One Sabbath morning the Pastor Thomas Pentycross, while preaching to his own congregation, was so entirely engrossed with the importance of his subject, that he exceeded his usual time, and the clock struck one. After pausing a moment he exclaimed with great energy, "Time reproves me; but eternity commends me!" and then resumed the discourse with much earnestness, continuing to preach for a considerable time longer in a very impressive manner.

Value Time

Melanchthon noted down the time lost by him that he might thereby reanimate his industry and not lose an hour. An Italian sculptor put over his door an inscription intimating that whosoever remained there should join in his labors. "We are afraid," said some visitors to Baxter, "That we break in upon your time." "To be sure you do," replied the disturbed and blunt man. Time was the estate out of which these great workers, and all other workers, carved a rich inheritance of thoughts and deeds for their successors. —*Smiles*

Time is Valuable

"This lifetime is too short to be squandered in vain and trifling diversion, in unprofitable visiting, in needless dressing for display, or in exciting amusements. We cannot afford to squander the time given us of God in which to bless others and in which to lay up for ourselves a treasure in heaven. We have none too much time for the discharge of necessary duties. We should give time to the culture of our own hearts and minds in order that we may be qualified for our lifework. By neglecting these essential duties and conforming to the habits and customs of fashionable, worldly society, we do ourselves and our children...a great wrong."*

"Satan takes the mind and turns it in a channel which is corrupt. A self-deception is upon many of the young. They think they are Christians, but they have never been converted. Until this work shall be wrought in them, they will not understand the mystery of godliness. There is no peace to the wicked. God requires truth and sincerity of heart. He sees and pities you, and all the youth who are eagerly following childish toys and wasting short, precious time for things of no value. Christ has bought you at a dear price, and offers you grace and glory if you will receive it; but you turn from the precious promise of the gift of everlasting life, to the meager and unsatisfactory pleasures of earth."**

*3 Testimonies 146
**2 Testimonies 289

Sing again the hymn, "'Tis Almost Time for the Lord to Come."

Time

It is related of the Duke of Wellington that he made an appointment with a city dignitary to meet at a certain hour on London Bridge. The dignitary was five minutes late, and finding the Duke watch in hand and upset, pleaded, "It is only five minutes, your grace." "Only five minutes!" he replied; "five minutes' unpunctuality would have, before now, lost me a battle." Next time the city magnate took care, as he thought, to be on the safe side. When the Duke appeared he greeted him rather triumphantly, "You see, your grace, I was five minutes before you this time." "Shows how little you know time's value," said the old Field Marshal. "I am here to the moment. I cannot afford to waste five minutes."

Time and Eternity

General Henry Lee once observed to the chief, "We are amazed, sir, at the vast amount of work that you accomplish." Washington replied, "Sir, I rise at four o'clock, and a great deal of my work is done while others are asleep"
—Little's Historical Lights

Why Her Time Lengthened

A venerable lady was once asked her age. "Ninety-three," was the reply. "The Judge of all the earth does not mean that I shall have any excuse for not being prepared to meet Him."

777 Sevens - 7777

Research
The Number Seven

"Be ye therefore perfect, even as your Father which is in heaven is perfect."
Matthew 5:48

Seven, in the Bible, reminds us of spiritual perfection. It is 6 (man's number) with 1 (God's number) added to it. Man can become spiritually perfect as God is <u>added</u> to (or indwells) him through the Holy Spirit. *"Be ye therefore perfect, even as your Father which is in heaven is perfect."*

God wants **alert** people to share the message about His first advent and His soon second coming. What is the best way to share this message? Live it! What does the verse above mean? How does it relate to Christ's second coming?

Reinforce
Color then read the meaning of the number seven. Learn to say seven in these languages.

French – sept (set)

Japanese – shichi (shee chee)

Spanish – siete (see EH teh)

Swahili – saba (SAH bah)

6 addend
+ 1 addend
7 sum

SEVEN - 7 = SPIRITUAL PERFECTION

The divine nature and the human nature combined (addition +) to give sinful man a Saviour.

7

Divine

Human

+

One Language

"And the whole earth was of one language, and of one speech."

Genesis 11:1

In the beginning of this world's history, all people spoke one language. It was so much easier to communicate to one another. After the Flood God confused their language to hinder the spread of sin. *"...Let us...confound their language, that they may not understand one another's speech."* Today, there are about 3,000 languages spoken on the <u>seven</u> continents. This does not include dialects (local form of a language). At Christ's first coming "one language was widely spoken, and was everywhere recognized as the language of literature."* Do you know what that language was? It was the Greek language! The English language is now recognized as the universal language. We must be **alert** for it is close to the time of Christ's second coming!

When all things are once again made perfect all the universe will speak one language. We are told: *"And every creature which is in heaven, and on the earth, and under the earth, and such as are in the sea, and all that are in them, heard I saying, Blessing, and honor, and glory, and power, be unto him that sitteth upon the throne, and unto the Lamb for ever and ever"* (Revelation 5:13).

"The great controversy is ended. Sin and sinners are no more. The entire universe is clean. <u>One pulse of harmony and gladness beats through the vast creation</u>. From Him who created all, flow life and light and gladness, throughout the realms of illimitable space. From the minutest atom to the greatest world, <u>all things</u>, animate and inanimate, in their unshadowed beauty and perfect joy, <u>declare that God is love</u>."** The perfect language of the whole universe at that time will be love to God and love to His created beings.

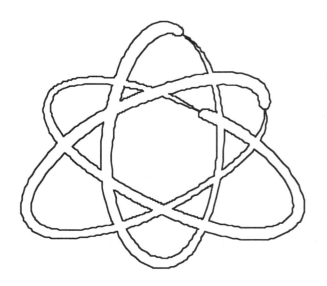

*The Desire of Ages 32 **The Great Controversy 678*

7 Remarkable Facts
Seven

• Seven occurs 287 times in the Old Testament (7 x 41). Seventh, the fractional part, occurs 98 times (7 x 14). Seven-fold occurs 7 times.

• Seventy occurs 56 times (7 x 8). Seventy in combination with other numbers, occurs 35 times (7 x 5).

• The two names Shem and Japheth, who received their father's blessing, occur together 7 times; but six of these are in connection with Ham whose posterity was cursed!

• The golden candlestick had 6 branches plus one central stem, making seven in all. What could this mean?

• Seven marks off the days of the week for eternity. (Read Isaiah 66:23.)

• Seven completes the colors of the spectrum and rainbow.

• Seven satisfies in music the notes of the scale. In each of these the eighth is only a repetition of the first.

• There were seven miracles wrought by Christ on the Sabbath day:
> –The withered hand (Matthew 12:9)
> –The unclean spirit (Mark 1:21)
> –Peter's wife's mother, (Mark 1:29)
> –The woman (Luke 13:11)
> –The man with dropsy (Luke 14:2)
> –The impotent man (John 5:8-9)
> –The man born blind (John 9:14)

Bible Search
Sevens

We have learned that six is the number stamped upon all things human, while seven speaks of things spiritual. These numbers are contrasting. The number seven (*savah*) means "to be full or satisfied, have enough of."

Place I - II - III

1. What is the seventh book in the Bible?

Note: This book shows what happens to people who do not strive for spiritual perfection.

2. What happened on the seventh day of creation week? (Genesis 2:1-3)

Note: In creation there is the six days of labor and the seventh of rest. Creation was full and complete, good and perfect. Nothing could be added to it or taken from it without marring it. Hence the word *shavath*—"to cease, desist, rest" and *Shabbath, Sabbath* day of *rest*—which eventually through the various languages comes to us in English as "seven."

Sanscrit – *saptan*   Gothic – *sibun*
Zend – *hapta*   German – *sieben*
Greek – *hepta*   English – *seven*
Latin – *seplem*

3. Who was the seventh man from Adam? (Genesis 5:24)

4. What went into the ark by sevens? (Genesis 7:2)

5. What happened 7 days before the Flood (Genesis 7:9-10)

6. Who worked 14 years (2 x 7) for a wife? Who did he work for? (Genesis 29:18-28)

7. What was Pharaoh's dream? (Genesis 41:17-21)

8. What was like blood for 7 days in Egypt? (Exodus 7:20, 25)

9. What were the 6 items listed as the food of Egypt? (Numbers 11:5) What are the Divine provisions of Emmanuel's land—seven in number? (Deuteronomy 8:8)

10. What city is remembered by the number seven? (Joshua 6:24)

11. Who cut seven locks of hair? (Judges 16:18-19)

12. What building took seven years to build? (I Kings 6:1, 38)

13. Who sneezed 7 times and why? (II Kings 4:35)

14. Who washed himself 7 times? (II Kings 5:9-14)

15. What king lived with the beasts for seven years? (Daniel 4:13-17; 28-34)

Place II - III

16. Who were the seven weak, human instruments mentioned in Judges that were raised up as deliverers of the people?

(1) 3:21 _____

(2) 3:31 _____

(3) 4:4 _____

(4) 4:21 _____

(5) 9:53 _____

(6) 7:20 _____

(7) 15:16 _____

Note: "*But God hath chosen the foolish things of the world to confound the wise; and God hath chosen the weak things of the world to confound the things which are mighty*' (I Corinthians 1:27). It was so in Apostolic days, and has been so in all ages. It was Luther, a miner's son, by whom God 'shook the world.' It was Calvin, a cooper's son in Picardy, by whom God built up His church in the Faith. It was Zwingle, a shepherd's son in the Alps, by whom God established the Reformation in Switzerland. It was John Knox, the son of a plain burgess* in a country town, who caused Scotland to be known as 'the Land of Knox.'

"And so through all the ages God has made it clear that it is He who is the worker, and that the instruments He chooses to use are nothing. He usually rejected man's firstborn, and chose a younger son. He took David, the youngest, from the sheepfold, to be ruler over His people, as He had chosen Gideon, the least member of the poorest family in Manasseh, to deliver Israel from the Midianite hosts." —*Number in Scripture* 175

17. List the events that happened with seven oak trees. (**1**–Genesis 35:4; **2**–Genesis 35:8; **3**-I Samuel 31:13; **4**–Joshua 24:16; **5**–II Samuel 18:9; **6**–Judges 6:11; and **7**–I Kings 13:14)

18. List the seven miracles in John:

(1) 2 _____

(2) 4:47 _____

(3) 5:4 _____

(4) 6 _____

(5) 9:1 _____

(6) 11 _____

(7) 21 _____

*a lesser town official

19. What food was used to feed 4,000 men, besides the women and children? (Matthew 15:34-36)

20. Who had seven devils cast out of her? (Mark 16:9)

21. What are the seven parables of Matthew 13?

22. Who were chosen to be the leaders in the early church? (Acts 6:3-5)

Place III

23. How often was the land of Israel to rest? (Leviticus 25:4)

24. When was the year of the Jubilee? (Leviticus 25:8-9) What is 7 x 7?

25. When was the day of atonement? (Leviticus 16:29)

26. What are the 6 pieces of armor in Ephesians 6:14-18?
What is the seventh that without, the others would be of little value?

27. What are the seven things that spiritually defile? (Matthew 15:19)

28. What are the seven gifts of Romans 12:6-8?

29. What are the seven unities of Ephesians 4:4-6?

30. What are the seven characteristics of wisdom? (James 3:17)

31. What are the seven graces of II Peter 1:5-7?

32. List all the different sevens in Revelation. Use *Strong's Concordance.*

Can you think of more sevens in the Bible?
How **alert** are you?

7 7 7 7 7 7 7

Reinforce

Each below = 100 Languages

= 1,000

= 1,000

= $\underline{1,000}$

3,000

6 (man) **+ 1** (God) **= 7** (Spiritual Perfection)

Remember

Store these facts in your mind.

7	7	7	7	7	7
+ 1	+ 2	+ 3	+ 4	+ 5	+ 6
8	9	10	11	12	13

7	7	7	7	7	7
+ 7	+ 8	+ 9	+ 10	+ 11	+ 12
14	15	16	17	18	19

One With Christ

"And this gospel of the kingdom shall be preached in all the world for a witness unto all nations; and then shall the end come."

Matthew 24:14

"During His ministry, Jesus had kept constantly before the disciples the fact that <u>they were to be one with Him</u> in His work for the recovery of the world from the slavery of sin. When He sent forth the Twelve and afterward the Seventy, to proclaim the kingdom of God, He was teaching them their duty to impart to others what He had made known to them. In all His work He was training them for individual labor, to be extended as their numbers increased, and eventually to reach to the uttermost parts of the earth. The last lesson He gave His followers was that they held in trust for the world the glad tidings of salvation."* This was why it was important for there to be a universal language—Christ's disciples could communicate with many people. The Holy Spirit also aided them in this work of speaking other languages.

> 6 + 1 = 7
> Man + God =
> Spiritual Perfection

Reinforce

Place I

Color this picture.

Jesus Sent Forth the Twelve and Then the Seventy.

The Acts of the Apostles 32

Review
Place I

1. As you find the sums, let them remind you of people all over the world listening to the message "Jesus is Coming Again."

7 + 1	7 + 2	7 + 3	7 + 4	7 + 5	7 + 6
7 + 7	7 + 8	7 + 9	7 + 10	7 + 11	7 + 12

2. Do these addition problems.

7 + 8	7 + 2	7 + 6	7 + 1	7 + 2	7 + 7
7 + 5	7 + 1	7 + 3	7 + 10	7 + 9	7 + 6
7 + 4	7 + 2	7 + 11	7 + 8	7 + 12	7 + 7
7 + 3	7 + 6	7 + 10	7 + 5	7 + 12	7 + 9

3. Write in the answers for these problems.

7 + 8 = _____   7 + 5 = _____   7 + 12 = _____

7 + 11 = _____   7 + 10 = _____   7 + 1 = _____

7 + 6 = _____   7 + 4 = _____   7 + 9 = _____

7 + 8 = _____   7 + 9 = _____   7 + 8 = _____

7 + 12 = _____   7 + 4 = _____   7 + 5 = _____

7 + 7 = _____   7 + 3 = _____   7 + 2 = _____

7 + 9 = _____   7 + 6 = _____   7 + 12 = _____

7 + 11 = _____   7 + 3 = _____   7 + 1 = _____

7 + 4 = _____   7 + 2 = _____   7+ 7 = _____

7 + 11 = _____   7 + 9 = _____   7 + 10 = _____

7 + 7 = _____   7 + 11 = _____   7 + 6 = _____

Learn to spell the word seven.
Write it at least seven times.

 _____   _____

 _____   _____

_____   _____

 _____

4. Think of all the languages there were in the world when Christ came the first time. Think of these sums as languages.

$$
\begin{array}{cccccc}
7 & 1 & 7 & 2 & 7 & 3 \\
+\,1 & +\,7 & +\,2 & +\,7 & +\,3 & +\,7 \\
\hline
\end{array}
$$

$$
\begin{array}{cccccc}
7 & 4 & 7 & 5 & 7 & 6 \\
+\,4 & +\,7 & +\,5 & +\,7 & +\,6 & +\,7 \\
\hline
\end{array}
$$

5. Which addend is missing in these addition problems?
Fill them in.

$$
\begin{array}{cccccc}
+\,1 & +\,2 & +\,3 & +\,4 & +\,5 & +\,6 \\
\hline
8 & 9 & 10 & 11 & 12 & 13 \\
\end{array}
$$

$$
\begin{array}{cccccc}
+\,7 & +\,8 & +\,9 & +\,10 & +\,11 & +\,12 \\
\hline
14 & 15 & 16 & 17 & 18 & 19 \\
\end{array}
$$

6. What is the sum of seven (7) languages
and seven (7) languages?

7. What is the sum of seven (7) languages
and nine (9) languages?

8. What is the sum of seven (7) languages
and three (3) languages?

9. What is the sum of seven (7) languages
and twelve (12) languages?

10. Review Ones through Sevens.

1 + 10	2 + 3	2 + 7	4 + 6	2 + 1	2 + 11
7 + 7	3 + 9	4 + 7	3 + 12	4 + 2	7 + 8
5 + 7	5 + 2	3 + 11	1 + 9	5 + 8	6 + 6
2 + 10	5 + 3	2 + 1	2 + 9	1 + 4	4 + 12
5 + 4	5 + 6	1 + 1	3 + 10	5 + 5	6 + 4
5 + 2	5 + 12	2 + 6	2 + 4	4 + 11	1 + 8
3 + 3	6 + 12	6 + 5	4 + 4	3 + 7	5 + 11
2 + 2	2 + 5	4 + 5	4 + 10	1 + 8	7 + 9

7 + 5	2 + 8	5 + 10	5 + 9	1 + 3	7 + 8
7 + 12	5 + 3	6 + 8	7 + 4	6 + 11	7 + 7
7 + 11	6 + 7	1 + 7	3 + 5	6 + 3	6 + 10
7 + 9	5 + 8	6 + 2	7 + 6	4 + 8	4 + 4
2 + 5	7 + 2	4 + 9	4 + 1	7 + 10	7 + 7
7 + 3	1 + 12	6 + 6	7 + 9	7 + 6	6 + 6
7 + 7	7 + 4	6 + 8	2 + 12	5 + 3	7 + 8
1 + 3	5 + 9	2 + 8	7 + 5	1 + 11	3 + 3

Review
Place II

When there are more than 24 hours or 12 months in the sum, we take it from hours or months and put it with days or years. Notice the examples below.

Example			
	1 day	11 hrs.	45 min.
	4 days	16 hrs.	30 min.
3 days 16 hours	5 days	27 hrs.	75 min.
+ 2 days 14 hours		- 24 hrs.	- 60 min.
5 days 30 hours	6 days	3 hr	15 min.
- 24		+ 1 hr	
6 days 6 hours	6 days	4 hrs.	15 min.

1. Add these units and convert where necessary.

L.   3 days 9 hours   3 weeks 4 days
     + 2 days 8 hours   + 2 weeks 6 days

A.   2 years 116 days   4 years 10 months
     + 1 year   214 days   + 2 years   6 month

N.   1 year 6 months   2 days 12 hours
     + 2 years 4 months   + 3 days 18 hours

G.   5 weeks 5 days   1 year 328 days
     + 1 week   4 days   + 1 year 224 days

Addition 1 –   Student – Page 199

U. 3 years 7 months 4 days + 1 year 6 months 5 days

A. 1 day 10 hours 45 minutes + 3 days 15 hours 25 minutes

G. 1 pound 15 ounces + 2 pounds 10 ounces

E. 8 quarts 2 pints + 1 quart 3 pints

The Number Seven

7

Seven is a number most complete:
Seven years composed the jubilee;
Seven days compose creation's week;
Seven attributes, the Deity.

7

Seven lamps branch from the golden bowl;
Seven burners shone from every one;
Seven eyes appeared on Joshua's stone,
Seven eyes at Zerubbabel's plumb.

7

Seven priests old Jericho compassed,
Seven trumpets of rams' horns to sound;
Seven days poured forth the threatening blast,
Seven brought the walls all to the ground.

7

Seven churches ancient Asia graced,
Seven candlesticks therein were placed;
Seven seals confined the mystic book,
Seven were by Judah's lion broke.

7

Seven horns were seen upon the Lamb;
Seven were the heads the dragon bore;
Seven angels flew at God's command,
Seven vials of His wrath to pour.

7

Seven times with oil the ancient priest
Sprinkled before the throne of God;
Seven times his finger, type of Christ,
Sprinkled the mercy-seat with blood.

Review
Column Addition
Place III

1. Find the sum, then check your work. Let your sums remind you of the many languages in the world.

L.

780	535	873	394	739	292
496	657	467	229	654	632
994	756	143	950	348	687

A.

364	271	618	163	605	877
823	522	212	842	497	382
119	721	874	811	552	629
724	241	297	324	968	336
837	367	762	679	875	336

N.

14476	76992	75936	58874	17888
5717	1577	29874	7197	8615
77126	24712	4765	40124	6427
8294	4820	7387	58181	4682
31326	8132	22997	7235	54367

G.

2750	6024	5519	3195	2612
131	4613	792	212	6764
400	174	3176	2673	757
5234	518	525	821	372

U.	7756	5227	2474	2612	8428
	3442	3075	3422	3716	7326
	2292	8353	4475	2818	7000
	7719	8932	8263	4227	3443
	6284	7978	3854	6682	5426
	3720	2887	7372	4673	8833

A.	41614	21322	82538	26318	91268
	41020	42226	52266	18741	64823
	62254	96745	80269	22382	23048
	87608	22353	42409	52861	32424
	58706	52803	62433	49493	74228
	35567	75240	67743	50998	33838

G. 30615 + 10234 + 62738 + 19753 + 91269 + 74824 =

E. 3676 + 75042 + 61812 + 2483 + 516 + 4526 =

π Review
Word Problems
Place I
Σ

Write out the numbers for each problem. Label the addends and the sums.

1. The language widely spoken during the time Christ came to this earth was Greek. The New Testament is believed to have been written in the Greek language. There are four (4) gospels (Matthew, Mark, Luke, and John). Add to these one (1) church history book which is *The Acts of the Apostles*. The sum is?

ß

———————   ———————————

———————   ———————————

———————   ———————————

2. Paul has written fourteen (14) epistles (writings). Then there are seven (7) general epistles and one (1) book of prophecy. How many epistles and books of prophecy are there?

———————   ———————————

———————   ———————————

———————   ———————————

3. There are five (5) books in the first part of the New Testament and twenty-two (22) in the last part of it. How many books are there in the New Testament?

Ω

———————   ———————————

———————   ———————————

———————   ———————————

Review
Word Problems
Place II

In areas where more than one language is spoken, it is necessary to have translators. Sometimes, in certain places in the United States, where there are many Spanish or Korean people attending a campmeeting, interpreters help the speakers, who do not speak those languages, by doing it for them so the people listening can understand.

1. One interpreter translated for the speaker for 2 hours and 15 minutes in the morning meetings, and 1 hour 45 minutes in the afternoon meeting. How much time did that interpreter spend helping the people understand?

2. In the evening a lady took over and helped until noon the next day. The night meeting lasted for 1 hour and 53 minutes. The next morning the meeting lasted the same amount of time as the previous day. How much time did she interpret?

3. How much total time was spent in the meetings helping the people understand the English speakers? Make this into an addition problem.

Work Area

"The true Interpreter must come."

The Desire of Ages 33-34

Review
Word Problems
Place III

1. Notice the example below of major language families in the world today. What is the total percentage?

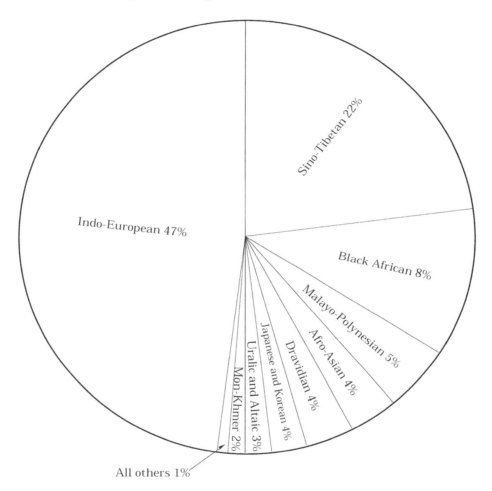

Sino-Tibetan 22%

Indo-European 47%

Black African 8%

Malayo-Polynesian 5%

Afro-Asian 4%

Dravidian 4%

Japanese and Korean 4%

Uralic and Altaic 3%

Mon-Khmer 2%

All others 1%

"Thus saith the Lord of hosts; In those days it shall come to pass, that ten men shall take hold out of all languages of the nations, even shall take hold of the skirt of him that is a Jew, saying, We will go with you: for we have heard that God is with you."
Zechariah 8:23

2. The Indo-European family is where the English language is listed. Total the major language families, and the families within each family. What is their total number?

Albanian

Armenian

Balto-Slavic
- Bulgarian
- Czech
- Latvian
- Lithuanian
- Polish
- Russian
- Serbo-Croatian
- Slovenian
- Slovak
- Ukrainian

Indo-European

Celtic
- Breton
- Irish (Celtic)
- Scots (Celtic)
- Welsh

Germanic
- Dutch
- English
- German
- Scandinavian
  - Danish
  - Icelandic
  - Norwegian
  - Swedish

Greek

Indo-Iranian
- Bengali
- Farsi
- Hindi
- Pashto
- Urdu

Romance
- French
- Italian
- Portuguese
- Romanian
- Spanish

Total _____ _____ _____ = _____

Reinforce

1. Doing a perfect job when folding the clothes, washing, ironing, knitting, washing the floor, dusting, or mowing the lawn, all witness for God. If you will be careful and **alert** to do your best in these little chores, He can trust you with greater responsibilities some day.

2. Read the poem, "Perfectly." Discuss it with your teacher.

3. Go on a nature walk and find sevens in creation. Make a list and think of spiritual lessons for the items you have found. Find a Bible verse to go with the lesson.

"God...make you perfect in every good work."
Hebrews 13:20-21

"His work is perfect."
Deuteronomy 32:4

7 Perfectly

I ask Thee for the daily strength,
    To none that ask denied—
A mind to blend with outward life,
    While keeping at Thy side:
Content to fill a little space,
    If thou be glorified.

And if some things I do not ask
    Among my blessings be,
I'd have my spirit filled the more
    With grateful love to Thee;
More careful not to serve Thee much—
But please Thee perfectly.

Remainder
A Home Christian

"Let us go on unto perfection...."
Hebrews 6:1

"The Lord requires perfection from His redeemed family. He calls for perfection in character-building. Fathers and mothers especially need to understand the best methods of training children, that they may cooperate with God. Men and women, children and youth, are measured in the scales of heaven in accordance with that which they reveal in their home life. A Christian in the home is a Christian everywhere. Religion brought into the home exerts an influence that cannot be measured.

"Our Saviour took up the true relationship of a human being as the Son of God. We are sons and daughters of God. In order to know how to behave ourselves circumspectly, we must follow where Christ leads the way. For thirty years He lived the life of a perfect man, meeting the highest standard of perfection."*

*5 Bible Commentary 1085-1086

"Know thou the God of thy father, and serve him with a perfect heart and with a willing mind."
1 Chronicles 28:9

Are you an **alert** family?

The home is the center where more kindness is shared, more give-and-take, more discussions, more listening, more communicating, and more love.

A Heart of Praise

A heart in ev'ry tho't renewed,
And full of love divine,
<u>Perfect</u>, and right, and pure, and good,
A copy, Lord of Thine.
—C. Wesley

"Perfection Is No Trifle"

"Perfection is no trifle where workmanship is craft and accuracy is law." It was in the dynamo room of a radio station that I saw this motto, conspicuously posted just above the superintendent's desk. Everything was in spotless, shining order, and meeting the **alert** young man himself and listening while he explained his fascinating domain, one could not doubt that he lived his creed strictly, conscientiously. One of the visitors remarked about it.

"And if he didn't, what do you suppose would happen up in the broadcasting room?" the manager, who was also our pilot, questioned in surprise. "Perfection—we must have it! That's the watchword of our whole organization."

How different a place this old world would be if this were the watchword of every individual one of us, no matter where we work or what sort of work we do. Suppose we right about-face from this I-should-worry, let-it-slide, it's-good-enough attitude, and nevermore let any duty pass from our hands until it is just as nearly perfect as 'tis possible to make it. It won't be easy, but—let's!

Remember the story about Michelangelo, the famous sculptor? One day as he worked on a marble statue, a friend, in passing paused to watch awhile. Finally he said: Angelo, this is the selfsame figure that you were working on three weeks ago. Pray tell me why you spend so much time on the nose? I'd say that nose was good enough for any statue. I wouldn't spend a minute more on it. It's but a trifle anyway." And the sculptor paused long enough in his careful work to turn and remark: "Recollect, my friend, that trifles make perfection, but perfection is no trifle." And indeed it isn't!

Once upon a time there was a poor lame man whose daily work it was to stand from dawn till dark in a hot, stuffy room, stitching harness. He could neither read nor write, and so had to be content with the humblest labor. But he felt dissatisfied with his lot, and bitterly complained.

Then one day there came a new minister into the parish, who stopped in at the shop one day, and talked with him while he worked.

"My good man," he said, "There is no work that cannot be made noble work. How do you know what great thing may someday depend upon these very stitches you are sewing? Certainly it is worth while to put each one of them in well, and with a strength that will hold. For if one should give way, will not another, and another, until finally the whole line of stitching is in a ravel? Let us be every day faithful in that which is least, for we know not at what time the Great Master is to take the work of the very humblest of His children, to test its worth and value."

The harness maker pondered long and earnestly what his pastor had said. And he began to see things differently.

Several months passed, and then one morning he heard a commotion in the street outside his window. Looking, he saw a horse dashing madly by, attached to a carriage in which sat a woman and a little girl. Just at the moment, a man rushed out, caught the horse by the bridle, and was dragged along by the infuriated animal. The harness stitcher started forward in sudden recognition. "My master," he cried, "that is my bridle; those are my stitches; suppose they do not hold!" But when he looked again, behold the horse stood panting in the middle of the street, the man's hand was still on the bridle, and the occupants of the carriage were safe. His stitches had held!

What a lesson to those of us who are sewing the fabric of our lives, stitch by stitch, day by day. Will your stitches hold in the time of stress? Will mine? Imperfect, crooked, careless ones will be sure to give way.

The Harness Stitcher Started Forward in Sudden Recognition

And, do you know, one of the most deadly enemies we have to meet along the highway of life is— But listen—

"I am more powerful than the combined armies of the universe.

"I have destroyed more men than all the wars of the world.

"I am more deadly than bullets, and I have wrecked more homes than the mightiest siege gun.

"I spare no one, and find my victims among the rich and poor alike.

"I loom to such proportions that I cast my shadow over every field of labor, from the turning of the grindstone to the moving of the swiftest train.

"I massacre thousands and thousands every year.

"I am relentless. I am everywhere—in the house, on the street, in the factory, at railroad crossings, on automobile wheels, and on the sea.

"I bring sickness, degradation, and death; yet few seek to avoid me.

"I destroy, crush, maim. I am heartless.

"I am your worst enemy.

"I AM CARELESSNESS!"

Several years ago friends began to tell me about "the best shoe repairer," whose place of business was "out on Carroll Avenue." But I didn't make his acquaintance until a necessary change of rooming places took me to that section of the city. Humble his work may be, but he is an artist in it. No half soles are quite so flexible and durable, no rubber heels are quite so perfectly fitted, as are his.

"You do fine work," I said one day while he was wrapping my package.

"Sure," and he looked up with a smile, "sure I do good-a work. Then peoples come-a back again! I been here eight-a year, and same peoples come-a one-two-tree—all-a time! Sure I do good-a work. Eet pay!"

Remember these words:
"Be ye therefore perfect,
even as your Father
which is in heaven is perfect."
Matthew 5:48

Twenty centuries ago a Sidonian crafts man inscribed upon a drinking glass these words: "Made by Ennion. Let the buyer remember." Are your common everyday tasks so perfectly performed that you would care to have them labeled with your name—and remembered?

—*Learning to Live*
Lora E. Clement

"Trifles make perfection, but perfection is no trifle."
Italian Proverb

Reflect

"The last lesson He gave His followers was that they held in trust for the world the glad tidings of salvation."

The Acts of the Apostles 32

888 Eights - 8888

Research
The Number Eight

"I can do all things through Christ which strengtheneth me."
Philippians 4:13

In the Bible, the number eight reminds us of a new beginning and means "one who abounds in strength; to make fat, cover with fat." *"I can do all things through Christ which strengtheneth me."*

Israel was looking forward to a time of new beginning when the <u>Deliverer</u> would come. They hoped the hated Romans would be overcome. But Jesus would come to give

Reinforce

Color then read the meaning of the number eight. Learn to say eight in these languages.

French – huit (weet)

Japanese – hachi (hah chee)

Spanish – ocho (OH choh)

Swahili – nane (NAH neh)

```
  7 addend
+ 1 addend
  8 sum
```

EIGHT - 8 = A NEW BEGINNING

The divine nature and the human nature combined (addition +) to give sinful man a Saviour.

8

them spiritual strength, not physical force to throw off the Roman yoke. There were many Jews scattered throughout the nations. Many from these countries would come to Jerusalem to attend the annual feasts and talk and hear about this time of new beginning. Some knew that it was almost time.

The new beginning they should have been **alert** to was overcoming sin in the life that they might abound in strength each day. Eight is the number associated with the resurrection from the dead. It symbolizes regeneration from spiritual sleep. *"Like as Christ was raised up from the dead by the glory of the Father, even so we also should walk in newness of life"* (Romans 6:4). The Jews were asleep in their sins. *"Awake thou that sleepest, and arise from the dead, and Christ shall give thee light"* (Ephesians 5:14).

Three times a year the Jews were required to gather at Jerusalem for religious feasts. These three main feasts were the Passover, Pentecost, and the Feast of Tabernacles. There were also other feasts that were celebrated at Jerusalem.

3 Main Feasts

Many of the feasts were to teach about the Messiah to come, and the strength He would give to overcome sin—a time of new beginnings!

Many Jews came to these feasts where they would hear about the Deliverer that would soon come.

7 feasts **+ 1** more feast added by the Jews (Purim - Esther 9:21-22, 26) = **8**

$$\begin{array}{r} 7 \\ + 1 \\ \hline 8 \end{array}$$

8 feasts **+ 1** more feast added by the Jews (Dedication - John 10:22) = **9**

$$\begin{array}{r} 8 \\ + 1 \\ \hline 9 \end{array}$$

Passover (Pesah) – The Passover reminded the Israelites of their freedom from the Egyptian bondage. It was so named because God passed over the houses of the Israelites and destroyed the firstborn of Egypt. The Passover feast began on the fifteenth of Nissan (March - April), and continued to the twenty-first. It was one of the most important feasts of all the Jewish celebrations. Today, it reminds us of our deliverance from the bondage of sin.

Pentecost (Shavuot) – The Pentecost was a feast of thanksgiving held at the close of the grain harvest, fifty days after the Passover. Everyone brought an offering to God who provides for all. Many Jews came home to Jerusalem from foreign countries for this feast. This can remind us of the many gifts God gives us daily.

The Feast of Tabernacles (Sukkot) – This feast signaled the close of the agricultural labors for the season. The choicest of the fruits were brought and displayed for all to see. The feast started on the first day of a week-long feast. This reminded Israel of their wanderings in the wilderness. Temporary booths were constructed for them to live in to remind them of their ancestors' forty-year life in temporary dwellings.

Eight is 7 plus 1. Hence it is the number specially associated with *Resurrection* and *Regeneration*, and the beginning of a new era or order.

When the whole earth was covered with the flood, it was Noah *"the eighth person"* who stepped out on to a new earth to commence a new order of things.

1. How many persons went into Noah's ark? Who were they? (II Peter 2:5; I Peter 3:20; Genesis 7:13)

2. What was performed on the eighth day after a birth of a son? (Genesis 17:12)

Note: This was the foreshadowing of the true _____ of the heart, that which was to be *"made without hands,"* even *"the putting off of the body of the sins of the flesh by the* _____ *of Christ"* (Colossians 2:11). This is connected with the new creation.

3. Who was the eighth son of Jesse? (I Samuel 16:6; 17:12)

4. Who rose from the dead on the eighth day? (Matthew 28:1-6)

Note: He rose from the dead on *"the first day of the week,"* that was of necessity the eighth day. And it is remarkable that the Bible contains the record of eight individual resurrections.

5. What eight individuals were resurrected from the dead in Scripture?

(1) I Kings 17:17-25 _____

(2) Luke 7:11-18 _____

(3) II Kings 4:32-37 _____

(4) Mark 5:35; Luke 8:49 _____

(5) II Kings 13:20-21 _____

(6) John 11 _____

(7-8) Acts 9:36-43; 20:7-12 _____

6. What feast lasted eight days? (Leviticus 23:34-36)

7. Elisha did 16 (2 x 8) miracles? What were they? (II Kings 2:14; 21; 24; II Kings 3:16-20; II Kings 4:1-7; 36-37; 38-41; 42-44; II Kings 5:1-19; 20-27; II Kings 6:1-7; 17; 18; 20; 30-33; II Kings 13:20-21)

Note: Remember he said, *"Let a double portion of thy spirit be upon me"* (II Kings 2:9).

8. There are many eights in the Bible —look up the list in the *Strong's Concordance.*

Remarkable Facts
Cube

Eight is the first cubic number, the cube of two, 2 x 2 x 2. We have seen that three is the symbol of the first plane figure, and that four is the first square. So here, is the first cube, we see something of transcendent perfection indicated, something, the length and breadth and height of which are equal.

This significance of the cube is seen in the fact that the *"Holy of Holies,"* both in the Tabernacle and in the Temple, were cubes. In the Tabernacle it was a cube of 10 cubits. In the Temple it was a cube of 20 cubits. In Revelation 22, the New Jerusalem is to be a cube of 12,000 furlongs.

$10^3 = 1,000$, The Tabernacle.

$20^3 = 8,000$, The Temple.

$12,000^3 = 1,28,000,000,000$, the New Jerusalem.

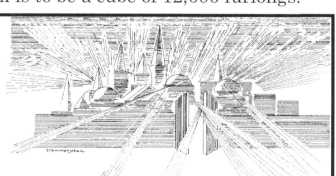

Reinforce

1 - 2 - 3 - 4 - 5 - 6 - 7 - 8
The Feast of Tabernacles lasted eight days.

7 (Week) **+ 1** (First Day) **= 8** (New Beginning)

Remember

Store these facts in your mind.

8	8	8	8	8	8
+ 1	+ 2	+ 3	+ 4	+ 5	+ 6
9	10	11	12	13	14

8	8	8	8	8	8
+ 7	+ 8	+ 9	+ 10	+ 11	+ 12
15	16	17	18	19	20

Reinforce

1. Cut a persimmon in half. How many lines go out from the center to make the flower? How many leaves are on the top?

2. Find things in nature that are designed with the number eight as you take a nature walk. (Example: A spider has 8 legs)

3. God's people left their homes and their crops, their sheep, their fishing boats, or their workshops, to take part in the yearly feasts. At first they went to Shiloh for these feasts, but after Solomon had built the Temple they went to Jerusalem.

As they made the journey, usually on foot, they sang Psalm 120 through 134. These songs were written for these pilgrim journeys. Read Psalm chapter 120 today, chapter 121 tomorrow, and a chapter for each day until this lesson is completed, or all Psalm 120-134 have been read.

Feasts

"Let your light so shine before men, that they may see your good works, and glorify your Father which is in heaven."
Matthew 5:16

Think of all the ceremonies the Jews went through at their feasts. Not all were from God. The Jews had added many, and they were burdensome to the people!

The feasts were meant to refresh and **alert** the people to that which was spiritual so they might return to their daily activities with vigor and a new beginning.

People had grown very weary of so many feasts and ceremonies. They wanted to overcome sin in their lives. They longed for the light about God. They were thirsty for knowledge of Him and for a new beginning.

Teachers in other countries told of the appearance of a <u>Deliverer</u>. "One after another, like stars in the darkened heavens, such teachers had arisen. Their words of prophecy had kindled hope in the hearts of thousands of the Gentile [people not of Israel] world."*

The Desire of Ages 33

Review
Place I

1. Find the sum for these problems. Let the sum remind you of the many people who traveled to Jerusalem for the feasts.

8 + 1	8 + 2	8 + 3	8 + 4	8 + 5	8 + 6
8 + 7	8 + 8	8 + 9	8 + 10	8 + 11	8 + 12

2. Do these addition problems.

8 + 6	8 + 2	8 + 4	8 + 1	8 + 8	8 + 7
8 + 6	8 + 9	8 + 3	8 + 10	8 + 1	8 + 5
8 + 8	8 + 7	8 + 11	8 + 4	8 + 12	8 + 2
8 + 5	8 + 6	8 + 12	8 + 3	8 + 10	8 + 9

3. Write in the answers for these problems.

8 + 1 = _____   8 + 5 = _____   8 + 10 = _____

8 + 11 = _____   8 + 12 = _____   8 + 8 = _____

8 + 6 = _____   8 + 4 = _____   8 + 9 = _____

8 + 8 = _____   8 + 9 = _____   8 + 8 = _____

8 + 12 = _____   8 + 4 = _____   8 + 7 = _____

8 + 5 = _____   8 + 3 = _____   8 + 2 = _____

8 + 9 = _____   8 + 2 = _____   8 + 12 = _____

8 + 11 = _____   8 + 3 = _____   8 + 1 = _____

8 + 4 = _____   8 + 6 = _____   8 + 7 = _____

8 + 11 = _____   8 + 9 = _____   8 + 10 = _____

8 + 7 = _____   8 + 11 = _____   8 + 6 = _____

Learn to spell the word eight.
Write it at least eight times.

_____   _____   _____

_____   _____   _____

_____   _____

4. Think of these problems as men who were like stars shining for Jesus in other countries as you fill in the addends.

$+1$	$+8$	$+2$	$+8$	$+3$	$+8$
9	9	10	10	11	11

$+4$	$+8$	$+5$	$+8$	$+6$	$+8$
12	12	13	13	14	14

**5. Which addend is missing in these addition problems?
Fill them in.**

$+1$	$+2$	$+3$	$+4$	$+5$	$+6$
9	10	11	12	13	14

$+7$	$+8$	$+9$	$+10$	$+11$	$+12$
15	16	17	18	19	20

6. Review Sevens and Eights.

8	8	6	8	8	7
+ 7	+ 12	+ 7	+ 4	+ 9	+ 6

7	8	8	8	7	1
+ 9	+ 11	+ 8	+ 5	+ 2	+ 8

8	7	7	9	7	7
+ 9	+ 10	+ 9	+ 8	+ 12	+ 8

3	8	8	8	8	7
+ 8	+ 7	+ 6	+ 8	+ 4	+ 12

5	7	8	6	8	7
+ 7	+ 11	+ 8	+ 8	+ 7	+ 9

6	7	5	8	8	8
+ 8	+ 7	+ 8	+ 9	+ 10	+ 8

7. Do these addition problems.

60 + 30	10 + 20	30 + 40	50 + 60	40 + 50	70 + 80
90 + 10	20 + 50	16 + 13	11 + 12	12 + 14	13 + 15
11 + 18	17 + 12	16 + 10	18 + 11	22 + 12	21 + 15

8. Find the sums for these addition problems.

2 + 4	2 + 11	8 + 9	5 + 7	3 + 10	7 + 3
8 + 8	8 +11	7 + 4	3 + 8	8 + 12	2 + 5
3 + 6	2 + 12	8 + 2	6 + 5	4 + 10	1 + 8
4 + 6	3 + 9	3 + 11	2 + 7	8 + 8	3 + 3

5	8	5	5	8	3
+ 12	+9	+ 10	+ 5	+ 9	+ 7

4	8	2	2	4	4
+ 11	+ 8	+ 3	+ 8	+ 12	+ 9

2	3	3	6	6	5
+ 6	+ 12	+ 4	+ 3	+ 12	+ 4

4	6	4	6	5	4
+ 8	+ 10	+5	+ 6	+ 11	+ 7

7	8	8	7	7	8
+ 5	+ 9	+ 8	+ 10	+ 12	+ 6

6	8	6	8	5	8
+ 11	+ 8	+ 7	+ 9	+ 8	+ 10

2	4	7	8	4	2
+ 9	+ 4	+ 11	+ 5	+ 3	+ 6

Addition 1 – Student – Page 225

Review
Place II

Remember, ones have a place, tens have a place,
and hundreds have a place.

Example

$$678 + 210 = 888$$

678	6 hundreds 7 tens 8 ones
+ 210	+ 2 hundreds 1 tens 0 ones
888	8 hundreds 8 tens 8 ones = 888

---

1. Find these sums. Make sure each sum is in its proper place. Each person who came up to the feast had a place to fill for God. Some did not take their place.

332	255	75	132	63	523
+ 57	+ 624	+ 821	+ 6	+ 613	+ 54

2. Place these addends in nice straight columns on a separate sheet of paper, keeping each number in its proper place.

F. 164, 20365, 8, 4192   39, 732, 4234

E. 232100, 3694, 76, 374   481, 5241, 22

A. 16, 432, 3, 162, 689   335267, 72866

S. 325876, 2347535, 39   63294, 31, 58

T. 3498, 378, 14874, 9   432, 78, 3624

Review
Place III

In this lesson you will be adding addends in column form. Add the tens as you did in horizontal addition. See the example below.

Example
49   Think   40 + 30 = 70
+ 35   9 + 5 = 14
84   70 + 14 = 84

This will take practice as you work one problem, then another, and add the two together. This will improve and train the mind to be **alert** and think.

Little incidents of everyday life may pass without our notice, but it is these that shape our character. Every event of life can be for good or for evil. The mind needs to be trained to **alertness** by daily tests, that it may acquire power to stand in any difficult position. In the days of trial and danger you will need to be prepared (**alert**) to stand firmly for the right, independent of those around you.

Alertness

Addition

Addition is the process
Of God's creative way,
For, in the very beginning,
He added to <u>evening</u>, day.

Addition is the answer
To the trouble man is in.
God's own light must be added
To save <u>darkened</u> souls from sin.

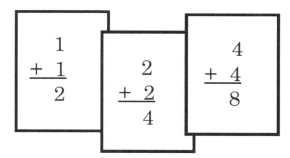

Checking
49   35
+ 35   + 49
84   84

Check by adding
in the opposite direction.

1. Add these numbers in your mind. Check by adding in an opposite direction. Let the sums remind you of the many people who traveled to Jerusalem for the feasts.

F.	42	93	30	17	26	31
	+ 84	+ 38	+ 61	+ 43	+ 72	+ 79

E.	85	75	64	76	24	59
	+ 54	+ 97	+ 49	+ 24	+ 78	+ 34

A.	20	67	82	54	61	75
	+ 82	+ 38	+ 26	+ 86	+ 21	+ 78

S.	64	43	47	22	34	54
	+28	+ 68	+ 58	+ 69	+ 36	+ 82

T.	74	82	53	25	52	70
	43	34	36	69	95	34
	+ 23	+ 57	+ 50	+ 32	+ 43	+58

S.	88	76	85	77	87	93
	92	42	62	54	52	37
	+ 81	+ 37	+ 79	+ 83	+ 92	+ 69

Review
Word Problems
Place I

We can think about the stars and their bright light. This brings to our minds the importance of being **alert** to the prophecies of the Bible. Write out the numbers for each problem below. Label the addend and the sum.

1. On a clear night you may see the seven (7) main stars of the Big Dipper and the seven (7) stars of the Little Dipper. How many stars do you see in both Dippers?

2. Have you seen the Ram with ten (10) main stars and the Crab with six (6) main stars? How many stars are there in them both?

3. The Archer has fourteen (14) stars with five (5) more in his bow. How many stars are there in the Archer and his bow?

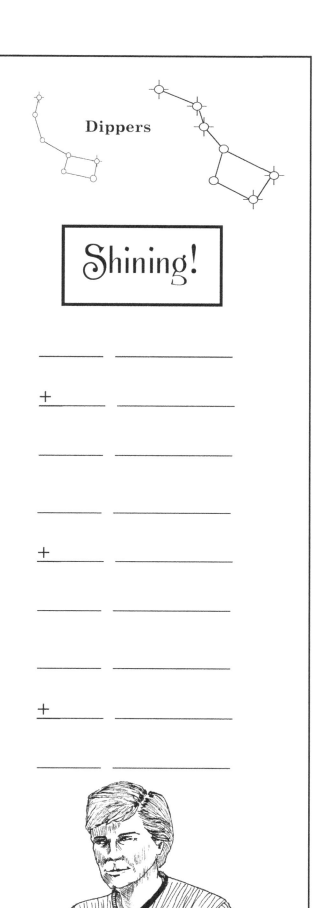

Dippers

Shining!

_____ _____

+ _____ _____

_____ _____

_____ _____

+ _____ _____

_____ _____

_____ _____

+ _____ _____

_____ _____

4. If there were eight (8) nations where men were telling about the coming Deliverer and three (3) more were added to it, how many nations would that be? Write the problem two different ways.

5. Do you know how many eight (8) stars and twelve (12) stars are? Write the problem two different ways.

6. There were **alert** teachers that gave people hope about the coming <u>Deliverer.</u> Eight (8) **alert** teachers and seven (7) **alert** teachers are how many **alert** teachers? Write this problem two different ways.

_____   _____

+ _____   + _____

_____   _____

_____   _____

+ _____   + _____

_____   _____

_____   _____

+ _____   + _____

_____   _____

Color this picture of <u>alert</u> teachers.

Review
Word Problems
Place II

Hebrew Alphabet

Khaph	Kaph	Yod	Teth	Heth	Zayin	Vav	He	Daleth	Gimel	Veth	Beth	Aleph

Tav	Sin	Shin	Resh	Koph	Tsadi	Feh	Peh	Ayin	Samekh	Nun	Mem	Lamed

1. In the Greek (eastern) language there are 24 letters, while in modern Hebrew there are 26 consonants. How many letters do we have in the English language? What is the total of all three alphabets?

2. Notice the following old Hebrew letters have the following numeric value כ 20, נ 50, ע 70, ק 100, ש 300, ת 400. Put these numbers in a column being sure all are in their proper place.

3. The Greek alphabet also has letters for numbers. Place these numeric values in columns: θ 9, λ 30, ο 70, σ 200, χ 600, and ω 800.

Add the columns together for problems two and three.

Greek Warriors

Greek Alphabet

Hebrew Young Man

Pilgrims

Review
Word Problems
Place III

The Bible was basically written in Hebrew and Greek. Both of these languages are unique, for they have no separate symbols for numbers like our Arabic figures of 1, 2, 3, etc. In their place, they make use of the letters of their alphabet. The Hebrew and Greek letters also stand for certain numbers, called the numeric value of the letter. See the charts on the next page. As each word consists of letters, the numeric value of a word is the sum of the numeric values of its letters.

By means of these numeric values, the Greeks and Hebrews performed their numeric operations. But, in Scripture an additional system is made use of for the purpose of numeric construction of the text, that of place values.

Work Area

Fill in the Greek and Hebrew letters for these problems.

1. What is the numeric value of these letters in the Greek ___ 17, ___ 41, and ___ 63. Add in your mind the total of the numeric value, and the value, and write the answer down.

2. These Hebrew letters have the following numeric values ___ 14, ___ 31, ___ 86, and ___ 119. Add in your mind the total of the numeric value, and the value, and write the answer down.

3. What is the total value of the name Jesus in Hebrew? See the charts on the next page.

The Hebrew and Greek letters stand for certain numbers and are called the numeric value of the letter.

Jesus

The name Jesus in Greek has the Value 975, Numeric Value is 888, and the Place Value is 87.

Greek Chariot

Greek Helmet

Greek Peasant

Hebrew

Place Value	Numeric Value	Value	
1.	1	2	א
2.	2	4	ב
3.	3	6	ג
4.	4	8	ד
5.	5	10	ה
6.	6	12	ו
7.	7	14	ז
8.	8	16	ח
9.	9	18	ט
10.	10	20	י
11	20	31	כ
12.	30	42	ל
13.	40	53	מ
14.	50	64	נ
15.	60	75	ס
16.	70	86	ע
17.	80	97	פ
18.	90	108	צ
19.	100	119	ק
20.	200	220	ר
21.	300	321	ש
22.	400	422	ת
	253	1495	1748

Greek

Place Value	Numeric Value	Value	
1.	1	2	α
2.	2	4	β
3.	3	6	γ
4.	4	8	δ
5.	5	10	ε
6.	7	13	ζ
7.	8	15	η
8.	9	17	θ
9.	10	19	ι
10.	20	30	κ
11.	30	41	λ
12.	40	52	μ
13.	50	63	ν
14.	60	74	ξ
15.	70	85	ο
16.	80	96	π
17.	100	117	ρ
18.	200	218	σ
19.	300	319	τ
20.	400	420	υ
21.	500	521	φ
22.	600	622	χ
23.	700	723	ψ
24.	800	824	ω
	300	3999	4299

Greek Woman

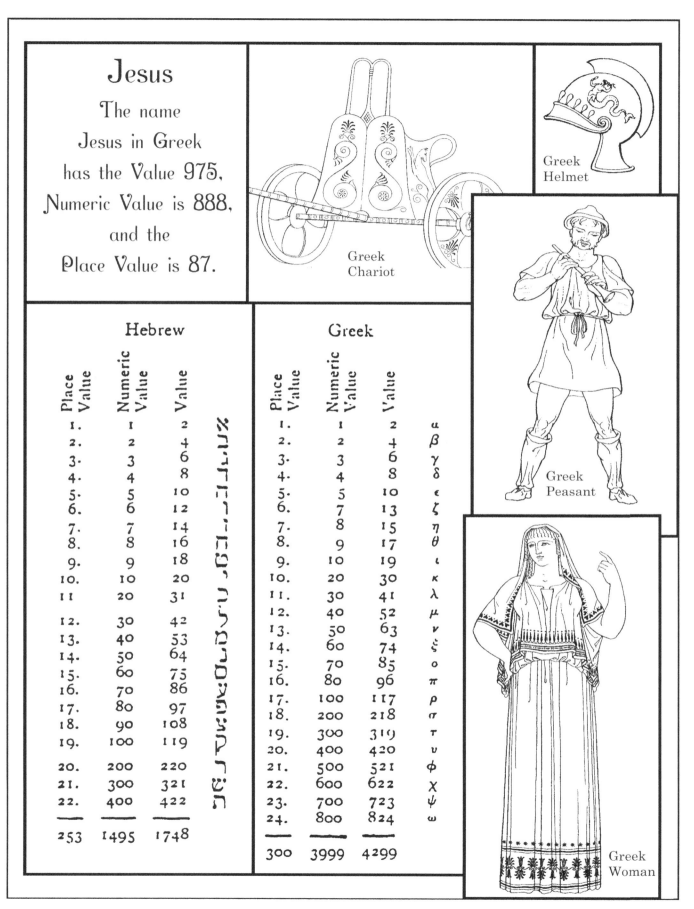

Reinforce

1. Have a special thanksgiving feast. Use foods that might have been eaten in Bible times for your menu. Invite friends or family to join you for this special occasion.

2. Use a Bible customs book and share with the guests some of the interesting things you have learned about customs at Bible feasts.

3. During the meal, see how many feasts you can remember that are recorded in the Bible. List them below. Some examples:

Esther's Feast
Marriage Feast at Cana

_____

_____

_____

_____

_____

_____

_____

_____

Some Bible Foods

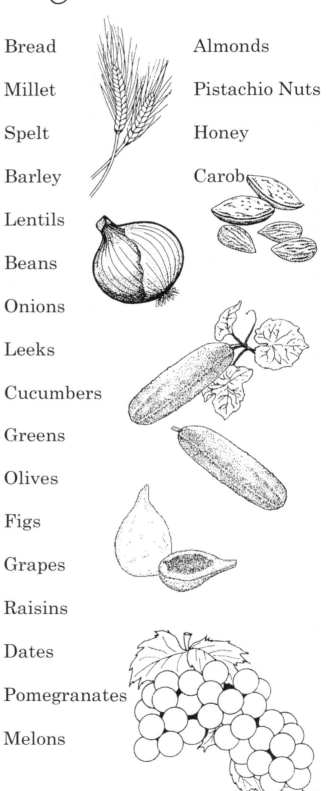

Bread

Millet

Spelt

Barley

Lentils

Beans

Onions

Leeks

Cucumbers

Greens

Olives

Figs

Grapes

Raisins

Dates

Pomegranates

Melons

Almonds

Pistachio Nuts

Honey

Carob

Remainder
Glad

"I was glad when they said unto me, Let us go into the house of the Lord.

"Our feet shall stand within thy gates, O Jerusalem.

"Jerusalem is builded as a city that is compact together:

"Whither the tribes go up, the tribes of the Lord,

unto the testimony of Israel, to give thanks unto the name of the Lord.

"For there are set thrones of judgment, the thrones of the house of David.

"Pray for the peace of Jerusalem: they shall prosper that love thee."

Psalm 122:1-6

Reinforce

Memorize
Psalm 122:1-6

Remarkable Facts About Psalm 118

• This chapter is the middle chapter of the entire Bible.

• Psalm 117 is the shortest chapter in the Bible, and Psalm 119 is the longest one.

• There are 594 chapters before Psalm 118 and 594 chapters after it.

• The sum of all the chapters without including Psalm 118 totals 1,188 chapters in the Bible.

• Psalm 118:8 is the middle verse of the entire Bible.

• What is its important message? *"It is better to take refuge in the Lord than to trust in man."*

Reinforce
Middle Verse of the Entire Bible
Memorize this verse. Color the letters.

"It is better to trust in the Lord than to put confidence in man."

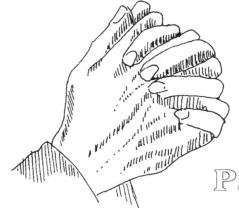

Psalm 118:8

9 99 Nines - 9 9 9 9

Research
The Number Nine

"And ye are complete in him, which is the head of all principality and power."
Colossians 2:10

In the Bible, the number nine reminds us of divine <u>completeness</u>. *"And ye are complete in him, which is the head of all principality and power."*

The number nine also means judgment. It can remind us how, when the time was <u>completely</u> fulfilled, all would pass judgment on themselves by how they responded to Christ. *"And Simeon... said unto Mary his mother, Behold, this child* [Jesus] *is set for the fall and rising again of many in Israel...that the thoughts of many hearts may be revealed"* (Luke 2:34-35).

When Jesus came as the Deliverer, many of the Jews rejected Him, while some of the more spiritually **alert** Gentiles honored Him.

Reinforce

Color then read the meaning of the number nine. Learn to say nine in these languages.

French – neuf (nŏof)

Japanese – ku (koo)

Spanish – nueve (NWEH beh)

Swahili – tisa (TEE sah)

8 addend
+ 1 addend
9 sum

NINE - 9 = DIVINE COMPLETE-NESS

The divine nature and the human nature combined (addition **+**) to give sinful man a Saviour.

9

Divine

Human →

+

"For hundreds of years the Scriptures had been translated into the Greek language, then widely spoken throughout the Roman Empire. The Jews were scattered everywhere, and their expectation of the Messiah's coming was to some extent shared by the Gentiles. Among those whom the Jews styled heathen were men who had a better understanding of the Scripture prophecies concerning the Messiah than had the teachers in Israel. There were some who hoped for His coming as a <u>Deliver</u> from sin. Philosophers endeavored to study into the mystery of the Hebrew economy. But the bigotry of the Jews hindered the spread of the light. Intent on maintaining the separation between themselves and other nations, they were unwilling to impart the knowledge they still possessed concerning the symbolic service. The True Interpreter must come. The One whom all these types prefigured must explain their significance."* The Gentiles were more **alert** to the Messiah's coming than were the Jews. Many Gentiles wanted to understand the Old Testament Scriptures.

1 – 2 – 3 – 4 – 5 – 6 – 7 – 8 – 9

The Desire of Ages 33-34

Nine in the Scriptures also reminds us of the end of the single digits. It can also remind us of the end of the Jewish and Gentile darkness. The <u>Deliverer</u> was coming. The Scriptures said it, and the Gentiles helped to proclaim it.

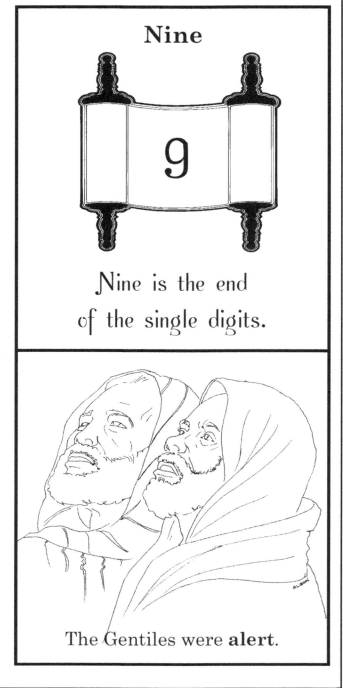

Nine

9

Nine is the end of the single digits.

The Gentiles were **alert**.

 # Bible Search

Nines

Nine is the last of the digits, and thus marks the end; and is significant of the conclusion of a matter.

It is akin to the number six, six being the sum of its factors (3 x 3 = 9, 3 + 3 = 6, and 3 + 3 + 3 = 9), and is thus significant of the end of man, and the summation of all his works. Remember, it is the number of finality or judgment. *"And hath given him authority to execute judgment also, because he is the Son of man"* (John 5:27). *"Because he hath appointed a day, in the which he will judge the world in righteousness by that man whom he hath ordained; whereof he hath given assurance unto all men, in that he hath raised him from the dead"* (Acts 17:31).

1. When is the word nine first used in the Bible? Use a concordance.

2. What is the ninth commandment? (Exodus 20:16)

3. What parable did Christ tell about 99? (Matthew 18:10-14; or Luke 15:1-7)

Note: Read *Christ's Object Lessons* pages 186-192.

4. What miracle did Jesus perform that included nine men? (Luke 17:11-19)

5. How long did the darkness of the land last at Jesus' death? (Matthew 27:45)

6. What did Jesus cry at the ninth hour? (Matthew 27:46)

7. Who came to Cornelius in the ninth hour and for what purpose? (Acts 10:3, 30)

8. What was the 9th stone on the foundation of the New Jerusalem? (Revelation 21:20)

Note: It is believed that Dan's (Judge) name was cut into the _____ stone on the high priest's breastplate. Dan failed to change his way and therefore his name is not found on any gate of the city of God. He is represented on his standard by a snake (Genesis 49:16-18). He was the fifth son of Jacob, and his first by Rachael's maid Bilhah (Genesis 30:3-6). Rachael giving her maid to Jacob brought more discord into Jacob's family.

9. There were nine persons stoned in the Bible, who were they?

(1) Leviticus 24:10, 14 _____   (2) Numbers 15:32, 36 _____

(3) Joshua 7:24-25 _____   (4) Judges 9:53 _____

(5) I Kings 12:18 _____   (6) I Kings 21:9-10 _____

(7) II Chronicles 24:20-21 _____   (8) Acts 7 _____

(9) Acts 14:19 _____

10. Who were the nine widows mentioned in the Bible?

(1) Genesis 38:11 _____   (2) II Samuel 14:4-5 _____

(3) I Kings 7:14 _____   (4) I Kings 11:26 _____

(5) I Kings 17:9 _____   (6) Mark 12:42 _____

(7) Luke 2:36-37 _____   (8) Luke 7:12 _____

(9) Luke 18:3 _____

9 9 9 9 9 9 9

11. Who were the nine people afflicted with blindness?

(1) Genesis 19:11 _____

(2) Genesis 27:1 _____

(3) Genesis 48:10 _____

(4) Judges 16:20-21 _____

(5) I Samuel 4:15 _____

(6) I Kings 14:4 _____

(7) II Kings 6:18 _____

(8) II Kings 25:7_____

(9) Acts 13:11 _____

12. What nine people were afflicted with leprosy in the Old Testament?

(1) Exodus 4:6 _____

(2) Numbers 12:10 _____

(3) II Kings 5:1 _____

(4) II Kings 5:27 _____

(5)-(8) II Kings 7:3 _____

(9) II Kings 15:5-6 _____

13. There are many nines in the Bible—look up the list in the *Strong's Concordance*.

Jesus the Great and Mighty Healer

Remarkable Facts
Nine

• Remember one of the sons of Jacob was Dan. It was prophesied of him, *"Dan shall judge his people, as one of the tribes of Israel. Dan shall be a serpent by the way, an adder in the path, that biteth the horse heels, so that his rider shall fall backward"* (Genesis 49:16-17). The name Dan means "judge." It is interesting that Dan, who should have been an arbiter of peace and equity, brought discontent and injustice.

Dan was like a serpent or horned adder. It is about 2 feet (.6 meters) long and the color of the sand in which it lies. This reptile waits in the dust of the road, watching for opportunity to sink its venomed fangs into the unwary prey. Jacob tells of this wily serpent biting the heel of a passing horse and causing it to rear up in terror, thus possibly throwing its rider, and either injuring or killing him. Gossip and talebearing is like this serpent's bite. *"He shall suck the poison of asps: the viper's tongue shall slay him"* (Job 20:16). The gematria* of the word "Dan" which means a judge, is 54 (9 x 6).

• The sum of the 22 letters of the Hebrew alphabet is 4995 or 5 x 999. It is stamped, therefore, with the numbers of grace and finality.

• The sum of the Greek alphabet is 3999.

Reinforce
Place I
Color this picture.

Place I - II - III

Go for a nature walk and find nines.

*a method of interpreting the Hebrew Scriptures by interchanging words whose letters have the same numerical value when added.

Reinforce
There are 39 Old Testament Books

9

10

10

<u>10</u>

39

1 (Christ) + 8 (New Beginning) = 9 (Complete in Him)

Remember
Store these facts in your mind.

9	9	9	9	9	9
+ 1	+ 2	+ 3	+ 4	+ 5	+ 6
10	11	12	13	14	15

9	9	9	9	9	9
+ 7	+ 8	+ 9	+ 10	+ 11	+ 12
16	17	18	19	20	21

Review
Place I

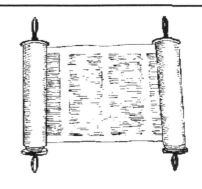

1. Find the sum for these addition problems. Think of the sums as being books in the Old Testament.

9	9	9	9	9	9
+ 1	+ 2	+ 3	+ 4	+ 5	+ 6

9	9	9	9	9	9
+ 7	+ 8	+ 9	+ 10	+ 11	+ 12

2. What is the sum for these addition problems?

9	9	9	9	9	9
+ 2	+ 6	+ 4	+ 7	+ 8	+ 1

9	9	9	9	9	9
+ 6	+ 3	+ 9	+ 10	+ 5	+ 1

9	9	9	9	9	9
+ 4	+ 2	+ 11	+ 8	+ 12	+ 7

9	9	9	9	9	9
+ 3	+ 9	+ 12	+ 5	+ 10	+ 6

3. Write in the answers for these problems.

9 + 6 = _____	9 + 4 = _____	9 + 10 = _____
9 + 11 = _____	9 + 11 = _____	9 + 9 = _____
9 + 1 = _____	9 + 9 = _____	9 + 8 = _____
9 + 9 = _____	9 + 5 = _____	9 + 2 = _____
9 + 11 = _____	9 + 2 = _____	9 + 7 = _____
9 + 5 = _____	9 + 4 = _____	9 + 8 = _____
9 + 8 = _____	9 + 3 = _____	9 + 10 = _____
9 + 12 = _____	9 + 6 = _____	9 + 7 = _____
9 + 7 = _____	9 + 9 = _____	9 + 1 = _____
9 + 11 = _____	9 + 3 = _____	9 + 12 = _____
9 + 4 = _____	9 + 12 = _____	9 + 6 = _____

Learn to spell the word nine.
Write it at least nine times.

_____ _____ _____

_____ _____ _____

_____ _____ _____

4. Think of these digits as books in the Old Testament as you do these problems.

9 + 1	1 + 9	9 + 2	2 + 9	9 + 3	3 + 9

9 + 4	4 + 9	9 + 5	5 + 9	9 + 6	6 + 9

9 + 7	7 + 9	9 + 8	8 + 9	9 + 9	9 + 9

5. Fill in the missing number.

+ 1 10	+ 2 11	+ 3 12	+ 4 13	+ 5 14	+ 6 15

+ 7 16	+ 8 17	+ 9 18	+ 10 19	+ 11 20	+ 12 21

6. Nine books and nine books are: _____

7. Nine books and one book are: _____

8. Nine books and two books are: +_____

    Books of the Old Testament = _____

9. Review the sevens, eights, and nines addition problems.

7 - 8 - 9

2 + 9	8 + 9	6 + 11	7 + 8	9 + 7	4 + 9
1 + 8	7 + 9	5 + 8	9 + 10	8 + 8	6 + 12
9 + 8	8 + 5	9 + 6	5 + 9	6 + 5	6 + 9
7 + 11	1 + 7	8 + 9	9 + 6	8 + 11	4 + 8
7 + 7	7 + 9	8 + 8	4 + 6	2 + 8	9 + 9
7 + 12	9 + 8	5 + 9	6 + 6	8 + 12	3 + 7
8 + 9	8 + 7	6 + 8	9 + 11	3 + 9	7 + 8
7 + 5	7 + 9	6 + 10	8 + 8	9 + 5	6 + 9

9 + 12	7 + 6	9 + 8	3 + 6	5 + 8	6 + 7
9 + 9	7 + 8	11 +7	1 + 9	5 + 7	8 + 8
7 + 10	5 + 9	8 + 6	8 + 9	3 + 7	4 + 8
4 + 7	12 + 9	9 + 9	6 + 8	3 + 8	7 + 9
2 + 6	7 + 8	4 + 9	9 + 8	9 + 12	8 + 2

Reflect

Nine is shaped like an upside down six, or you could say six is an upside down nine. Remember that 6 is the number of man. Man needs the divine nature added to his physical nature. Nine represents the part that completes man's nature. If you put a nine on top of a six you have Jesus' number which represents a completely balanced character.

  8

10. Think of all the Bible promises about Jesus' first coming as you review these addition facts.
Write some references for the Bible promises on the scroll to the right.

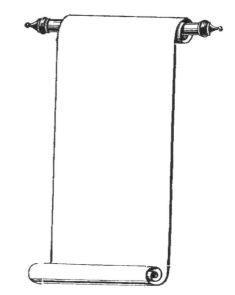

| Jesus Promised |
| He Would Come Again. |

| 2 | 7 | 9 | 10 | 7 | 11 |
| + 6 | + 7 | + 5 | + 6 | + 3 | + 7 |

| 6 | 9 | 12 | 4 | 7 | 8 |
| + 6 | + 9 | + 6 | + 8 | + 8 | + 9 |

| 6 | 8 | 6 | 10 | 7 | 8 |
| + 5 | + 8 | + 7 | + 7 | + 2 | + 8 |

| 7 | 8 | 9 | 3 | 8 | 9 |
| + 12 | + 7 | + 6 | + 8 | + 11 | + 4 |

| 6 | 9 | 8 | 7 | 11 | 4 |
| + 8 | + 3 | + 10 | + 5 | + 9 | + 6 |

| 9 | 7 | 6 | 12 | 8 | 9 |
| + 8 | + 9 | + 8 | + 8 | + 2 | + 7 |

11. Add up these columns of numbers.
Remember to stay in the right place.

90	60	50	70	90	70
+ 80	+ 70	+ 90	+ 80	+ 60	+ 80

40	40	60	40	60	80
+ 80	+ 70	+ 60	+ 90	+ 80	+ 70

30	90	100	400	300	200
+ 90	+ 90	+ 600	+ 500	+ 700	+ 400

500	600	800	900	1000	2000
+ 200	+ 300	+ 800	+ 100	+ 2000	+ 9000

Israel

World

Israel's place was to be <u>alert</u> to enlighten the whole world about Christ's first coming.

12. Fill in the missing numbers.

6	8	6	10	7	8
+___	+___	+___	+___	+___	+___
11	16	13	17	9	16

7	8	9	3	8	9
+___	+___	+___	+___	+___	+___
19	15	15	11	19	13

6	6	9	8	7	5
+___	+___	+___	+___	+___	+___
13	14	11	17	15	13

9	9	11	3	9	7
+___	+___	+___	+___	+___	+___
21	15	17	9	19	11

2	7	9	10	7	11
+ 8	+ 14	+ 14	+ 16	+ 10	+ 17
6	9	12	4	7	8
+ 12	+ 18	+ 18	+ 12	+ 15	+ 17
6	9	8	7	11	4
+ 14	+ 12	+ 18	+ 12	+ 20	+ 10
9	7	6	12	8	9
+ 17	+ 16	+ 14	+ 20	+ 10	+ 16

Review
Place II

Carrying means bearing, conveying, removing, and transporting. The children of Israel were carrying important information about the <u>Deliverer</u>, but were not **alert** to sharing it. This lesson will help you when carrying in addition. Study the example below.

Example

325 = 3 hundreds 2 tens 5 ones = 300 + 20 + 5
<u>434 = 4 hundreds 3 tens 4 ones = 400 + 30 + 4</u>
759   7 hundreds 5 tens 9 ones = 700 + 50 + 9 = 759

---

1. Write out the breakdown of these numbers as shown in the example. This will help you while learning to carry.

348	914	650	735	623	526
+ 540	+ 84	+ 328	+143	+ 373	+ 273

When a place has a sum greater than 9, it is to be carried to the digit to the left which is the next greater place. Look at the example below.

Example

29 = 2 tens   9 ones = 20 +   9
<u>48 = 4 tens   8 ones = 40 +   8</u>
77   6 tens ⑴7 ones = 60 + ⑴7

7 tens   7 ones = 70 +   7 = 77

---

2. Breakdown, add and carry.

28	45	27	56	69	78	24
+ 97	+ 76	+28	+ 58	+ 36	+ 24	+ 26

Breakdown the numbers in your mind, then write the answers down.
Carry the tens' digits to the tens' place.

Example

$$\begin{array}{r} 36 \\ + 49 \\ \hline 85 \end{array}$$

Add 9 + 6 = 15
Think: 15 is 1 ten and 5 ones.
Carry the 1 to tens' place and
write the 5 in the ones' place.
Then add 3 + 4 + 1 = 8.

---

3. Break down, add and carry.

B.

29	39	58	65	46	37
+ 32	+ 25	+ 49	+ 27	+ 46	+ 24

I.

37	68	69	49	36	25
+ 26	+ 32	+ 54	+ 29	+ 24	+ 48

B.

39	69	78	48	27	17
+ 43	+ 48	+ 29	+ 35	+ 47	+ 36

L.

47	76	59	36	19	59
+ 59	+ 49	+ 38	+ 68	+ 68	+ 36

E.	47 + 58	77 + 49	59 + 38	25 + 68	19 + 69	26 + 57
B.	38 + 65	67 + 39	58 + 48	45 + 68	39 + 77	76 + 59
O.	37 + 54	59 + 29	75 + 39	48 + 48	29 + 65	38 + 36
O.	74 + 68	45 + 66	84 + 49	37 + 88	49 + 77	69 + 46
K.	96 + 46	25 + 55	37 + 26	26 + 54	37 + 36	25 + 76
S.	59 + 48	29 + 68	37 + 39	75 + 55	89 + 37	49 + 59

Review
Place III

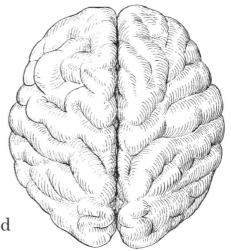

The brain is a wonderful organ God has given us. It can remember many things. The most important thing to remember is the Scriptures. Have you memorized the promises concerning the second coming of Jesus? Did the Jews know the Scriptures concerning the first advent? Did the Jewish leaders understand them?

1. Work these problems in your mind, check your work then write the answers down.

S.	25 + 66	78 + 34	94 + 26	45 + 69	28 + 98	88 + 65

C.	45 + 95	96 + 59	86 + 87	57 + 22	98 + 74	14 + 66

R.	78 74 39	25 96 58	84 98 55	38 78 75	34 68 66	79 74 65

I.	63 86 45	98 59 43	92 66 45	34 76 49	64 85 46	32 42 37

P.	66 38 62	86 36 29	79 80 27	34 94 39	65 37 78	68 46 85

"The brain is as strong as its weakest think"

T.	55	74	16	88	41	16
	67	19	48	54	85	52
	84	81	77	42	21	68

U.	97	45	23	58	67	92
	98	62	48	37	96	75
	75	57	67	43	93	39

R.	38	62	22	28	21	32
	95	61	15	78	65	79
	83	98	94	45	24	96

E.	72	55	35	73	42	68
	46	78	47	91	82	90
	84	63	64	29	68	23

"You are today where your thoughts
have brought you;
You will be tomorrow
where your thoughts take you."
James Allen

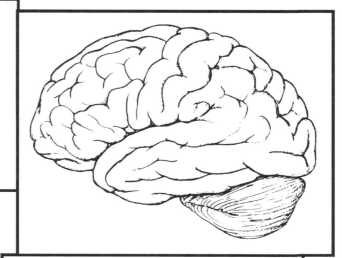

"For as he thinketh in his heart,
so is he;
Eat and drink,
saith he to thee;
but his heart is not with thee."
Proverbs 23:7

"They are never alone
that are accompanied
with noble thoughts."
Philip Sidney

Research
Conditional

"And I will bring them,
and they shall dwell
in the midst of Jerusalem:
and they shall be my people,
and I will be their God,
in truth and in righteousness."
Zechariah 8:8

"This promise of blessing should have met fulfillment in large measure during the centuries following the return of the Israelites from the lands of their captivity. It was God's design that the whole earth be prepared for the first advent of Christ, even as today the way is preparing for His second coming. At the end of the years of humiliating exile, God graciously gave to His people Israel, through Zechariah, the assurance: *'I am returned unto Zion, and will dwell in the midst of Jerusalem: and Jerusalem shall be called a city of truth; and the mountain of the Lord of hosts the holy mountain.'* And of His people He said, *'Behold...I will be their God, in truth and in righteousness'* (Zechariah 8:3, 7-8).

"These promises were conditional on obedience. The sins that had characterized the Israelites

Reinforce
Read this poem.

Coming

Jesus will soon appear.
We see the signs fulfilled
That speak His coming near,
Our troubled hearts to still.

O children will we share
In that bright world to come?
Let us in meekness bear
Our trials while we roam.

'Tis but a little while—
His word attests it true.
Alert children free from guile
Their coming King will view.

"These [blessings] promises
were conditional
on obedience."

prior to the captivity, were not to be repeated. *'Execute true judgment,'* the Lord exhorted those who were engaged in rebuilding; *'and show mercy and compassions every man to his brother: and oppress not the widow, nor the fatherless, the stranger, nor the poor; and let none of you imagine evil against his brother.' 'Speak ye every man the truth to his neighbor; execute the judgment of truth and peace in your gates'* (Zechariah 7:9-10; 8:16).

"Rich were the rewards, both temporal and spiritual, promised those who should put into practice these principles of righteousness. *'The seed shall be prosperous,'* the Lord declared; *'the vine shall give her fruit, and the ground shall give her increase, and the heavens shall give their dew; and I will cause the remnant of this people to possess all these things. And it shall come to pass, that as ye were a curse among the heathen, O house of Judah, and house of Israel; so I will save you, and ye shall be a blessing'* (Zechariah 8:12-13).

"By the Babylonish captivity the Israelites were effectually cured of the worship of graven images. After their return, they gave much attention to religious instruction and to the study of that which had been written in the book of the law

Reinforce

"...The vine shall give her fruit, and the ground shall give her increase, and the heavens shall give their dew...."

Zechariah 8:12

Color this picture.

and in the prophets concerning the worship of the true God. The restoration of the temple enabled them to carry out fully the ritual services of the sanctuary. Under the leadership of Zerubbabel, of Ezra, and of Nehemiah they repeatedly covenanted to keep all the commandments and ordinances of Jehovah. The seasons of prosperity that followed gave ample evidence of God's willingness to accept and forgive, and yet with fatal shortsightedness they turned again and again from their glorious destiny and selfishly appropriated to themselves that which would have brought healing and spiritual life to countless multitudes.

"This failure to fulfill the divine purpose was very apparent in Malachi's day. Sternly the Lord's messenger dealt with the evils that were robbing Israel of temporal prosperity and spiritual power. In his rebuke against transgressors the prophet spared neither priests nor people. *'The burden of the word of the Lord to Israel'* through Malachi was that the lessons of the past be not forgotten and that the covenant made by Jehovah with the house of Israel be kept with fidelity. Only by heartfelt repentance could the blessing of God be realized. *'I pray you,'* the prophet pleaded, *'beseech God that he will be gracious unto us'* (Malachi 1:1, 9).

"Not by any temporary failure of Israel, however, was the plan of the ages for the redemption of mankind to be frustrated. Those to whom the prophet was speaking might not heed the message given, but the purposes of Jehovah were nevertheless to move steadily forward to their complete fulfillment. *'From the rising of the sun even unto the going down of the same,'* the Lord declared through His messenger, *'My name shall be great among the Gentiles; and in every place incense shall be offered unto my name, and a pure offering: for my name shall be great among the heathen'* (Malachi 1:11)."*

"O magnify the Lord with me and let us exalt his name together."
Psalm 34:3

"From the rising of the sun even unto the going down of the same, My name shall be great among the Gentiles..."

*Prophets and Kings 703-706

Review
Word Problems
Place I

1. Jesus would come to explain the Scriptures correctly. There are two (2) books in the first half of the Old Testament and there are three (3) in the last half that are especially quoted from. How many books are especially quoted from in the Old Testament?

2. There are seventeen (17) important quotes in the Psalms, and eleven (11) important quotes in the book of Isaiah about the <u>Deliverer</u>. How many quotes are there in the Psalms and in the book of Isaiah?

3. There are eleven (11) other important quotes from other books. The book of Zechariah has six (6). How many does that add up to be?

4. What is the total of the important quotes about the Deliverer?

_____
+ _____
_____

_____
+ _____
_____

_____
+ _____
_____

_____
+ _____
_____

"Till I come, give attendance to reading."
1 Timothy 4:13

5. Sing the song, "Like a Little Candle."

(1) Jesus bids us shine with a pure, clear light,
(2) Like a little candle burning in the night;
(3) In this world of darkness we must shine,
(4) You in your corner, I in mine.

Review
Word Problems
Place II

6. There are nine (9) words in the first line of the above song. Then there are eight (8) in the second line. What is the sum of words in the first two lines?

7. The third line of music has eight (8) words and the fourth line has nine (9) words. How many words are there in the third and fourth lines?

8. What is the sum of problem one and two above?

"A burning and
a shining light."

John 5:35

1. Reading through the Bible is a fun project for a family. Once you have completed the first 39 books, it does not take long to finish the last 27 books. When you have finished reading, how many books have you read?

2. The Psalms (songs) are sometimes called the Psalter. It was the hymn book and prayer book of Israel. The Psalms were written by different authors. David wrote seventy-three and seventy-seven were written by other authors. How many songs to the glory of God are there?

3. The longest Psalm is Psalm 119. It goes through the Hebrew alphabet as titles in each section. The first eleven sections have 88 verses while the last eleven sections have 88 verses. How many verses are there in Psalm 119? If you read one section each day you could complete Psalm 119 in 22 days. How many verses are in each section?

Review
Word Problems
Place III

Make a chart of prophecies about the second coming of Jesus.
Use your Bible and concordance. See the sample.
Mark your Bible in a chain reference fashion.

Example	
Prophesied	**Prophecy**
John 14:3	"I will come again"

1. How many verses did you find?

2. How many books in the Bible
did you use?

Revelation

The last book of the Bible was penned by John, the author of the fourth Gospel
and the 3 Epistles of John.

Revelation is the only book in the New Testament that is essentially all prophecy.
Its theme is the unfolding of the future events related to the church and the
world, ending in the triumph of our Lord. These revelations are given to John
through Jesus, who received them from the Father (chapter 1:1).

By one estimate, there are 300 symbols used in Revelation, each with a definite
meaning. Jesus is referred to as a Lamb, referring to His sacrifice for His people,
more than 25 times.

Reinforce

1. As you clean all the light fixtures and replace bulbs, be reminded how Israel should have been an **alert** light to the Gentiles. All levels sing the song, "Like a Little Candle."

2. Find Bible verses about being a light by using your *Strong's Concordance*. Copy them neatly on a piece of paper, decorate it, then hang it on the wall for all to see.

3. Turn your porch light on if it is dark outside during family worship every evening.

"They looked unto Him and were lightened."
Psalm 34:5

"Ye are the light of the world. A city that is set on an hill cannot be hid.
"Neither do men light a candle, and put it under a bushel,
but on a candlestick;
and it giveth light unto all that are in the house.
"Let your light so shine before men, that they may see your good works,
and glorify your Father which is in heaven."

Matthew 5:14-16

4. Sing the hymn, "How Shall We Stand in the Judgment."

Remainder
Coming

"If my people, which are called by my name, shall humble themselves,

and pray, and seek my face, and turn from their wicked ways;

then will I hear from heaven, and will forgive their sin, and will heal their land."

II Chronicles 7:14

"For more than a thousand years the Jewish people had awaited the coming of the promised Saviour. Their brightest hopes had rested upon this event. For a thousand years, in song and prophecy, in temple rite and household prayer, His name had been enshrined; and yet when He came, they did not recognize Him as the Messiah for whom they had so long waited. *'He came unto his own, and his own received him not'* (John 1:11). To their world-loving hearts the Beloved of heaven was *'as a root out of a dry ground.'* In their eyes He had *'no form nor comeliness;'* they discerned in Him no beauty that they should desire Him (Isaiah 53:2).

"The whole life of Jesus of Nazareth among the Jewish people was a reproof to their selfishness, as revealed in their unwillingness to recognize the just claims of the Owner of the vineyard over which they had been placed as husbandmen. They hated His example of truthfulness and piety; and when the final test came, the test which meant obedience unto eternal life or disobedience unto eternal death, they rejected the Holy One of Israel and became responsible for His crucifixion on Calvary's cross."*

Remember, the number nine means judgment. It reminds us how, when the time was <u>completely</u> fulfilled, all would pass judgment on themselves by how they responded to Christ.

"For more than a thousand years the Jewish people had awaited the coming of the promised Saviour."

*Prophets and Kings 710

Reinforce
1. Judgment

One must always be **alert** for all will pass judgment on themselves
by how they responded to Christ this very day.
The number nine can help us remember this.
Read these stories about judgment.

Christ our Advocate in the Judgment Day

When he lay down on his bed, during his last illness, one asked him how he was now. He answered, "I lie here in the everlasting arms of a gracious God." "Are you not afraid," said the friend, "to appear at the tribunal of God?" He replied "Were I looking to give the account in my own person, considering my sins, indeed I might be terrified; but then I view Christ the Judge as my Advocate and my Accountant, and I know that I do not owe more debt than He has paid."

—*Life of John Brown, of Haddington*

Ready for Judgment Day

There was an young Scotch lad at the time of the great meteoric shower of November 1833. When on every side men and women were that night in terror at the thought that the hour of final doom had come, this lad's mother aroused him from his sleep with a cry, "Sandy, Sandy, get up, will you? The day of judgment has come." Instantly the boy was alive to that call, and was on his feet, shouting, "Glory to God! I'm ready."

No Difference

It was my sad lot to be in the Chicago fire. As the flames rolled down our streets, destroying everything in their onward march, I saw the great and the honorable, the learned and the wise, fleeting before the fire with the beggar and the thief and the harlot. All were alike. As the flames swept through the city it was like the judgment day. The Mayor, nor the mighty men, nor wise men could stop these flames. They were all on a level then, and many who were worth hundreds of thousands were left paupers that night. When the day of judgment comes there will be no difference. When the Deluge came there was no difference; Noah's ark was worth more than all the world. The day before it was the world's laughing-stock, and if it had been put up to auction you could not have got anybody to buy it except for firewood. But the Deluge came, and then it was worth more than all the world together. And when the day of judgment comes Christ will be worth more than all this world— more than ten thousand worlds.

—*Moody*

How to be Occupied

When a minister of the gospel was spending a few weeks in Edinburgh, there came, on business, to the house where he was a man of the world. He was introduced to the preacher in the following manner—"This is Mr._____ , an acquaintance of mine, who, I am sorry to add, never attends public worship." "I am almost tempted to hope," replied the minister, "that you are bearing false witness against your neighbor." "By no means," said the infidel, "for I always spend my Sabbath in settling accounts." The minister immediately replied, "You will find, sir, that the day of judgment will be spent in exactly the same manner."

No Evasion in Judgment

I will tell you a dream of one of quality, related to myself by the dreamer himself. Said he, "I dreamed the day of judgment was come, and all men appeared before Christ. Some were white, others spotted. Me-thought," said he, "I was all white, saying that I had one black spot upon my breast, which I covered with my hand. Upon the separation of these two sorts I got among the white on the right hand.

Glad was I; but at last a narrow search was made, and one came and plucked away my hand from my breast; then appeared my spot, and I was thrust away among the spotted ones.

—*Thomas Larkham*

God's Judgments Misunderstood

"Do you not perceive, Mr. Milton," Charles II, is said to have said to the sightless old poet, "that your blindness is a judgment of God for taking part against the late King, my father?" "Nay," is said to have said Milton, calmly; "if I have lost my sight through God's judgment, what can you say of your father, who lost his head?"

—*Francis Jacox*

Thought of Judgment

Jerome said that the trumpet of the last day seemed to be always sounding in his ear, saying, "Arise, ye dead, and come to judgment."

"In judgment be ye not too confident, even as a man who will appraise his corn when standing in a field, ere it is ripe."

—*Dante* (1300-21)

2. Color and read these words.

"And Simeon... said unto Mary his mother, Behold, this child [Jesus] is set for the fall and rising again of many in Israel... that the thoughts of many hearts may be revealed."
Luke 2:34-35

10 10 Tens - 10 10 10

Research
The Number Ten

"...Nevertheless when the Son of man cometh, shall he find faith on the earth?"
Luke 18:8

The number ten reminds us of the perfection of divine order; the completeness of order, marking a whole cycle. From the first sin to Jesus' first coming is one complete cycle. From His first coming to His second coming is another complete cycle. "...*Nevertheless when the Son of man cometh, shall he find faith on the earth?*"

"Christ would have averted the doom of the Jewish nation if the people had received Him. But envy and jealousy made them implacable. They determined that they would not receive Jesus of Nazareth as the Messiah. They rejected the Light of the world, and henceforth their lives were surrounded with darkness as the darkness of midnight. The doom foretold came upon the Jewish nation. Their own fierce passions, uncontrolled, wrought their ruin. In their blind rage they destroyed one another. Their

Reinforce

Color then read the meaning of the number ten. Learn to say ten in these languages.

French – dix (dees)

Japanese – ju (joo)

Spanish – diez (dee EHS)

Swahili – kumi (kOO mee)

$$\begin{array}{r} 10 \text{ addend} \\ + 10 \text{ addend} \\ \hline 20 \text{ sum} \end{array}$$

TEN - 10 = PERFECT DIVINE ORDER

The divine nature and the human nature combined (addition +) to give sinful man a Saviour.

10

Divine
Human →
+

rebellious stubborn pride brought upon them the wrath of their Roman conquerors. Jerusalem was destroyed, the temple laid in ruins, and its site plowed like a field. The children of Judah perished by the most horrible forms of death. Millions were sold to serve as bondmen in heathen lands.

"That which God purposed to do for the world through Israel, the chosen nation, He will finally accomplish through His church on earth today. He has *'let out his vineyard unto other husbandmen,'* even to His covenant-keeping people, who faithfully *'render him the fruits in their seasons.'* Never has the Lord been without true representatives on this earth who have made His interests their own. These witnesses for God are numbered among the spiritual Israel, and to them will be fulfilled all the covenant promises made by Jehovah to His ancient people."*

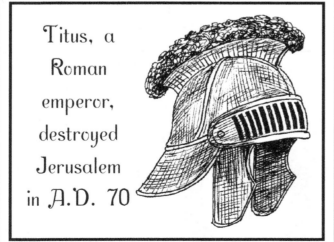

Titus, a Roman emperor, destroyed Jerusalem in A.D. 70

Prophets and Kings 712-714

Reflect
The Church = God's Faithful People

"The church is God's fortress. His city of refuge, which He holds in a revolted world. Any betrayal of the church is treachery to Him who has bought mankind with the blood of His only-begotten Son. From the beginning, faithful souls have constituted the church on earth. In every age the Lord has had His watchmen, who have borne a faithful testimony to the generation in which they lived. These sentinels gave the message of warning; and when they were called to lay off their armor, others took up the work. God brought these witnesses into covenant relation with Himself, uniting the church on earth with the church in heaven."

The Acts of the Apostles 11

Bible Search 10

Tens

The first decade is the representative of the whole numeral system, and originates the system of calculation called "decimals," because the whole system of numeration consists of so many tens, of which the first is a type of the the whole.

Completeness of order, marking the entire round of anything, is, therefore, the ever-present signification of the number ten. It implies that nothing is wanting; that the number and order are perfect; that the whole cycle is complete.

1. Where is the Ten Commandments found in the Bible?

2. What is the tithe? (Leviticus 27:32-33; Malachi 3:8-11)

3. The redemption money was ten gerahs. What is a gerah? (Exodus 30:13; Numbers 3:47) Use a Bible Dictionary to answer this question.

Note: Every male that was numbered, over 20 years of age, must pay this sum and meet God's claim. But the first-born were to pay ten times as much; for when God took the Levites instead of the first-born of Israel, there were found 22,273 first-born males, but only 22,000 Levites. So that 273 had to pay the ransom money, which amounted to ten times ten gerahs. Thus, though the five shekels looked like a variation, the significance of ten is sustained, for the five shekels were ten times the "half shekel." (See Numbers 3:12-13, 40-51.)

4. To complete the circle of God's judgment what came upon Egypt of old? What will finally come upon the whole world? (Exodus 9:14; Revelation 15)

5. What formed the foundations of the Tabernacle that were 10 x 10? They were made of silver. Silver is significant of redemption (I Peter 1:18-19). (Exodus 38:27)

6. What ten people said, "I have sinned?" (**1**–Exodus 9:27, 10:16; **2**–Numbers 22:34; **3**–Joshua 7:20; **4**–I Samuel 15:24, 30, 26:21; **5**–II Samuel 12:13, 24:10, 17,

I Chronicles 21:8, 17, Psalm 41:4, 51:4; **6**–II Samuel 19:20; **7**–II Kings 18:10, 17; **8**–Job 7:2; **9**–Micah 7:9; **10**–Nehemiah 1:6)

7. Why could an Ammonite or Moabite not enter the congregation of the Lord; even to their tenth generation? (Deuteronomy 23:3-5; Nehemiah 13:1)

8. What ten parables are listed in Matthew 13, 22, and 25?

9. What parable includes 10 people? (Matthew 25:1-13)

10. What ten Passovers are recorded in Scripture? (**1**–Exodus 12; **2**–Numbers 9:5; **3**–Joshua 5:10; **4**–II Chronicles 30:1; **5**–II Chronicles 35:1; **6**–Ezra 6:19; **7**–Luke 2:41; **8**–John 2:13; **9**–John 6:4; and **10**–Matthew 26:2)

11. What ten deaths were occasioned by women? (**1**–Judges 4:21; **2**–Judges 9:52-53, II Samuel 11:21, **3**–II Samuel 20:1, 21-22; **4**–I Kings 3:19; **5**–I Kings 18:4; **6**–I Kings 21:9-10; **7**–II Kings 6:29; **9**II Kings 11:1; Esther 9:13-14; and Matthew 14:8)

12. There are many tens in the Bible—look up the list in the *Strong's Concordance*.

What women for question 11 could these women represent?

Remarkable Facts
Ten

• Noah completed the antediluvian age in the tenth generation from Adam.

• The Ten Commandments contains all that is necessary for man to be like God, both as their number and content.

• The Lord's Prayer is completed in ten clauses.

> The first, God's sovereignty.
> The second, Jehovah's manifested Name.
> The third, the realization of God's kingdom.
> The fourth first mentions the earth.
> The fifth, the gift of grace supplying our need.
> The sixth treats of man's sin.
> The seventh pleads for spiritual guidance.
> The eighth pleads for final deliverance from all evil.
> The ninth sums up the divine glory (3), while
> The tenth completes the eternal cycles.

• Abraham's faith was proved by a completed cycle of ten trials:

> (1) His departure from Haran.
> (2) His flight to Egypt from the famine.
> (3) In the seizure of Sarah.
> (4) In his war to rescue Lot.
> (5) In his taking Hagar.
> (6) In his circumcision.
> (7) In the second seizure of Sarah at Gerar.
> (8) In the expulsion of Ishmael.
> (9) In the expulsion of Hagar.
> (10) In the offering of Isaac.

• Ten instances in the Old Testament of younger sons being preferred before the elder:

(1) Abel,
(2) Shem,
(3) Abraham,
(4) Isaac,
(5) Jacob,
(6) Judah,
(7) Joseph,
(8) Ephraim,
(9) Moses, and
(10) David.

• The image in Daniel 2:41 had ten toes symbolizing ten kingdoms as did the ten horns of the fourth beast of Daniel's vision in Daniel 7 and Revelation 12, 13, and 17.

• Fire came down from heaven ten times, six of which were in judgment:

(1) Sodom (Genesis 19:24),
(2) On the first offerings (Leviticus 9:24),
(3) On Nadab and Abihu (Leviticus 10:2),
(4) On the murmurers at Taberah (Numbers 11:1),
(5) On Korah and his company (Numbers 16:35),
(6) On Elijah's offering at Carmel (I Kings 18:38),
(7) On Elijah's enemies (II Kings 1:10),
(8) On Elijah's enemies (II Kings 1:12),
(9) On David's sacrifice (I Chronicles 21:26), and
(10) On Solomon's sacrifice (II Chronicles 7:1).

Reinforce

Take a nature walk and find tens or a combination of ten in creation.

Reinforce

Cycle means:

"a complete round of events that repeat themselves."

First Sin—
Christ's
First Advent

Christ's
First Advent—
Christ's
Second
Coming

"...This same Jesus,

which is taken up from you into heaven,

shall so come in like manner

as ye have seen him go into heaven."

Acts 1:11

9 (Conclusion) **+ 1** (God) **= 10** (Complete)

Remember

Store these facts in your mind.

10 + 1 11	10 + 2 12	10 + 3 13	10 + 4 14	10 + 5 15	10 + 6 16
10 + 7 17	10 + 8 18	10 + 9 19	10 + 10 20	10 + 11 21	10 + 12 22

A Few

"The eyes of your understanding being enlightened;
that ye may know what is the hope of his calling,
and what the riches of the glory of his inheritance in the saints."
Ephesians 1:18

In Israel there were a few **alert**, faithful people who longed for the Deliverer to come. They read the promises from the Scriptures and believed them. One such promise was, *"The sceptre shall not depart from Judah, nor a lawgiver from between his feet, until Shiloh come"* (Genesis 49:10).

There are seventeen (17) words in the above promise that add up several ways but all come up to the same sum.

"The fullness of the time had come."* Man had become more and more sinful as time passed. Satan had taught the people wrong ideas about God and His law. Many now served Satan. "The bodies of human beings, made for the dwelling place of God had become the habitation of demons."** The first cycle, marking Christ's first advent, was completed. People needed a <u>Deliverer</u>.

10	8	9	7	8
+ 7	+ 9	+ 8	6	8
17	17	17	+ 4	+ 1
			17	17

"THE FULLNESS OF THE TIME HAD COME."

Place I Color these words.

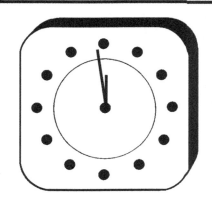

*The Desire of Ages 34 **Ibid 36

Remember how many times Jesus healed people controlled by demons? As the heart pumping blood throughout the body is vital to the physical life, so the mind working correctly is vital to the spiritual life. Sometimes people call the mind the heart. We can be **alert** to allow God's Spirit to control us and not allow Satan's suggestions.

Reinforce

Place I
Trace the words,
"Love to God," and
"Love to Man."

God desires His law
to be written
in our heart (mind).

Law of Love

1.

2. Love

3. to

4. God

5.

6. Love

7. to

8. Man

9.

10.

$$4 + 6 = \_\_\_\_$$

"I delight
to do thy will,
O my God:
yea, thy law
is within
my heart."
Psalm 40:8

"O how love
I thy law!
it is my
meditation
all the day."
Psalm 119:97

Review

Place I

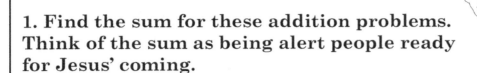

1. Find the sum for these addition problems. Think of the sum as being alert people ready for Jesus' coming.

10	10	10	10	10	10
+ 1	+ 2	+ 3	+ 4	+ 5	+ 6

10	10	10	10	10	10
+ 7	+ 8	+ 9	+ 10	+ 11	+ 12

2. What is the sum for these addition problems?

10	10	10	10	10	10
+ 8	+ 6	+ 1	+ 7	+ 2	+ 4

10	10	10	10	10	10
+ 9	+ 3	+ 1	+ 10	+ 5	+ 6

10	10	10	10	10	10
+ 11	+ 8	+ 4	+ 2	+ 12	+ 7

10	10	10	10	10	10
+ 12	+ 9	+ 3	+ 5	+ 6	+ 10

> "Great peace have they which love thy law:
> and nothing shall offend them."
> Psalm 119:165

3. Write in the answers for these problems.

10 + 6 = _____   10 + 4 = _____   10 + 10 = _____

10 + 11 = _____   10 + 3 = _____   10 + 9 = _____

10 + 1 = _____   10 + 9 = _____   10 + 8 = _____

10 + 9 = _____   10 + 5 = _____   10 + 2 = _____

10 + 11 = _____   10 + 2 = _____   10 + 7 = _____

10 + 5 = _____   10 + 4 = _____   10 + 8 = _____

10 + 8 = _____   10 + 3 = _____   10 + 10 = _____

10 + 12 = _____   10 + 6 = _____   10 + 7 = _____

10 + 7 = _____   10 + 9 = _____   10 + 1 = _____

10 + 11 = _____   10 + 3 = _____   10 + 12 = _____

10 + 4 = _____   10 + 12 = _____   10 + 6 = _____

Ten
Commandments

I   V
         VI
II   VII
III   VIII
         IX
IV   X

Learn to spell the word ten.
Write it at least ten times.

_____   _____   _____   _____

_____   _____   _____

10 10   _____   _____   10 10

10 10   10   10
        10   10

4. Fill in these blanks with the right number.

10 + _____ = 14   10 + _____ = 17   10 + _____ = 12

10 + _____ = 11   10 + _____ = 16   10 + _____ = 21

10 + _____ = 19   10 + _____ = 22   10 + _____ = 20

10 + _____ = 13   10 + _____ = 15   10 + _____ = 18

Reflect

$$1 + 9 = 10$$

Nine reminds us of DIVINE COMPLETENESS.

God is the ONE

I am the ZERO

His power makes me COMPLETE!

10 - 10 - 10

Remember, "I can of my own self do nothing (0)...."
John 5:30

Review
Place II
Many problems require carrying to more than one place.
See the example below.

Example

```
498 =    4 hundreds  9 tens  8 ones =   400 +  90 +  8
+ 757 = + 7 hundreds  5 tens  7 ones = + 700 +  50 +  7
         11 hundreds 14 tens 15 ones   1100 + 140 + 15
         11 hundreds 15 tens  5 ones   1100 + 150 +  5
         12 hundreds  5 tens  5 ones   1200 +  50 +  5
```

1 thousand 2 hundreds 5 tens 5 ones = 1255

---

1. Break down these numbers. Find the sum of these problems.

947	736	852	794	693	582
+ 593	+ 690	+ 785	+ 872	+ 964	+ 953

569	489	674	593	749	395
+ 486	+ 539	+ 589	+ 839	+ 573	+ 989

Now carry in your mind without writing the problem out.

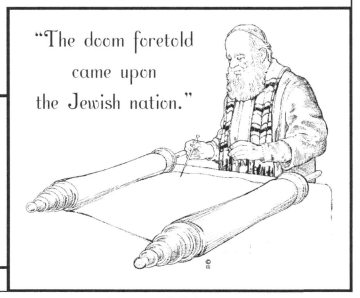

"The doom foretold came upon the Jewish nation."

"Christ would have averted the doom of the Jewish nation if the people had received Him."

Example

```
  697
+ 789
 1486
```

Add 9 + 7 = 16.
Write down the 6 and carry the 1 to tens' place.
Add 8 + 9 + 1 = 18.
Write down the 8 and carry the 1 to the hundreds' place.
Add 7 + 6 + 1 = 14.
Write down the 4 and put the 1 in thousands' place.

2. Find these sums.

P.	398 + 659	549 + 894	684 + 797	395 + 859	494 + 948	688 + 766
R.	849 + 584	684 + 794	918 + 396	962 + 968	536 + 995	399 + 773
O.	796 + 818	923 + 979	479 + 974	944 + 998	247 + 678	980 + 825
M.	580 + 253	484 + 763	218 + 765	446 + 39	836 + 786	787 + 799

"That which God purposed to do for the world through Israel,
the chosen nation, He will finally accomplish
through His church on earth today."

I.	468 + 538	542 + 634	963 + 985	387 + 368	725 + 968	931 + 778
S.	379 + 788	553 + 488	676 + 779	682 + 666	836 + 875	469 + 767
E.	797 + 659	764 + 889	967 + 466	707 + 969	573 + 749	545 + 689
S.	369 + 937	457 + 697	659 + 494	777 + 547	478 + 657	566 + 968

Reflect

"Never has the Lord been without true representatives
on this earth who have made His interests their own.
These witnesses for God are numbered among the spiritual Israel,
and to them will be fulfilled all the covenant promises
made by Jehovah to His ancient people."

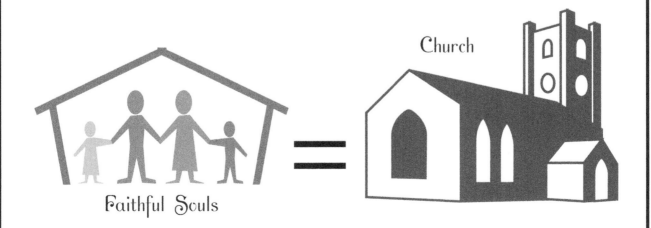

Faithful Souls = Church

Review
Place III

1. Add these problems in your mind then write the sum down. Think of the sum as being Bible promises about Jesus' second coming.

S.	25 + 66	78 + 34	94 + 26	55 + 69	28 + 98	68 + 63
E.	45 + 95	96 + 58	86 + 87	57 + 35	98 + 76	24 + 68
C.	79 + 84	35 + 96	73 + 46	26 + 78	75 + 26	56 + 39
O.	94 58 44	38 78 73	44 68 76	79 84 65	73 86 45	86 59 44
N.	82 67 54	44 66 48	64 85 46	42 52 37	74 38 52	86 35 19
D.	79 70 17	43 84 37	65 37 78	68 46 67	56 67 73	74 19 82

C.	16	87	43	36	97	45
	48	76	87	54	89	62
	79	44	30	89	75	57
O.	33	58	77	84	38	62
	48	37	86	66	87	64
	67	43	93	57	63	98
M.	35	37	23	32	92	55
	26	77	67	70	48	78
	94	36	53	98	86	65
I.	35	73	42	16	79	42
	47	98	62	77	93	26
	64	29	68	60	65	76
N.	31	74	57	63	75	89
	58	38	28	90	48	80
	93	56	52	81	15	34
G.	45	67	41	31	24	96
	17	34	25	72	36	74
	84	91	77	59	54	38

"From the beginning,
faithful souls have constituted the church on earth."

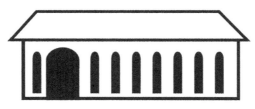

Review
Word Problems
Place I

1. The adult heart weighs from nine (9) to eleven (11) ounces (255 to 312 grams). It helps keep the physical body **alert** and working well. One person has a heart weighing ten (10) ounces and another person has a heart weighing nine (9) ounces. How much do both hearts weigh together?

2. The human brain (heart) has twelve (12) pairs of nerves that directly connect it with other parts of the body. How many nerves would one (1) person have that connects his brain to the rest of his body?

3. A baby's heart beats 130 - 150 beats per minute. A six year old - 100 beats per minute. A 10 year old - 90 beats per minute. An adult man 70 beats per minute. An adult woman 78 beats per minute. How fast would both the ten year old and the adult woman's heart beat per minute?

_____ + _____ = _____

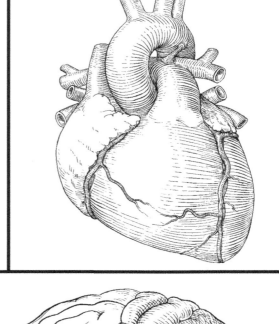

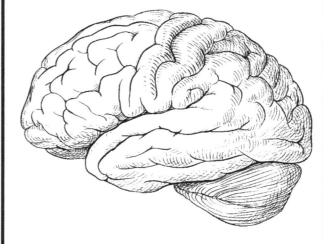

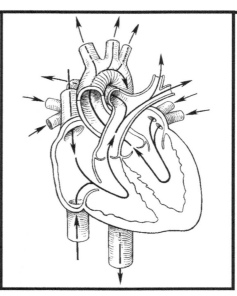

4. The thought in *The Desire of Ages* 32 (a memory verse) that has been included in your memory verses has twenty (20) words in it. Write out in the square to the right three problems that have the sum of twenty.

5. We have many promises about Christ's second coming. What does Matthew 24:42 remind us to do? It has twelve (12) words in it. In the square make several problems that have the sum of twelve (12).

6. Another promise about Christ's second coming is found in Revelation 1:7. Trace this promise (below) with a colored pencil or crayon as you read it.

"BEHOLD, HE COMETH WITH CLOUDS;
AND EVERY EYE SHALL SEE HIM,
AND THEY ALSO WHICH PIERCED HIM:
AND ALL KINDREDS OF THE EARTH
SHALL WAIL BECAUSE OF HIM.
EVEN SO, AMEN."

REVELATION 1:7

Review
Word Problems
Place II

1. The Reynolds family made a study of Christ's second coming from the Scriptures. They found many Bible promises. See the chart.

C.   How many Bible promises did they find from Genesis through Isaiah?

O.   The remaining books of the Old Testament have how many promises about Jesus' coming?

M.   Matthew, Mark, Luke and I and II Corinthians have beautiful promises. What do they add up to?

E.   The rest of the books plus Revelation equal? _____

2. What is the total number of verses the Reynolds family found in the Bible about the second coming?

Book	# of References
Ge	2
Ex	2
Job	2
Ps	4
Isa	20
Jer	1
Eze	3
Da	9
Joe	4
Am	2
Na	6
Hab	2
Zec	1
Mal	1
Mt	18
Mr	2
Lu	11
I Co	1
II Co	2
Eph	1
I Th	3
II Th	1
I Ti	3
II Ti	2
He	1
Jas	2
II Pe	3
Re	34

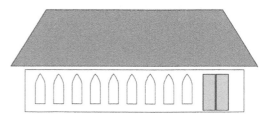

Review
Word Problems
Place III

1. See the chart on previous page. How many Bible promises did the Reynolds family find on the second coming from Isaiah, Daniel, Matthew, Luke and Revelation?

2. It is helpful to have good study tools. See the chart below to see the cost of some valuable tools.

Wide Margin KJV Bible	$79.95
Strong's Concordance	39.99
New Englishman's Concordance—Hebrew	39.95
New Englishman's Concordance—Greek	34.95
Treasury of Scripture Knowledge	25.97
Lexicon—Hebrew	24.95
Lexicon—Greek	19.95
Noah Webster's 1828 Dictionary	65.00
Bible Dictionary	45.95
Atlas of the Bible Lands	12.95

How much does a wide margin Bible and a *Strong's Concordance* cost?

What do the first 5 items cost?

How about the last 5 items?

What is the total of all the materials?

Work Area

Reinforce

1. Be **alert** to complete rounds of events that repeat themselves. For example: can you think of some time events that repeat themselves (weekly cycle, Sabbath)? What cycles can you see in nature (seasons)? in families (birth - death)?

2. Every evening in private prayer, review the complete round of events making up your day. Can you see any bad cycles of behavior (actions that tend to repeat themselves) that you need to stop? Pray for forgiveness and cleansing. God will help you "turn over a new leaf" and start a whole new cycle of victorious living. Do not forget to <u>add</u> up God's blessings during the day and thank Him for them. Do you see cycles in His blessings? What about the sun rising every day?

"The Lord's mercies...

are new every morning:

great is thy faithfulness."

Lamentations 3:22-23

Spring

Summer

Autumn

Winter

Remainder
Beautiful Descriptions of Christ's Coming
Read these descriptions of Christ's first and second Coming.

Christ's First Coming	Christ's Second Coming
Read Isaiah 53:2-7	Read Revelation 19:11-16
Describe the lamb and sheep.	**Describe the horse.**

Reinforce

1. Find things in nature that remind you of either Christ's first coming or His second coming. (Example: field of hay–stable; dark cloud)

2. Color the words and be reminded of what the number ten means.

The number ten reminds us of the perfection of divine order; the complete-ness of order, marking a whole cycle.

11 11 Elevens - 11 11 11

Research
The Number Eleven

"And ye are complete in him, which is the head of all principality and power."

Colossians 2:10

In the Bible, the number eleven reminds us of incompleteness, disorder, and imperfection. This can help us remember how imperfect Israel needed the <u>Deliverer</u>. People who were not **alert** had become very sinful. "Satan had been working to make the gulf deep and impassable between earth and heaven. By his falsehoods he had emboldened [encouraged or made bold] men in sin. It was his purpose to wear out the forbearance [patience] of God, and to extinguish [put out] His love for man, so that He would abandon [leave] the world..."* and let Satan have it. Men were incomplete and needed a Saviour to be complete! *"And ye are complete in him, which is the head of all principality and power."*

The Desire of Ages 34-35

Reinforce
Color then read the meaning of the number eleven. Review the numbers 1-10 in French, Japanese, Spanish, and Swahili.

```
  11 addend
+ 11 addend
  22 sum
```

ELEVEN - 11 = IN-COMPLETE-NESS

The divine nature and the human nature combined (addition +) to give sinful man a Saviour.

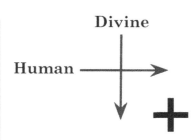

Bible Search 11

Elevens

Ten is the number which marks the perfection of Divine order, then eleven is an addition of it, and undoes that order. While twelve is the number which marks the perfection of Divine government, and eleven falls short of it. Whether we consider it 10 + 1, or 12 − 1, it is the number which marks disorder, disorganization, imperfection, and disintegration.

1. Who were the eleven in Genesis 36:40-43?

2. What was missing that made only 11? (Genesis 42:32)

3. From Horeb to Kadesh Barnea was how long of a journey? (Deuteronomy 1:2)

Note: One more day would have carried them to the complete administration of all those wonderful laws which God had given them.

4. Who reigned for only 11 years when Nebuchadnezzar came up and began his disintegrating work on Jerusalem? (II Kings 23:36, 24:1; II Chronicles 36:5-6)

5. Who ruled when Nebuchadnezzar completed the work by putting an end to Israel's rule in Jerusalem? (II Chronicles 36:11; Jeremiah 52:1-2)

6. Who prophesied against Tyre and Egypt in the eleventh year? (Ezekiel 26:1, 30:20, 31:1)

7. Who was missing from the 12, making only eleven apostles? Who replaced him? (Acts 1:25-26)

8. What are considered the "Eleventh Hour" parables? (Matthew 22:1-14; Luke 14:15-24; Matthew 20:1-16)

9. How long was Christ's life on earth? (Daniel 9:26)

10. What eleven kings and rulers were offended with God's servants for telling the truth? (**1**–Exodus 10:28; **2**–Numbers 24:10; **3**–I Kings 13:4; **4**–I Kings 22:26-27; **5**–II Kings 5:11-12; **6**–II Chronicles 16:10; **7**–II Chronicles 24:21; **8**–II Chronicles 26:19; **9**–Jeremiah 26:21; **10**–Jeremiah 32:3; and **11**–Matthew 14:3)

11. Do this problem and then answer this question: He was 30 years of age when he stood before Pharaoh (Genesis 41:46). He was 17 years old when sold (Genesis 37:2, 36). He was 2 years in prison (Genesis 42:1). How many years did he serve a master? What is his name?

12. There are many elevens in the Bible—look up the list in the *Strong's Concordance*.

Remarkable Facts
Other Numbers

• The only 15-letter word that can be spelled without repeating a letter is uncopyrightable.

• Addul Kassem Ismael, Grand Vizier of Persia in the 10th century, carried his library with him wherever he went. The 117,000 volumes were carried by 400 camels trained to walk in alphabetical order.

• A jiffy is an actual unit of time for 1/100th of a second.

• The smallest unit of time is the yoctosecond.

• There are 293 ways to make change for a dollar.

• It costs more to buy a new car in America today than it cost Christopher Columbus to equip and undertake three voyages to and from the New World.

• The world's termites outweigh the world's humans by 10 to 1.

• About 11% of the people in the world are left-handed.

• A jellyfish is 95% water.

• The average raindrop falls at 7 miles per hour.

• If the information contained in the DNA could be written down, it would fill a 1,000 volume encyclopedia. Calculating DNA length for each person, would stretch across the diameter of the solar system.

• You blink over 10 million times a year.

Reinforce

"It is Time"

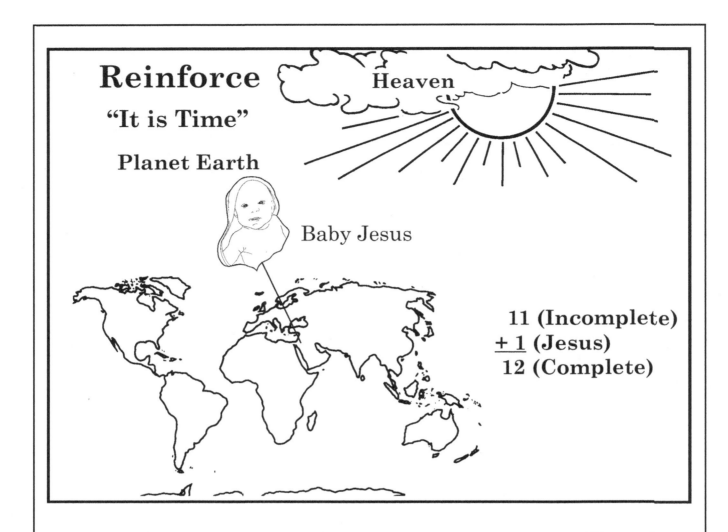

Heaven

Planet Earth

Baby Jesus

11 (Incomplete)
+ 1 (Jesus)
12 (Complete)

Remember

Store these facts in your mind.

11	11	11	11	11	11
+ 1	+ 2	+ 3	+ 4	+ 5	+ 6
12	13	14	15	16	17

11	11	11	11	11	11
+ 7	+ 8	+ 9	+ 10	+ 11	+ 12
18	19	20	21	22	23

The Interpreter

"If there be a messenger with him,
an interpreter,
one among a thousand,
to shew unto man his uprightness:

"Then he is gracious unto him,
and saith, Deliver him from going
down to the pit:
I have found a ransom."
Job 33:23-24

The Scriptures had been misunderstood. "The true Interpreter must come. The One whom all the types [symbols] prefigured [told about] must explain their significance [importance]."*

People need to know how to be complete in Christ, the Interpreter of all the symbols.

List below some of the symbols that represent Christ in the Bible.

_____

_____

_____

_____

*The Desire of Ages 33-34

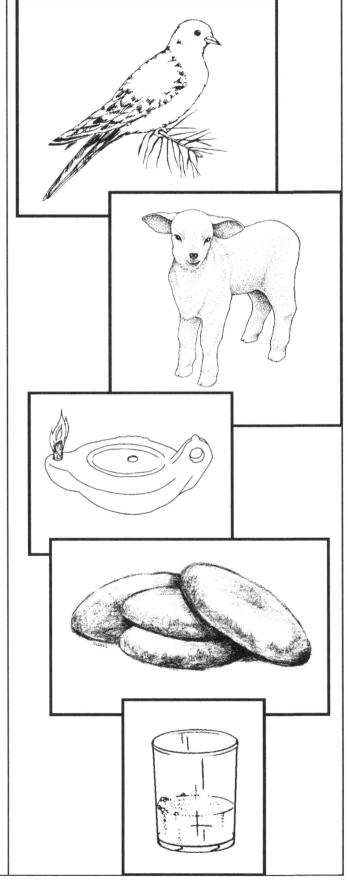

Omega

LAMB

Review

WATER

High Priest

Place I

Light

1. Find the sum for these addition problems.
Think of the sums as symbols representing Christ.

Alpha

11	11	11	11	11	11
+ 1	+ 2	+ 3	+ 4	+ 5	+ 6

11	11	11	11	11	11
+ 7	+ 8	+ 9	+ 10	+ 11	+ 12

2. What is the sum for these addition problems?

Seed

11	11	11	11	11	11
+ 1	+ 6	+ 4	+ 7	+ 2	+ 8

11	11	11	11	11	11
+ 11	+ 3	+ 12	+ 10	+ 5	+ 9

11	11	11	11	11	11
+ 4	+ 7	+ 11	+ 2	+ 3	+ 8

11	11	11	11	11	11
+ 5	+ 9	+ 12	+ 1	+ 10	+ 6

Bread   Angel   Lion   DOVE

3. Write in the answers for these problems.

11 + 4 = _____   11 + 6 = _____   11 + 10 = _____

11 + 12 = _____   11 + 11 = _____   11 + 9 = _____

11 + 9 = _____   11 + 1 = _____   11 + 8 = _____

11 + 2 = _____   11 + 5 = _____   11 + 9 = _____

11 + 11 = _____   11 + 7 = _____   11 + 2 = _____

11 + 5 = _____   11 + 4 = _____   11 + 8 = _____

11 + 3 = _____   11 + 8 = _____   11 + 12 = _____

11 + 10 = _____   11 + 7 = _____   11 + 6 = _____

11 + 1 = _____   11 + 7 = _____   11+ 9 = _____

11 + 12 = _____   11 + 4 = _____   11 + 11 = _____

11   11   Learn to spell the word eleven.   11   11
   11   Write it at least eleven times.   11

_____   _____   _____   _____

_____   _____   _____   _____

11 _____   _____   _____   11
     11   11   11

4. With intense interest heaven must have watched to see if Jehovah would arise, and sweep away the inhabitants of the earth. *"And when the fullness of the time had come,"* God did not destroy the sinful world but gave His Son to it! **As you do these sums, think of the answers as those in heaven watching Jesus coming to this world.**

11	11	11	11	11	11
+ 5	+ 8	+ 10	+ 7	+ 9	+ 6

11	11	11	11	11	11
+ 4	+ 1	+ 3	+ 11	+ 2	+ 12

5. Fill in the missing number.

11	7	5	11	11	4
+ __	+ __	+ __	+ __	+ __	+ __
13	18	16	12	22	15

11	6	11	11	8	11
+ __	+ __	+ __	+ __	+ __	+ __
14	17	21	20	19	23

Reinforce

Take a nature walk and find eleven in creation or combinations of eleven (6 + 5; 7 + 4).

**6. Print each word below for the following numbers.
See the example on number twelve.**

1 _____ 2 _____ 3 _____

4 _____ 5 _____ 6 _____

7 _____ 8 _____ 9 _____

10 _____ 11 _____ 12 _twelve_____
                                          (example)

7. Find all the number names in this word search.

1   4   3   6   11

```
E T W O I V E O N X I
L S F N E V E S E S I I
F I V E I N I N E V E
V X E E G E L E V E N
F O U R H E V L E W T
V E N H T E N T W E L
T H E T F O U S R T H
```

12   5   2

7   8   9   10

Interpreter

Addition 1 – Student – Page 301

Review
Place II

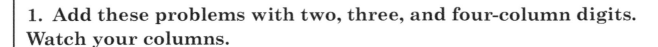

When there are several numbers to be added,
be careful they are in the right place.
Christ was always in the right place at the right time.

**1. Add these problems with two, three, and four-column digits.
Watch your columns.**

C.

386	492	378	496	832	749
537	643	539	642	584	482
625	736	934	827	825	736
234	439	637	475	428	631

O.

4681	9423	7745	4937	1591
6476	3948	3263	3632	1272
4363	1275	2364	1652	8292
1126	3435	4327	4132	3832

M.

19	46	36	84	34	62
42	58	43	59	80	37
53	64	75	34	97	72
36	33	26	72	36	35
63	47	61	72	21	27
44	72	74	13	25	71

P.

2723	8234	4586	5924	8357
3463	3957	5326	6256	7434
9258	2485	3769	2035	6463

L.	786	792	546	743	761	418
	243	468	698	871	395	367
	135	833	872	353	767	495
	671	958	513	634	481	828
	826	314	749	168	876	638
	<u>794</u>	<u>359</u>	<u>423</u>	<u>964</u>	<u>254</u>	<u>265</u>

E.	3170	4365	7126	5736	4329
	5703	4625	1478	4372	3562
	2106	3153	2614	7284	6493
	5520	4133	6623	3536	6734
	<u>4493</u>	<u>2152</u>	<u>3764</u>	<u>9485</u>	<u>5385</u>

T.	33561	43957	62436	53948	72813
	45384	85392	43785	63827	59644
	62731	45123	37639	48383	63723
	<u>38293</u>	<u>56397</u>	<u>46824</u>	<u>56372</u>	<u>83759</u>

E.	55126	80343	24694	4782	91993
	71373	87166	4961	1696	74258
	42743	12435	4646	2374	17998
	<u>82174</u>	<u>70998</u>	<u>5638</u>	<u>5392</u>	<u>75278</u>

Reflect

Mr. Moody said, in preaching on "Christ as a <u>Deliverer</u>:" "I remember preaching on this subject, and walking away, I said to a Scotchman, 'didn't finish the subject.' 'Ah man! you didn't expect to finish, did ye? It'll take all eternity to finish telling what Christ has done for man.'"

Review
Place III

When we are complete in Christ, we will be in harmony (line) with all the other worlds in the universe. When adding decimals, be sure to keep the decimal points in line, in the addends and in the sum. Continue to add just as you do with whole numbers. Add zeros in "short" decimal places to keep your numbers lined up correctly. See the example below.

Example

$$4.93 + 359.4 + 15.367 = c$$

$$
\begin{array}{r}
4.930 \\
359.400 \\
+ 15.367 \\
\hline
379.697
\end{array}
$$

$$c = 379.697$$

1. Copy these numbers in columns, add, then check.

C.   68.5, 54.3, 95.9   35.9, 5.3, 63.8

O.   5,288.9, 85   8.7, 47.8, 8.9

M.   83.7, 78, 43.5   21.3, 59.6, 7

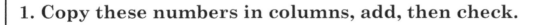

2. Add zeros in these columns and find the sum. Do not forget to put in the decimal point.

P.
$$
\begin{array}{r}
71.1 \\
63.46 \\
32.81 \\
\underline{53.67}
\end{array}
\qquad
\begin{array}{r}
39.35 \\
75.94 \\
48.3 \\
\underline{82.14}
\end{array}
\qquad
\begin{array}{r}
62.84 \\
85 \\
4.15 \\
\underline{45.8}
\end{array}
\qquad
\begin{array}{r}
8.78 \\
64.20 \\
41.17 \\
\underline{4.3}
\end{array}
\qquad
\begin{array}{r}
31.6 \\
8.01 \\
23.54 \\
\underline{88.7}
\end{array}
$$

L.

961.58	19.18	382.7	8.83
56.341	577.5	6.716	413.11
105.25	65	217.268	2.286
68.134	552.267	56.3	68.687

3. Copy these numbers in columns, add, then check.

E. $47.125 + 66.54 + 649 + 98.8 = \mathbf{w}$

  $91.44 + 15.7 + 24.859 = \mathbf{o}$

T. $26.16 + 79 + 44.487 + 7.32 = \mathbf{r}$

  $573.596 + 89 + 23.14 = \mathbf{l}$

E. $76 + 52.41 + 106.8 + 34.077 = \mathbf{d}$

  $24.85 + 9 + 7.681 + 259 = \mathbf{s}$

Reflect
Christ a Pattern

As I stood beside one of the wonderful Aubosson tapestries (woven pictures), I said to the gentleman in charge, "How is this done?" He showed me a small loom, with a partly finished web upon it, and said that the weaver stands behind his work, with his materials by his side, and above him the picture which he is to copy, exactly thread for thread, and color for color. He cannot vary a thread or a shade without marring his picture. It is a glorious thing for us to have a perfect life for example by which to form our lives. And we cannot vary a hair-breadth from that example without injuring our lives.

—*Eugene Stock*

Research
Worlds Without End

"...There shall come a Star out of Jacob...."
Numbers 24:17

Can you imagine how many worlds there are in the universe? There are so many that man cannot count that far. God knows their number, just like He knows each person that lives on this earth. He came from His beautiful heavenly home to live on this earth for over 33 years.

What will it be like to be in heaven with Christ? "Many seem to have the idea that this world and the heavenly mansions constitute the universe of God. Not so. The redeemed throng will range from world to world, and much of their time will be employed in searching out the mysteries of redemption. And throughout the whole stretch of eternity, this subject will be continually opening to their minds. The privileges of those who overcome by the blood of the Lamb and the word of their testimony are beyond comprehension."*

*7 Bible Commentary 990

"Praise ye him, sun and moon: praise him, all ye stars of light."
Psalm 148:3

"I shall see him, but not now: I shall behold him, but not nigh: there shall come a Star out of Jacob, and a Sceptre shall rise out of Israel,..."
Numbers 24:17

"I am the root and the offspring of David, and the bright and morning star."
Revelation 22:16

Review

Word Problems
Place I

1. **Make problems on the following pages and label your answers. See the sample and go as far as you can.**

Examples

11 worlds	11 worlds
+ 1 world	+ 2 worlds
12 worlds	13 worlds

"One such soul saved

is of more value than worlds.

Gold and earthly treasure can

bear no comparison

to the salvation

of even one poor soul."

1 Testimonies 513

Read the stories in the next column.

Reinforce

Read these stories.

"While We Were Yet Sinners"

A Roman servant, knowing that his master was sought for to be put to death, clothed himself in his master's garments that he might be taken for him: he was taken, and put to death in his stead; in memory of which, his master caused his statue in brass to be erected, as a monument of gratitude for the poor servant's fidelity and affection. What monument, then should Christians erect for Jesus Christ, who, when we lay condemned, descended from heaven and died to effect our salvation? For a good man, some would even dare to die; and greater love than this cannot be shown, that a man should lay down his life for a friend; but behold! God manifested His love to us, in that while we were yet enemies, Christ died for us.

Christ Died for the Ungodly

A Christian mother told me that her son, whom she had advised to unite with Christ had a difficulty. "I don't see, mother, the great merit in Christ's dying for me. If I could save a dozen men by dying for them, I think I would. Much more if there were millions of them." "But my son, would you die for a dozen grasshoppers?" That set him thinking. After a few days he came to her with his doubts all cleared. "I don't know about the grasshoppers; they are a pretty clever kind of insect. But if it was a million mosquitoes, I think I should let them die." There are older heads than his that need the same hint.

—*Dr. Ray Palmer*

Review
Word Problems
Place II

It is not known how many galaxies there are. On a single photograph made with the telescope at Mount Palomar (think of the pictures from Hubble), more than 10,000 galaxies were detected! Did you know there are over 30,000,000,000 stars estimated in our galaxy, the Milky Way? Note the list on the next page of our local group of galaxies.

Find the list of words in the puzzle below.

Word List

TELESCOPE
MOUNT
PALOMAR
GALAXIES
MILKY
WAY
STARS
EARTH
WORLDS
JESUS
SOUL
SAVED
ATOM
SINLESS

```
S  R  A  T  S  R  L  M  I  L  K  Y
O  T  E  L  E  S  C  O  P  E  J  E
U  A  A  W  I  D  S  U  A  T  O  M
L  D  R  O  X  S  U  N  L  S  O  U
S  E  T  W  A  Y  O  T  O  L  A  V
T  V  H  E  L  P  A  L  O  M  A  R
R  A  T  A  A  S  I  J  E  S  U  S
S  S  H  R  G  N  W  O  R  L  D  S
S  I  N  L  E  S  S  L  E  T  O  M
```

Make a column of these addends, then find the sum.

1. 392, 187, 268, 179

2. 429, 614, 957, 843, 288

3. 7777, 8462, 3461, 4622

Addition 1 – Student – Page 310

Our local group of galaxies

Leo I
Leo II
Large Magellanic Cloud
Sculptor
Fornax
Milky Way
Small Magellanic Cloud
NGC6822

NGC185
1C1613
Wolf-Lundmark
Triangulum
NGC147
M32
Andromeda
NGC205

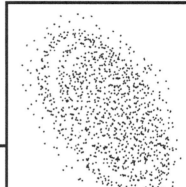

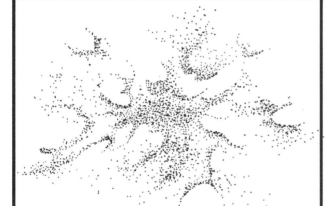

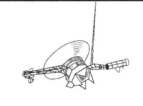

Reinforce
Read this story.

Does Jesus Dwell in This House?

Pastor Nettleton, while passing the residence of a gentleman in one of his walks, went up to the door and knocked. A young woman came to the door, of whom he inquired if Jesus dwelt there. Quite astonished, she made no reply. Again he asked, "Does Jesus Christ dwell in this house?" "No, sir," said she, and invited him to come in. "Oh no," said he, very sadly; "if Christ is not here, I can't come in, and he turned and went away. The next time he preached in that city, a young woman met him as he was leaving the church, and with tears in her eyes, asked if he recollected inquiring at a house, if Christ dwelt there. "Yes," said he, "I do." "I am that person," said she, "of whom you inquired and it has blessed my soul" (*—H. L. Hastings*). The question I would ask you is: Does Jesus live in your life? Your home?

Review
Word Problems
Place III

Heavenly beings travel to the many worlds, it seems, with the speed of thought. When we drive an automobile or send a rocket up into space, we need fuel.

1. Joseph's father bought the following amounts of gasoline on his trip: 11.2 gallons, 15.1 gallons, 9.2 gallons, and 13.9 gallons. What was the total amount of gasoline bought?

2. When we travel, we drive miles (kilometers). On a recent field trip the Daniels family and friends drove to several historic spots. They drove 43.8 miles, 8.4 miles, 13.1 miles, 2.5 miles, and 7.3 miles. How many miles did they drive?

3. When the Daniels returned home it only took 36.5 miles to get there. What was the total number of miles driven that day?

Bible Travel
In the Time of Jesus
and His Disciples

"In journeyings often,
in perils of waters,
in perils of robbers,
in perils by mine own countrymen,
in perils by the heathen,
in perils in the city,
in perils in the wilderness,
in perils in the sea,
in perils among false brethren;

"In weariness and painfulness,
in watchings often,
in hunger and thirst,
in fastings often,
in cold and nakedness."
ii Corinthians 11:26-27

In Bible times travel was expensive, uncomfortable, and dangerous. Therefore, it was done only when absolutely necessary. Paul's travels tell of the hardships of journeying in the East as the verses on the previous page describe.

Whenever possible men would travel in large groups for protection from wild animals and robbers. Sometimes a guide or someone who knew the way, especially the location of wells or other sources of water, was invaluable to travelers.

Most travelers were traders and merchants going from village to village. Their tempting wares were piled high on their donkeys or camels. They planned their route to arrive in the larger towns in time for the feasts and local fairs.

Walking was a common way to get from place to place. When the way was wet and slippery, most travelers took off their sandals for better footing. This also conserved their valuable footwear from the abuse they would receive on the primitive roadways.

The rich or soldiers would ride on the backs of horses, mules, or donkeys, and when traveling in the desert, camels were used. In order to avoid the intense heat of the desert and to escape detection by robber tribes, traveling was often

Walking was a common way to get from place to place.

done by night. The guide would use the stars to get his direction.

For a long journey the donkey was often the mount used. It had a solid footing on the stoney, muddy roadways. It could carry a large load, and maintain an even pace no matter what the terrain.

The camel was considered the long-distance freight vehicle of the day. They were known for their bad temperament. The camel was a delicate beast and required proper attention and care. Enabled to retain both food and water, it could go for days without either. When it could eat, its staple food was grass, bushes, and wild flowers. Its droppings were used for fuel and the female camel's milk for food.

Pack and riding saddles were made of leather sacking, stuffed

with padding attached to a wooden frame. The saddle cover was made of sheepskin with more cushions and horns. Saddle bags were often hung at the side.

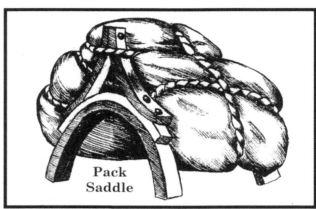

Pack
Saddle

Many of the ancient trade routes passed through Palestine, which was where Europe, Asia, and Africa met. Merchants with their heavy-laden camel caravans from many lands could be seen traveling these historical routes.

The horse was usually used for war to pull chariots. They were used for working on a farm, however, when the need arose (Isaiah 28:28).

Food was taken by travelers going a distance, which included bread, parched grain, and dried fruit (Joshua 9:4-6; Judges 19:19). Normally food was taken for about two days. That is why Jesus was aware that crowds who had been following Him for three days had nothing to eat (Matthew 15:32).

When nighttime overtook a traveler far from a village or inn, it usually meant sleeping by the roadside. He would use a stone for a pillow and wrap his mantle around his body for warmth.

The inn was rare and very primitive, often they were simply walled enclosures with dirty, unfurnished rooms along the outer walls. The courtyard in the center housed a well and stable for the traveler's animals. The inn provided only minimum protection against elements, wild animals, and thieves. They were most unpleasant!

Wheeled vehicles were not unknown in Palestine, but they had a limited use. The rough hilly country proved unsuitable for large wheeled vehicles. They were used on level coastal plains. When the Romans made paved roads they were used more extensively then.

Roman roads became the lifeline of the trade centers and capitals throughout the empire. They were the finest road builders. The roads were the responsibly of the army. They built them and kept them in good repair.

Sea travel was also dangerous. Roman merchant ships sailed the Mediterranean Seas with cargo of grain and passengers, and linked land caravans and travelers with the vast empire.

Most Jewish merchants hired Greek, Phoenician and Roman vessels to handle their shipments. Caesarea and Joppa were the major parts from which one could enter or leave Palestine during the first century.

Sea travel was dangerous. Paul was once in a storm at sea.

Illustration
Roman Roads

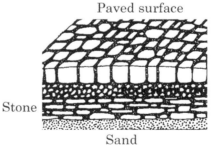

Paved surface

Stone

Rock set in concrete

Sand

The bottom level was made of sand, then came stone and rock set in concrete, next crushed stone in concrete, and finally the paved surface.

Remind

1. Satan tries to wear out our patience with people today like he tried to wear out God's patience with Israel. Be as patient with those who sin against you as you want God to be in your case! *"Overcome evil with good,"* remembering how God sent Jesus to help sinful men. Remember, Satan will try "to make the gulf deep and impassable" between you and those who have treated you wrong. Do not let him harden your heart toward any person no matter what they have done. Because you have been injured by them, you have a special chance to show God's selfless love for them that others may not have the same opportunity to show. (The contrast will be greater.) In practical terms this means love your enemies, turn the other cheek, do good to those that hate you.

2. Try to complete whatever job mother gives you. What if Jesus had gotten discouraged and failed to complete the plan to save sinful men? If sister is having a hard time completing her job of drying the dishes, help her finish her task.

Many of the ancient trade routes passed through Palestine, which was where Europe, Asia, and Africa met.

Remainder
One Fallen World

"...I came not to call the righteous, but sinners to repentance."
Mark 2:17

This world is just a small atom in God's vast dominion over which He presides. Yet this fallen world is very precious in His sight. Christ, the most beloved commander in the heavenly courts, went from His high estate, and laid aside His glory to save men. He left all the sinless worlds that loved Him to come to this earth, to be *"wounded"* and *"bruised"* (Isaiah 53:5). God gave Himself in His Son that He might have the joy of bringing this world back into the heavenly fold.

"He [Christ] might have gone to the pleasant homes of the unfallen worlds, to the pure atmosphere where disloyalty and rebellion had never intruded; and there He would have been received with acclamations of praise and love. But it was a fallen world that needed the Redeemer. *'I came not to call the righteous,'* said He, *'but sinners to repentance.'*"*

Alert people who are incomplete can be complete in Christ.

*5 Bible Commentary 1088

Reflect

"Jesus did not count heaven a place to be desired while we were lost."
The Desire of Ages 416

"...Ye are complete in him..."
Colossians 2:10

Reinforce
Remember

1. In the Bible, the number eleven reminds us of incompleteness, disorder, and imperfection—like this earth, today.

2. Color this picture as you think about how complete this earth will be when Jesus recreates it.

12 12 Twelves - 12 12 12

Research
The Number Twelve

"And, behold, I come quickly; and my reward is with me, to give every man according as his work shall be."

Revelation 22:12

In the Bible, the number twelve reminds us of perfection of government. At the right <u>time</u> God sent Jesus to show **alert** people on earth Heaven's perfect government.

"When the fullness of the time had come, the Deity [Father, Son, Holy Spirit] was glorified by pouring upon the world a flood of healing grace that was never to be obstructed or withdrawn till the plan of salvation should be fulfilled."*

Soon, the <u>time</u> will come for Jesus to come the second time. Someday, God will have a perfect government on this earth.

The Desire of Ages 37

Reinforce
Color then read the meaning of the number twelve. Review the numbers 1-10 in French, Japanese, Spanish, and Swahili.

6 addend
+ 6 addend
12 sum

TWELVE - 12
PERFECTION
OF
GOVERNMENT

The divine nature and the human nature combined (addition +) to give sinful man a Saviour.

+

12

Divine

Human

+

The number twelve is found as a multiple in all that has to do with rule. Twelve is the product of 3 (the perfectly Divine and heavenly number) and 4 (the earthly, the number of what is material and organic).

While seven is composed of 3 added to 4, twelve is 3 multiplied by 4 (3 x 4 = 12) and hence denotes organization—signifying perfection of government.

1. How many sons did Jacob have? (Genesis 35:22)

2. Describe the breastplate of the high priest. (Exodus 39:8-14)

3. What was to be made into 12 cakes and where was it to be kept? (Leviticus 24:5-6)

4. What did Israel find at Elim? (Numbers 33:9)

5. What were the children of Israel to take out of the Jordan as they crossed over it? for what purpose? (Joshua 4:2-3, 9)

6. What did Elijah take to build his alter on Mount Carmel? (I Kings 18:31-32)

7. What was Elisha doing when Elijah called him? (I Kings 19:19)

8. What did Jesus do when He was twelve years of age? (Luke 2:42)

9. What did Jesus call unto Himself? (Matthew 10:1)

10. What was left after Jesus fed the five thousand? (Matthew 14:20)

11. Who was the girl Jesus raised from the dead that was 12 years of age? (Luke 8:41, 54)

12. List the twelves from Revelation:

(1) 7:4-8 _____

(2) 12:1 _____

(3) 21:12 _____

(4) 21:12 _____

(5) 21:12 _____

(6) 21:14 _____

(7) 21:14 _____

(8) 21:21 _____

(9) 22:2 _____

13. There are many twelves in the Bible—
look up the list in the *Strong's Concordance*.

Remarkable Facts
Twelve

• The sun which "rules" the day, and the moon and stars which "govern" the night, do so by their passage through the 12 constellations which completes the great circle of the heavens of 360 (12 x 30) degrees or divisions, and thus govern the year.

• There were twelve patriarchs from Seth to Noah and his family, and twelve from Shem to Jacob.

• There are never more then 12 sons of Israel named in any one list in Scripture.

• There were 12 judges raised up in the times of apostasy and rebellion.

Othniel	Gideon	Ibzan
Ehud	Tola	Elon
Shamgar	Jair	Abdon
Barak	Jephthah	Samson

The Judges period ends under Samuel.

• The temple of Solomon has the number twelve as the predominating factor, in contrast with the Tabernacle, which had the number five. This agrees with the grace which shines in the Tabernacle, and with the glory of the kingdom which is displayed in the Temple.

• The measurement of the New Jerusalem will be 12,000 furlongs square, while the wall will be 144 (12 x 12) cubits (Revelation 21:16-17).

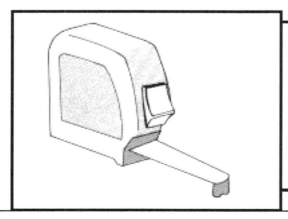

Reinforce

Read the article, "Throwing Away Diamonds" on the next page.

Throwing Away Diamonds

Time

Lost! One golden hour, set with sixty diamond minutes. No reward is offered, for it is gone forever! Yet how often and how many of us thoughtlessly and carelessly waste not only our own time, but the time of others.

A young man was five minutes late in keeping an appointment. "You have wasted an hour of our time," said the chairman severely, when he appeared. Surprised, the young man exclaimed: "I am only *five minutes* late." "True," came the answer, "but there are twelve of us."

Time is the warp and the woof of that precious thing called life. But do we really care for each hour as though it were a golden treasure? Do we guard each minute as though it were a priceless diamond? Do we realize that to "waste" a minute is to destroy a very real part of human life? That it is possible heedlessly to fritter away enough of ourselves, and others, to equal the destroying of a whole human life?

Rather a startling thought, isn't it? A minute seems such a very little scrap of time to throw away, when it stands all by itself!

The story is told of a certain student who seemed actually frightened lest he should lose a single precious moment. When questioned as to the reason for his carefulness, he replied: "I have but one candle, and when it has burned, I am through."

Really, come to think of it, we simply can't afford to spare even our *spare* time, can we? "The race of life," says Thomas Carlyle, "has become intense; the runners are treading on each other's heels; woe to him who stoops to tie his shoestrings."

How about it? Are you stooping?

"What is the price of that book?" asked a man who had been dawdling for an hour in the front store of Benjamin Franklin's newspaper establishment.

"One dollar," replied the clerk.

"One dollar," echoed the lounger; "can't you take less than that?"

"One dollar is the price," was the answer.

The would-be purchaser looked over the books on sale awhile longer, and then inquired: "Is Mr. Franklin in?"

"Yes," said the clerk; "he is very busy in the pressroom."

"Well, I want to see him," persisted the man.

The proprietor was called and the stranger asked: "What is the lowest, Mr. Franklin, that you can take for that book?"

"One dollar and a quarter," was the prompt rejoinder.

"One dollar and a quarter! Why, your clerk asked me only a dollar just now."

"True," said Franklin, "and I could have better afforded to take a dollar than to leave my work."

The man seemed surprised; but wishing to end a parley of his own seeking, he demanded: "Well, come now, tell me your lowest price for this book."

"One dollar and a half," replied Franklin.

"One dollar and a half! Why, you yourself offered it for a dollar and a quarter, just a moment ago."

"Yes," responded Benjamin Franklin coolly, "and I could better have taken that price then than a dollar and a half now. Time is money."

The man silently laid the money on the counter, took his book, and left the store, having received an impressive lesson from a master in the art of translating time into either wealth or wisdom.

One of the most common expressions we hear today is, "I haven't time." Why not? We have—all of us—all the time there is, haven't we? The real trouble is that we have wasted, or are wasting, the precious minutes. "Every human being is just a bundle of habit, tied with the string of time." And he can form what habits he will. Are those of thrift or of extravagance having their way in your life?

Abraham Lincoln studied by the light of a pine knot in the fireplace of his father's rude log cabin, and thus prepared for a life which stands out as one of the world's masterpieces. Elbert Hubbard was unschooled. But the Pennsylvania train took forty-five minutes to cover the distance between his home town and Buffalo, New York, where he worked each day. Other young businessmen played cards during those forty-five minutes. He spent them reading, studying. Madame Schumann-Heink trained for her wonderful musical career after she and her seven children had been deserted by husband and father. She could never have done it had she not been a past master in the systematic, careful use of time. Harriet Beecher Stowe wrote "Uncle Tom's Cabin" in the midst of pressing household cares. Longfellow translated "The Inferno" by snatches of ten minutes a day while waiting for meals, persisting over a period of years till the work was done. Robert Burns wrote many beautiful poems after doing a full day's work on a farm.

The author of "Paradise Lost" was a busy man, and had time to work on his sublime poetry only when he could spare a few minutes from the pressing duties of state. John Stuart Mill did much of his best work while clerking in a store. Galileo was a surgeon; yet to the improvement of his spare moments the world owes some of its greatest discoveries. Fritz Kreisler, having given a concert in a Michigan city, was driving across country to another appointment sixty miles away. The great violinist and his accompanist occupied the back seat of the car. A piece of sheet music was open before them, their attention fixed thereon. As they neared their destination Mr. Kreisler said to his accompanist, "Well, Carl, we can do that now!" In the two hours they had memorized practically sixty pages of music. And this list of odd-minute achievements might be indefinitely prolonged.

Yes, without a doubt time is precious. And there is no escaping the fact that *tempus fugit* (time flies), and that once gone, it is gone forever. The Persian poet, Omar Khayyam, truthfully says:

"The moving finger writes; and having writ,
Moves on; nor all your piety nor wit
Shall lure it back to cancel half a line,
Nor all your tears wash out a word of it."

What are you doing with the minutes, the hours, the days, as they come and go? Are you improving them? Investing their untold wealth wisely and well?

"Yesterday is dead," says Poor Richard; "tomorrow doesn't exist; to-day is here—*use it!*"

And why don't you?

"Upon the right improvement of our time depends our success in acquiring knowledge and mental culture. The cultivation of the intellect need not be prevented by poverty, humble origin, or unfavorable surroundings. Only let the moments be treasured."
Christ's Object Lessons 343

Reinforce
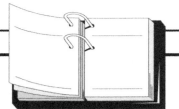

When the "Fullness of the <u>Time</u>" had come
Jesus came from His heavenly family to His earthly family.

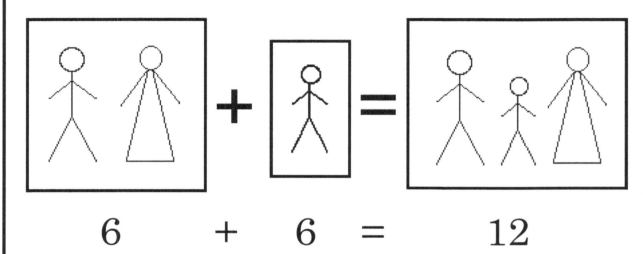

$$6 \quad + \quad 6 \quad = \quad 12$$

6 (Man) **+ 6** (Jesus Became A Man) **= 12** (Perfect Family Government)

Remember
Store these facts in your mind.

12	12	12	12	12	12
+ 1	+ 2	+ 3	+ 4	+ 5	+ 6
13	14	15	16	17	18

12	12	12	12	12	12
+ 7	+ 8	+ 9	+ 10	+ 11	+ 12
19	20	21	22	23	24

Our Time

"Redeeming the time,
because the days are evil."

Ephesians 5:16

It was <u>time</u> for Jesus to be born. Most people were not **alert** to the <u>time</u> of His coming. Today it is <u>time</u> once more for Him to come. Are you **alert** to the <u>time</u>? It is important that we use our <u>time</u> wisely as we prepare for this important event.

"Our <u>time</u> belongs to God. Every moment is His, and we are under the most solemn obligation to improve it to His glory. Of no talent He has given will He require a more strict account than of our <u>time</u>.

"The value of <u>time</u> is beyond computation. Christ regarded every moment as precious, and it is thus that we should regard it. Life is too short to be trifled away. We have but a few days of probation in which to prepare for eternity. We have no <u>time</u> to waste, no <u>time</u> to devote to selfish pleasure, no <u>time</u> for the indulgence of sin. It is now that we are to form characters for the future, immortal life. It is now that we are to prepare for the searching judgment."*

Christ's Object Lessons 342

Reinforce

"We are admonished to redeem the time. But time squandered can never be recovered. We cannot call back even one moment. The only way in which we can redeem our time is by making the most of that which remains, by being co-workers with God in His great plan of redemption."

Christ's Object Lessons 342

Sing the hymn,
"Joy to the World."

Review

Place I

1. Find the sum for these addition problems. Think of the sum as seconds on a clock, ticking by as we anticipate our Lord's return.

12	12	12	12	12	12
+ 1	+ 2	+ 3	+ 4	+ 5	+ 6

12	12	12	12	12	12
+ 7	+ 8	+ 9	+ 10	+ 11	+ 12

2. What is the sum for these addition problems?

12	12	12	12	12	12
+ 2	+ 1	+ 8	+ 6	+ 4	+ 7

12	12	12	12	12	12
+ 6	+ 9	+ 3	+ 10	+ 5	+ 1

12	12	12	12	12	12
+ 4	+ 8	+ 11	+ 7	+ 12	+ 2

12	12	12	12	12	12
+ 5	+ 9	+ 12	+ 6	+ 10	+ 3

"Every man and woman who is truly converted will be a diligent worker."
Christ's Object Lessons 343

3. Write in the answers for these problems.

12 + 6 = _____	12 + 4 = _____	12 + 10 = _____
12 + 11 = _____	12 + 11 = _____	12 + 9 = _____
12 + 1 = _____	12 + 9 = _____	12 + 8 = _____
12 + 9 = _____	12 + 5 = _____	12 + 2 = _____
12 + 11 = _____	12 + 2 = _____	12 + 7 = _____
12 + 5 = _____	12 + 4 = _____	12 + 8 = _____
12 + 8 = _____	12 + 3 = _____	12 + 10 = _____
12 + 12 = _____	12 + 6 = _____	12 + 7 = _____
12 + 7 = _____	12 + 9 = _____	12 + 1 = _____
12 + 11 = _____	12 + 3 = _____	12 + 12 = _____
12 + 4 = _____	12 + 12 = _____	12 + 6 = _____

12 12 12 Learn to spell the word twelve. 12 12
Write it at least twelve times. 12 12
12

_____ _____ _____ _____

_____ _____ _____ _____

_____ _____ _____ _____

12   12   12   12   12

Be **alert**, and do each of these problems correctly the first <u>time</u>, so you do not have to waste <u>time</u> doing them again.

4. Add 12 to each number on the clock as you write out your problems. Go clockwise, from left to right starting with 2 o'clock.

```
 12
+ 1      +___     +___     +___
 13
```

```
+___     +___     +___     +___
```

```
+___     +___     +___     +___
```

5. Find the sum of these addition problems.

```
  12        7        11        12
+  2      + 12      + 12      +  5
```

```
  12        3         9        12
+  1      + 12      + 12      +  6
```

```
  12        4        12        10
+ 12      + 12      +  2      + 12
```

60 seconds = 1 minute

30 minutes = 1/2 hour

60 minutes = 1 hour

24 hours = 1 day

"Every moment is freighted
with eternal consequences.
We are to stand as minute men,
ready for service at a moment's notice.
The opportunity that is now ours
to speak to some needy soul
the word of life may never offer again.
God may say to that one,
'This night thy soul
shall be required of thee,'
and through our neglect
he may not be ready (Luke 12:20).
In the great judgment day,
how shall we render our account to God?"
Christ's Object Lessons 343

Review
Place II

Remember how important it is to keep the decimals
in the proper place in the columns.

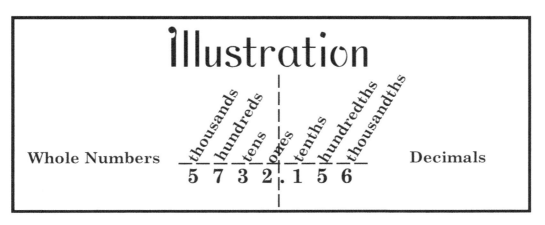

1. **Add the following problems. Add zeros where needed in the problems. Put the sums in the proper place.**

R.	53.40	74.20	.573	4.36	.14	71.30
	7.48	53.10	43.100	32.60	2.34	5.42
	31.10	4.07	3.260	.23	.548	3.10

I.	6.120	19.20	.541	6.52	32.20	25.12
	23.560	7.40	16.200	3.61	2.32	5.20
	.234	2.53	4.350	.06	6.53	20.46

2. **Put these numbers correctly in columns then add.**

G.   73.5, 46.21, 259.7   4.33, 87.41, 21.34

H.   7.4, 561.6, 32.29   27.4, 2.12, 93.5

T.   24.52, 3.3, 81.2   41.25, 7.46, 12.5

"It is the duty
of every Christian
to acquire habits
of order, thoroughness,
and dispatch."
Christ's Object Lessons 344

T.   6.6, 23.42, 0.29   2.62, 12.0, 27.34

I.   22.7, 9.26, 0.35   27.4, 2.32, 2.4

M.   2.43, 4.13, 0.16   4.31, 9.24, 0.121

"He [Jesus] had come
into the world
as the character builder,
and as such
all His work was perfect."
Christ's Object Lessons 345

E.

32.20	3.16	7.100	0.076	0.32	9.52
5.26	47.10	0.572	1.500	0.41	3.20
0.12	2.20	12.300	6.430	2.50	0.45

"Thou shalt arise,
and have mercy upon Zion:
for the <u>time</u> to favour her,
yea, the set <u>time</u>, is come."

Psalm 102:13

Coming

I'll come again,
  The very same,
As when I went away.
  My signs I'll show,
That you may know,
  The nearness of that day.

"Whatever the line of work
in which we engage,
the word of God teaches us to be
'not slothful in business;
fervent in spirit; serving the Lord....'
"Knowing that of the Lord ye shall
receive the reward of the inheritance;
for ye serve the Lord Christ'
(Romans 12:11; Ecclesiastes 9:10;
Colossians 3:24)."
Christ's Object Lessons 346

Review
Place III

Many countries use the decimal system for money. The digits left of the decimal are dollars, and those to the right are cents. When showing numbers with a decimal be sure to put them in the proper column.

1.   Add these sums and check your work.

G.	$3.98	$6.56	$2.09	$7.32	$4.99
	5.95	2.15	5.24	2.88	7.69
	2.50	9.72	3.62	4.51	6.20

O.	$31.79	$64.79	$47.55	$26.87	$37.34
	69.95	23.64	85.38	3.71	83.74
	44.12	88.80	8.31	54.51	52.87
	95.67	70.66	28.47	92.24	7.17

V.	$40.15	$7.32	$35.72	$68.23	$76.88
	6.58	56.30	64.21	4.36	19.35
	28.86	67.68	8.82	47.97	7.85
	29.42	81.75	58.83	37.54	45.69
	36.37	8.43	82.68	9.17	56.05

E.	$427.78	$310.38	$288.59	$26.46
	636.28	201.82	676.89	743.99
	441.02	19.82	33.53	350.25
	35.46	351.82	79.32	672.06
	781.52	951.39	628.50	83.92
	392.02	2.76	324.25	585.27

"The life of Christ from His earliest years was a life of earnest activity."*

"He lived not to please Himself. He was the Son of the infinite God, yet He worked at the carpenter's trade with His father Joseph."*

"Into all His secular labor He brought the same perfection as into the characters He was transforming by His divine power. He is our pattern."
*Christ's Object Lessons 345

2. Copy these problems in columns and add.

R. $62.64 + $28 + $27.89 = p

N. $26 + $53 + $1.39 + 89¢ = e

M. $43.40 + $0.98 + $6.39 = r

E.   69¢ + $3.30 + $14 + 56¢ = f

N. $65 + $91 + $406.79 = e

T. $3.29 + 54¢ + 6¢ + 75¢ = c

S. $89.32 + 98¢ + $12.34 + $1.27
      + 44¢ = t

Time is more precious than money.

"When one is always at work
and the work is never done,
it is because mind and heart
are not put into the labor.
The one who is slow and who works
at a disadvantage should realize that
these are faults to be corrected.
He needs to exercise his mind
in planning how to use the time
so as to secure the best results.
By tact and method, some will
accomplish as much in five hours
as others do in ten. Some who are
engaged in domestic labor are always
at work not because they have
so much to do but because they do not
plan so as to save time.
By their slow, dilatory ways
they make much work out of very little.

But all who will, may overcome these fussy, lingering habits.
In their work let them have a definite aim. Decide how long a time is required
for a given task, and then bend every effort toward accomplishing the work in
the given time. The exercise of the will power will make the hands move deftly."
Christ's Object Lessons 344

Research
Moments Are Precious

"Remember how short
my time is…"
Psalm 89:47

God regards each moment as precious. We have only a little <u>time</u> before Jesus will return. We do not have much <u>time</u> left to prepare. It is important that we are **alert** and ready to meet Him. How do we do this? By letting Him perfect our characters. **Alertness** is one character quality that is very important. Let us not waste any <u>time</u> as we develop this most important quality.

In the true history of our world, <u>time</u> is divided into two parts. The years before the birth of Christ are referred to as B.C. (before Christ). The years after Christ's birth are called A.D. (anno Domini—in the year of our Lord).

Soon

Jesus soon is coming;
This is my song—
Cheers the heart
When joys depart,
And foes are
Pressing strong."
—*Anonymous*

Illustration
B.C.—A.D.

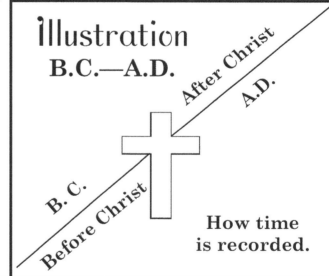

How time
is recorded.

"By many children and youth, time is wasted that might be spent in carrying home burdens, and thus showing a loving interest in father and mother. The youth might take upon their strong young shoulders many responsibilities which someone must bear."
Christ's Object Lessons 345

Review
Word Problems
Place I

Do these three addition problems in the boxes provided for them.

1. Four (4) years A.D. and twelve (12) more are how many years A.D.?

2. Twelve (12) years B.C. (Before Christ) can be made into several addition problems. Do several below using twelve (12) as the sum. Remember that the years before Christ start higher and decrease as they come to the year of His birth.

3. Seven (7) A.D. plus what makes nineteen (19) A.D.?

1.	2.	3.

4. Like time, the heart is also divided into two (2) major parts, called chambers. The chambers divide the heart lengthwise and the valves divide it crosswise, each side has two (2) parts and _____ parts altogether. Blood goes from the right side of the heart to the lungs. It then returns to the left side, and from there it is pumped out to the body. The normal heart beats about 72 times a minute (6 [man] sets of 12 [perfect government])

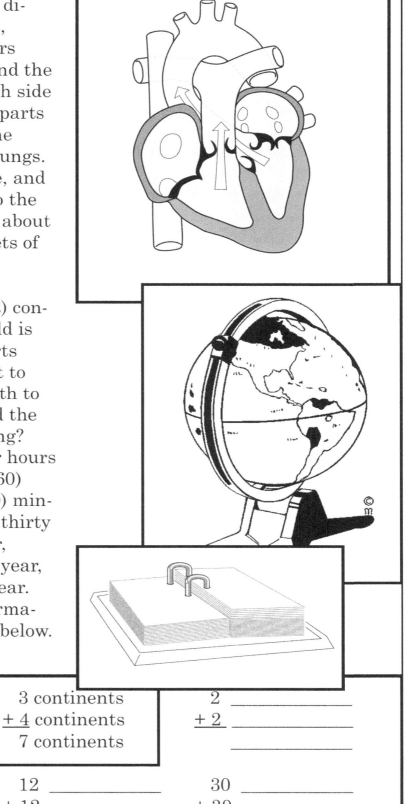

5. There are seven (7 - perfect) continents in the world. The world is divided into two (2) major parts (like time), latitude, from east to west, and longitude, from north to south. How many parts would the world be cut into for measuring? _____ There are twenty-four hours in a day (2 sets of 12). Sixty (60) seconds in a minute, sixty (60) minutes in an hour (5 sets of 12), thirty (30) minutes in one half-hour, twelve (12) months in one (1) year, and six (6) months in half a year. Make problems from the information above to fit the numbers below. Label the problems.

Example of Labeling Numbers	3 continents + 4 continents 7 continents	2 _____ + 2 _____ _____

6 _____ + 6 _____ _____	12 _____ + 12 _____ _____	30 _____ + 30 _____ _____

Review
Word Problems
Place II

1. Time should be used wisely. In one day Peter spent 2.5 hours in Bible study, 1.0 hour in prayer, 3.4 hours doing his school work, 7.3 hours exercising, and 2.0 hours in eating. How much time did Peter use doing useful things that day?

2. Shopping for food and household needs can take time. It saves time and money to make a list and only buy what is on the list. At the grocery store mother purchased 3 heads of lettuce at 89¢ each, crackers at $5.12, almonds at $3.98, and a dozen apples at $1.29. How much did mother spend at the store?

3. It takes time to sew, but sewing is a useful way to use your time. Mother bought material for two dresses for herself and Rebecca plus a shirt fabric for father. She paid $9.59 for one piece, $5.40 for another, and $4.35 for the third piece. How much was spent on material?

Reflect
Time is a Talent!

"Is there not an appointed time to man upon earth?"
Job 7:1

"You can't make footprints in the sands of time sitting down."

"Time gives good advice."
Maltese Proverb

"Dost thou love life? Then do not squander time, for that's the stuff life is made of."
Benjamin Franklin

"All the treasures of earth cannot bring back one lost moment."
French Proverb

"Time is the wisest of all counselors."
Plutarch

Review
Word Problems
Place III

1. Using time wisely can involve planting a garden. This also saves money for the family budget and provides good exercise for all. Mark planted a garden and in the late summer opened a vegetable stand. He sold tomatoes, lettuce, cucumbers, squash, and potatoes. He made $3.16 in the first hour, later in the day he made $2.34, and $5.20. Just as he was closing one more customer came and spent 95¢. How much did Mark make that first day his vegetable stand was open? Mark paid $12.29 for seed. Did he pay for his seed the first day?

2. By watching for sales, grocery money can be saved for materials to help others find out about Jesus' soon return. John went grocery shopping for his family. He spent $56.48 on needed items that were on sale then he drove to another grocery store where he spent $1.98, $2.89, and $2.46. How much was spent on groceries that day?

3. Mother bought peanut butter at $12.50 for one gallon, 6 pounds of apples at 59¢ a pound, a bag of popcorn at 98¢, and a ten-pound watermelon for $1.98. She only had $20.00 to spend. Did mother have enough money?

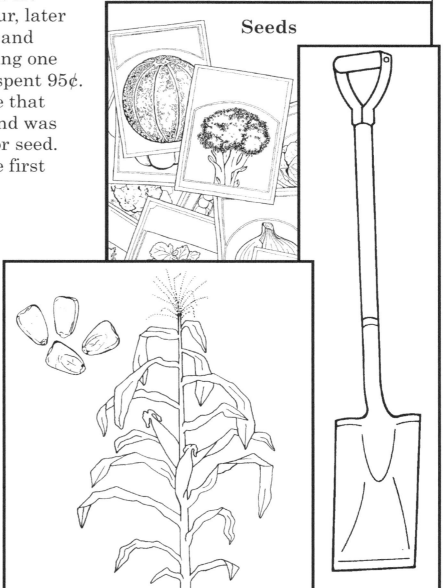

Seeds

Research
Redeem

"It is time for thee, Lord, to work...."

Psalm 119:126

You can see <u>time</u> is very important. We are encouraged to redeem the <u>time</u>. *"Walk in wisdom toward them that are without, redeeming the <u>time</u>"* (Colossians 4:5). Redeem means to buy back, or make good. Now, how can we redeem the <u>time</u> we have wasted by using it incorrectly? Remember, the only way is to make the best use of that <u>time</u> which we still have left to us. We can be **alert** to *"The Fulness of the <u>Time</u>,"* and prepare for what is about to come upon this earth. We can also **alert** others to the fact that Jesus is coming soon. *"It is <u>time</u> for thee, Lord, to work...."*

Reinforce

Use a watch with a second hand. Time yourself while you count to sixty and see if you are through when the second hand goes around once.

1-2-3-4-5-6-7-8-9-10-11-12-13-14-15-16-17-18-19-20-21-22-23-24-25-26-27-28-29-30-31-32-33-34-35-36-37-38-39-40-41-42-43-44-45-46-47-48-49-50-51-52-53-54-55-56-57-58-59-60

O Brother, Be Faithful

Sing this hymn.

O brother be faithful! soon Jesus will come, For Whom we have waited so long;

O, soon we shall enter our glorious home, And join in the conqueror's song.

O brother, be faithful! for why should we prove Unfaithful to Him who hath shown

Such deep, such unbounded and infinite love—Who died to redeem us His own?

—Unknown

Review
Place I

1. Review your addition problems.
Think of the sum as seconds going by,
by taking us closer to Jesus' coming.

4 + 8	11 + 9	8 + 10	10 + 5	12 + 10	7 + 1
12 + 11	9 + 4	12 + 6	6 + 11	12 + 12	9 + 7
1 + 11	12 + 7	12 + 1	2 + 7	11 + 7	12 + 2
5 + 8	7 + 10	8 + 11	6 + 10	9 + 5	12 + 9
10 + 1	6 + 8	2 + 12	12 + 8	11 + 2	7 + 10
12 + 8	7 + 3	12 + 3	11 + 8	7 + 11	6 + 9
7 + 9	3 + 11	4 + 7	1 + 9	12 + 7	2 + 10

3 + 12	1 + 8	12 + 9	8 + 10	4 + 12	11 + 9
9 + 8	12 + 10	7 + 5	11 + 4	2 + 8	10 + 3
8 + 7	10 + 9	2 +9	4 + 12	10 + 11	12 + 5
5 + 12	8 + 9	11 + 12	10 + 4	10 + 11	9 + 10
5 + 11	8 + 7	9 + 3	8 + 3	12 + 11	7 + 12

O brother, be faithful! He soon will descend,

Creation's omnipotent King,

While legions of angels His chariot attend,

And palm wreaths, of victory bring.

O brother, be faithful! and soon shalt thou hear

Thy Saviour pronounce the glad word,

Well done, faithful servant, thy title is clear,

To enter the joy of thy Lord.

—Unknown

Review
Place II

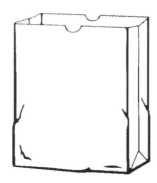

1. Copy the item amounts from the family's last grocery bill. Break it into 2 or 3 problems if the columns are very long. Add up each column. Add the columns together. What is the total? Does it match the grocery slip?

2. Place these amounts in columns.

3.53 + 2.25 =	2.06 + 3.85 =	6.30 + 9.86 =
1.36 + 24.3 =	12.49 + 2.1 =	7.52 + 0.49 =
3.67 + 0.432 =	3.22 + 2.25 =	12.5 + 4.16 =
0.791 + 0.102 =	53.5 + 78.3 =	8.92 + 53.2 =
7.42 + 62.3 =	0.621 + 42.3 =	75.3 + 6.58 =
34.7 + 0.347 =	8.94 + 32.2 =	24.5 + 6.32 =
9.57 + 4.63 =	38.2 + 29.7 =	0.596 + 0.423 =
1.341 + 31.5 =	3.32 + 35.5 =	17.1 + 0.139 =
0.35 + 34.0 =	0.234 + 3.54 =	54.6 + 3.26 =

Review

Place III

1 - 2 - 3 - 4 - 5 - 6
7 - 8 - 9 - 10 -
11 - 12

1. **What does each number mean in Scripture?**

    1 = _____

    2 = _____

    3 = _____

    4 = _____

    5 = _____

    6 = _____

    7 = _____

    8 = _____

    9 = _____

    10 = _____

    11 = _____

    12 = _____

2. **What does alert mean?**

3. **Describe the children of Israel just before Christ came.**

4. **Mark your Bible. See page 347.**

4. Mark your Bible. See page 347.

Reinforce

Go on a nature hunt
for twelves or numbers
that make up twelve,
(Example: 3 + 3 + 3 + 3 = 12)
out in the woods.

Reinforce

The number twelve reminds us of perfect government. Practice letting God govern your life now. A government always has laws. This week be **alert** to follow God's time laws.

1. Are you eating at the same regular times for meals every day and every meal?

2. Are you getting up at the same time every day, including weekends?

3. Are you ready for bed every night on time?

4. Are you ready for church and not making others wait on you?

Our daily preparation often reflects our preparation for Christ's second coming. If you are in the habit of hurrying to get things done at the last minute, most likely your character preparation will not be completed either by the time Christ returns. God can help you overcome in this area if you have a problem with not being ready on time.

"Parents cannot commit a greater sin than to allow their children to have nothing to do."
Christ's Object Lessons 345

Twelve =
Perfect
Family
Government

"Parents should teach their children the value and right use of time."
Christ's Object Lessons 345

"Teach them that to do something which will honor God and bless humanity is worth striving for. Even in their early years they can be missionaries for God."
Christ's Object Lessons 345

Remainder
Christ's First Coming

"But when the fulness of the time was come, God sent forth his Son, made of a woman, made under the law,

"To redeem them that were under the law, that we might receive the adoption of sons" (Galatians 4:4-5).

Christ's Second Coming

"...And they shall see the Son of man coming in the clouds of heaven with power and great glory,

"...It is near, even at the doors.

"Watch therefore: for ye know not what hour your Lord doth come.

"Therefore be ye also ready: for in such an hour as ye think not the Son of man cometh" (Matthew 24:30, 33, 42, 44). **Alert** people will be ready to welcome Christ.

Prophecies About the Deliverer
Place III

Prophesied	Prophecy	Fulfilled
Genesis 3:15	Seed of a Woman	Galatians 4:4
Genesis 12:3	Seed of Abraham	Matthew 1:1
Genesis 17:19	Seed of Isaac	Luke 3:34
Numbers 24:17	Seed of Jacob	Matthew 1:2
Genesis 49:10	From Tribe of Judah	Luke 3:33
Isaiah 9:7	Heir to David's Throne	Luke 1:23, 33
Micah 5:2	Born in Bethlehem	Luke 2:4
Daniel 9:25	Time for Birth	Luke 2:1-2
Isaiah 7:14	Born of a Virgin	Luke 1:26-27, 30-31
Jeremiah 31:15	Slaughter of Innocents	Matthew 2:16-18
Hosea 11:1	Flight to Egypt	Matthew 2:14-15
Malachi 3:1	Proceeded by a Forerunner	Luke 7:24, 27
Psalm 2:7	Declared Son of God	Matthew 3:17

Prophesied	Prophecy	Fulfilled
Isaiah 9:1, 2	Galilean Ministry	Matthew 4:13-16
Deuteronomy 18:15	A Prophet	Acts 3:20, 22
Psalm 78:2	To Teach in Parables	Matthew 13:34-35
Isaiah 61:1-3	To Heal the Broken-hearted	Luke 4:16-21
Isaiah 53:4	A Healer	Matthew 8:16-17
Isaiah 53:3	Rejected by His Own People, the Jews	John 1:11
Psalm 110:4	Priest After the Order of Melchizedek	Hebrews 5:5-6
Zechariah 9:9	Triumphal Entry	Matthew 21:1-11 Mark 11:7, 9, 11
Psalm 41:9	Betrayed by a Friend	Luke 22:47-48 John 13:18-19, 26
Zechariah 11:12	Sold for Thirty Pieces of Silver	Matthew 26:14-16
Zechariah 11:13	How Money Was Used	Matthew 27:3-8
Zechariah 13:7	Disciples Forsake	Matthew 26:31
Psalm 35:11	Accused by False Witnesses	Mark 14:57-58

Prophesied	Prophecy	Fulfilled
Isaiah 53:7	Silent to Accusations	Mark 15:4-5 Matthew 27:12-14
Micah 5:1	Smitten With a Rod	Matthew 27:30
Isaiah 50:6	Spat Upon and Smitten	Matthew 26:67
Psalm 35:19	Hatred Without Reason	John 15:24-25
Isaiah 53:5	Sacrifice	Romans 5:6, 8
Isaiah 53:9, 12	Crucified With Malefactors	Mark 15:27-28 Luke 23:33
Psalm 22:1	Agonizing Cry	Matthew 27:46, 25
Zechariah 12:10 Psalm 22:16	Pierced Through Hands and Feet	John 20:27
Psalm 22:7-8	Scorned and Mocked	Matthew 27:39, 41-44 Luke 23:35
Psalm 69:21	Given Vinegar and Gall	Matthew 27:34 John 19:28-30
Psalm 109:4	Prayer for Enemies	Luke 23:34
Psalm 22:17-18	Soldiers Gambled for His Coat	Matthew 27:35-36 John 19:23-24
Psalm 34:20	No Bones Broken	John 19:32-33, 36

Prophesied	Prophecy	Fulfilled
Zechariah 12:10	His Side Pierced	John 19:34
Isaiah 53:9	Buried With the Rich	Matthew 27:57-60
Psalm 16:10 Psalm 49:15	To Be Resurrected	Mark 16:6 Acts 2:30-31 I Corinthians 15:4
Psalm 68:18 Psalm 24:7-10	His Ascension to God's Right Hand	Mark 16:19 Ephesians 4:8 I Peter 3:22

Reinforce

Place I

Color
this picture.

Outline of School Program

Age	Grade	Program
Birth through Age 7	Babies Kindergarten and Pre-school	*Family Bible Lessons* (This includes: Bible, Science–Nature, and Character)
Age 8	First Grade	*Family Bible Lessons* (This includes: Bible, Science–Nature, and Character) + Language Program (*Writing and Spelling Road to Reading and Thinking* [WSRRT])
Age 9-14 or 15	Second through Eighth Grade	*The Desire of all Nations* (This includes: Health, Mathematics, Music, Science–Nature, History/Geography/Prophecy, Language, and Voice–Speech) + Continue using WSRRT
Ages 15 or 16-19	Ninth through Twelfth Grade	9 – *Cross and Its Shadow I** + Appropriate Academic Books 10 – *Cross and Its Shadow II** + Appropriate Academic Books 11 – *Daniel the Prophet** + Appropriate Academic Books 12 – *The Seer of Patmos** (Revelation) + Appropriate Academic Books *or you could continue using *The Desire of Ages*
Ages 20-25	College	Apprenticeship

Made in the USA
Monee, IL
21 August 2022